Lonely Planet

BEST BIKE RIDES

AUSTRALIA

BEST DAY TRIPS ON TWO WHEELS

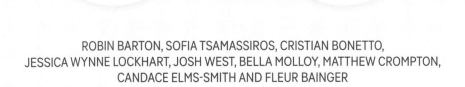

ROBIN BARTON, SOFIA TSAMASSIROS, CRISTIAN BONETTO,
JESSICA WYNNE LOCKHART, JOSH WEST, BELLA MOLLOY, MATTHEW CROMPTON,
CANDACE ELMS-SMITH AND FLEUR BAINGER

Contents

DOWNLOADABLE DIGITAL RIDE MAPS

Download GPX or KML files of the
rides in this book so you can take
the route with you on your ride.

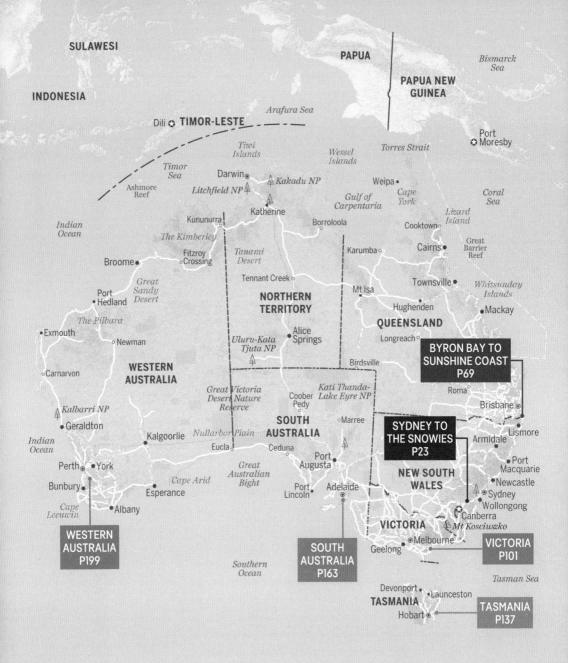

SULAWESI

INDONESIA

PAPUA

PAPUA NEW GUINEA

Bismarck Sea

Arafura Sea

Dili ⬡ TIMOR-LESTE

Timor Sea

Tiwi Islands

Wessel Islands

Torres Strait

Port ⬡ Moresby

Ashmore Reef

Indian Ocean

Darwin ◉ ⛺ *Kakadu NP*

Litchfield NP ⛺

Katherine

Kununurra

The Kimberley

Fitzroy ◦ Crossing

Broome •

Port • Hedland

Great Sandy Desert

The Pilbara

Exmouth •

Newman •

Carnarvon ◦

Tanami Desert

Tennant Creek ◦

NORTHERN TERRITORY

Uluru-Kata Tjuta NP ⛺

Alice ◉ Springs

Borroloola ◦

Gulf of Carpentaria

Karumba •

Weipa •

Cape York

Cooktown ◦

Lizard Island

Coral Sea

Great Barrier Reef

Cairns •

Mt Isa •

Townsville •

Hughenden •

Whitsunday Islands

Mackay •

QUEENSLAND

Longreach ◦

Birdsville ◦

BYRON BAY TO SUNSHINE COAST P69

Roma ◦

Brisbane ◉

Lismore •

WESTERN AUSTRALIA

Great Victoria Desert Nature Reserve

SOUTH AUSTRALIA

Coober ◦ Pedy

Kati Thanda-Lake Eyre NP

Marree •

SYDNEY TO THE SNOWIES P23

Armidale •

Port • Macquarie

Kalbarri NP ⛺

Geraldton •

Indian Ocean

Perth ◉ ◦ York

Bunbury •

Kalgoorlie ◦

Nullarbor Plain

Eucla ◦

Ceduna ◦

Great Australian Bight

Port Augusta ◦

Port Lincoln ◦

Adelaide ◉

NEW SOUTH WALES

Newcastle •

⛺ Sydney

Wollongong •

Canberra ⬡

Mt Kosciuszko ⛰

Cape Arid

Esperance •

Albany •

Cape Leeuwin

WESTERN AUSTRALIA P199

Southern Ocean

VICTORIA

Melbourne ◦

VICTORIA P101

SOUTH AUSTRALIA P163

Geelong ◦

Tasman Sea

Devonport • ◦ Launceston

TASMANIA

Hobart ◦

TASMANIA P137

0 — 1000 km
Ⓝ 0 — 600 miles

Welcome to Australia

Searing sunlight. The medicinal tang of tea tree in the warm air. Fast-moving flashes of colour as parrots fly through the trees, screeching to each other as they go. Yes, cycling in Australia is a revelation for the senses. But the diverse bike rides in this book also take in much more than Australia's natural splendour. You can coast through cities, such as Canberra, Melbourne or Sydney, on waterside cycle paths, stopping for sightseeing and coffee as you please. Or explore the nation's heritage on several traffic-free rail trails that usher riders through layers of history, all the way back to the traditional custodians of the country.

Other trails, around Clare in South Australia or Tasmania's Bruny Island, offer a sustainable way of touring regions renowned for their food and wine. Adrenaline-seekers can try some of the new mountain-biking trails that are revitalising towns like Derby and Melrose. Being on a bicycle unlocks countless memorable experiences on this vast continent.

Trail near Geelong (p102)

My Perfect Bike Ride

Robin Barton

LILYDALE TO WARBURTON RAIL TRAIL

P114

Yes, bike rides are as much about the journey as the destination, but the rail trail from Lilydale leads riders to Warburton, which is one of my favourite places in the world. The unpretentious town lies at the foot of Victoria's Yarra Ranges, surrounded by ferns and forest. Around 160km of mountain bike trails are about to be built in Warburton, making it Australia's next cycling hotspot. And you can start by taking a train to Melbourne's outskirts and hopping on the gravel rail trail from Lilydale Station.

Beechworth (p128)

Sofia Tsamassiros

GOLDEN VALLEY ASCENT

P161

I'm pretty biased when it comes to my favourite ride in Australia by choosing a ride in my own state, and that is the Golden Valley Ascent in Tasmania. This ride most definitely isn't for everyone, but one thing that makes me love riding so much, and this ride showcases brilliantly, is the opportunity to surrender yourself to the environment in which you are travelling. To me, this is the beauty of nature, knowing and feeling how, at times, insignificant humans can be within our surrounding environment.

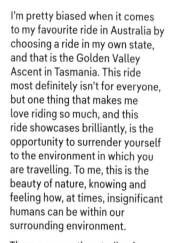

Cristian Bonetto

MURRAY TO MOUNTAINS RAIL TRAIL

P128

There are countless trails of extraordinary beauty in Australia but my heart belongs to the ride from Beechworth to Bright in Victoria's High Country. It encapsulates everything that I love about my home state: gripping history, beautiful gold-rush architecture, fabulous food and wine, and a palpable Italian influence. Especially beautiful in autumn, the trail makes for a cosy, relaxing weekend away, punctuated by bike rides, lazy winery lunches and evening wind-downs by a crackling fire.

Top 5 Scenic Rides

 1
Murray to Mountains Rail Trail
A 'best of' version of this trail.

 2
Hanging Rock Firetrail
Beginner-friendly introduction to the Blue Mountains.

3
Bruny Island
Diverse environments and world-class produce.

 4
Wadandi Track
One of the world's biodiverse hotspots.

 5
Riesling Trail
Rail trail past world-class vineyards.

Lilydale to Warburton Rail Trail
near Launching Place (p119)

Jessica Wynne Lockhart

BRISBANE
MINI RIVER
LOOP

P76

The meandering nature of the Brisbane River makes it difficult to orientate yourself as an outsider. I've lived in Queensland for two years, but it was only after doing the Brisbane Mini River Loop that I began to understand the lay of the land. It's also just a super-fun and scenic inner-city bike ride, with the added bonus of beer and pizza at the Howard Smith Wharves near the finish line.

Josh West

BAROSSA
TRAIL

P182

As a Barossa Valley native, I unknowingly cycled much of the Barossa Trail while adventuring South Australia's backcountry in my youth, though it wasn't until years later that I developed a deeper appreciation for the region's natural splendour. While the Barossa is renowned for its exceptional wines, the valley's rolling countryside, bordering ranges and rich biodiversity keep me pedalling back. Nowadays, each ride feels like I'm exploring the landscape anew, complete with obligatory cellar door visits.

MYPHOTOBANK.COM.AU/SHUTTERSTOCK ©

Cyclists near Tanunda (p183), Barossa Valley

Bella Molloy

MURRAY TO MOUNTAINS RAIL TRAIL

P128

Cycling on the Murray to Mountains Rail Trail is always guaranteed to bring a smile to my face. The trail is perfectly situated in the Ovens valley and, from the town of Bright, the views out towards Mt Buffalo have never failed to impress. In autumn, the colours of the falling leaves on the trees bordering the trail are spectacular. Even better, there are great local food spots and wineries conveniently located right along the route.

Matthew Crompton

THREE BRIDGES

P26

Even after a decade in Sydney, doing the Three Bridges ride on a sunny day always makes me fall in love with the city once again. I love cycling beneath the geometric beauty of the Anzac Bridge cables, and seeing the glitter of Darling Harbour and Barangaroo from the Pyrmont Bridge. Ultimately, though, nothing beats the trip across the Sydney Harbour Bridge – seeing Luna Park across the water and all the sailboats moored in Lavender Bay never fails to delight.

Top 5 Urban Rides

1 Capital City Trail
Quirky, inner-city loop through Melbourne.

2 Brisbane Mini River Loop
Showcases the best of Brissie.

3 River Torrens Linear Park Trail
Australia's longest hills-to-coast track.

4 Swan River Loop
Leisurely ride along Perth's riverfront.

5 Three Bridges
Urban tour of Sydney's harbour.

Candace Elms-Smith

MURRAY TO MOUNTAINS RAIL TRAIL

P128

The Murray to Mountains Rail Trail in Victoria is my all-time favourite bike ride in Australia. The eclectic landscape from Beechworth to Bright holds you captive as you ride through verdant valleys and alongside the peaceful Ovens River, catching intermittent glimpses of the rugged Mt Buffalo range. But the best part is, you can begin with a delicious treat from the famous Beechworth Bakery and end with a refreshing pint of local craft beer at Bright Brewery!

Fleur Bainger

SWAN RIVER LOOP

P202

I didn't expect the city I've lived in for the past 16 years to harbour any more surprises, especially so many hovering under my nose. Bird-packed wetlands in the shadow of skyscrapers? Check. Kangaroos on their own private island? Check. A hidden cycleway tucked into the side of a bridge? Yep, that too. Riding the Swan River Loop in Perth was like ticking off a list of first-time activities that I didn't know I needed to have.

Our Picks

BEST COASTAL RIDES

Cooling sea breezes, ocean views and plenty of places for a picnic add up to some of the appeal of a bike ride along a coast. There's also a good chance that regional authorities have planned a cycle or shared path along their waterfronts, and many of the rides featured in this book use such traffic-free routes. But what really sells a good coastal ride is dipping your toes in the ocean at the end.

TOP TIP

Oceanside rides are more likely to be flat if they follow a shoreline. Enjoy coasting along without gravity holding you back.

 1

Sunshine Coastal Pathway

Bask on Mooloolaba's beachfront, then explore the Sunshine Coast on this shared-use path.

P72

 2

Indian Ocean Explorer

Pedal along Perth's Pacific coast from the hip harbour town of Fremantle to Cottesloe.

P208

 3

Coast Park Path

Amble through Adelaide's handsome beachfront neighbourhoods before catching a train back to town.

P170

 4

South Coast Cycleway

South of Sydney, Wollongong's coast is blessed with beaches and best explored by bicycle.

P46

 5

St Helens Foreshore & Townlink

Play on St Helens' mountain bike trails via this ride beside beautiful Georges Bay.

P156

Alexandra Headlands, Sunshine Coast (p71)

Cottesloe Beach (p211), Perth

TOP TIP

Take note of the wind direction. You might find that breezes are stronger by the ocean and more favourable in one direction.

TOP TIP

Be seen and don't be too bashful to wear high-vis, such as a bright gilet or socks. It makes all the difference for safety.

Our Picks

BEST CITY ROUTES

Gliding through urban Australia on bike-friendly trails and roads is the best way to experience a city. You'll have the freedom to stop and explore where you wish and to see the parts that cars can't reach. A city reveals its personality more readily – from Melbourne's bluestone laneways to Sydney's stellar sights – to a bike-riding flaneur. And there's always the bonus of parking the bike for a beer or coffee with friends.

TOP TIP

Watch for car doors being opened in your path and kids or pets jumping out without warning. Give parked cars a wide berth.

 1

Lake Burley Griffin

See Canberra's landmarks and visit galleries and museums on this circuit of Lake Burley Griffin.

P56

2

Capital City Trail

Leisurely flow with the Yarra River through Melbourne's captivating neighbourhoods, taking in their different personalities.

P104

River Torrens Linear Park Trail (p166)

 3

Swan River Loop

You'll never stray from the Swan River as you skirt Perth's CBD on this traffic-free trip.

P202

 4

River Torrens Linear Park Trail

Adelaide's leafy suburbs reveal their charms as you follow the Torrens River to the ocean.

P166

 5

Three Bridges

Spy world-famous sights as you cross Sydney Harbour Bridge and Darling Harbour on this ride.

P26

Yarra River (p108), Melbourne

Our Picks

BEST FOOD & DRINK ROUTES

Blessed with many fine food and wine regions to explore, Australia rewards the epicurean cyclist who likes to ride on the mild side. Rather than rack up kilometres, good-time riders can tick off wineries in the Clare Valley or Bellarine Peninsula, cheese producers on Bruny Island, waterfront cafes in New South Wales and craft breweries almost everywhere. Touring by bicycle rather than car allows some extra liberties and some regions have routed bike paths past places to eat and drink. But ride responsibly, nevertheless.

TOP TIP

Cycling while intoxicated with alcohol is illegal; penalties vary across the states and territories but often feature a hefty fine.

Riesling Trail

Weave around Australia's most charming wine region, Clare Valley, on this purpose-built trail.

P186

Coast to Vines Rail Trail

Ride from Adelaide's southern suburbs to McLaren Vale's cellar doors along the old Willunga railway.

P176

Bruny Island

Work up an appetite on this challenging exploration of Bruny Island and its many tasty pit stops.

P144

Bellarine Rail Trail

Ride from Geelong to historic Queenscliff on the coast via the Bellarine's wineries.

P124

Shores of Newcastle

Sample up-and-coming Newcastle's exciting eateries on this short tour of its waterfront.

P42

Ploughmans lunch, McLaren Vale (p176)

Our Picks

BEST OFF-THE-BEATEN-TRACK ROUTES

Cycling is all about the freedom to roam and many of these routes open up some less frequented areas. You might explore the bushland of Margaret River, a car-free Tasmanian island or the bucolic scenery of eastern Victoria. Everywhere, you'll find that wildlife is less shy and more abundant. But even though you might meet fewer people off the beaten track, the welcome offered in small-town Australia will be as warm and helpful as ever.

TOP TIP

Navigation is key: carry a paper map (or take a photo of a map) as a back-up for any app you use.

Wombat, Maria Island (p148)

 1

Wadandi Track

Swap the vineyards for natural bushland as you ride through sunny Margaret River.

P228

2

Maria Island

Meander into Maria Island National Park to meet the wildlife at the edge of Australia.

P148

 3

Great Southern Rail Trail

Southeast of Melbourne, this rail trail takes in Gippsland's farming communities and quiet countryside.

P120

 4

Lilydale to Warburton Rail Trail

Warburton lies on the edge of wild, misty forests and has little of the touristy-ness of neighbouring towns.

P114

 5

Valley Ponds Trail

Cycle on gravel tracks through forests between two quiet Tasmanian towns.

P152

Our Picks

BEST MOUNTAIN ROUTES

The e-bike is a great leveller and allows people of all cycling abilities to experience the wonders of Australia's mountains. And there's a lot to enjoy. Rail trails lead into Victoria's High Country, cooler in summer and suffused with colour in autumn. Explore the national parks of Kosciuszko or the Blue Mountains on easy-going tracks. Or rent a mountain bike to try the trails around Melrose in the Flinders Ranges.

TOP TIP

If you're working up more of a sweat, wear appropriate clothing made from technical, wicking fabric (not cotton) to minimise chafing.

INPROGRESSIMAGING/SHUTTERSTOCK ©

Thredbo Valley Track

Plan for an adventure in Kosciuszko National Park on this off-road trail that is suitable for beginners.

P50

Melrose MTB Trails

Shred these brilliant community-managed mountain bike trails in the foothills of Mt Remarkable, partway along the Mawson Trail.

P192

Hanging Rock Firetrail

Follow the ridgeline track to Hanging Rock in the Blue Mountains National Park.

P38

Murray to Mountains Rail Trail

The beauty of this ride is that you see the mountains but you don't ride up them.

P128

Mt Coot-tha Loop

Circumnavigate Mt Coot-tha on the outskirts of Brisbane as many times as you can manage.

P82

FILEDIMAGE/SHUTTERSTOCK ©

Thredbo Valley Track (p50)

Hanging Rock (p39),
Blue Mountains National Park

TOP TIP

Carry a windproof jacket if cycling outside the summer months, when the weather can be wet and windy in the mountains.

When to Go

Whatever the time of year, there will be somewhere in Australia with prime conditions for cycling...and other places where it's a hot mess.

The vast size of Australia means there is huge climatic variation across the continent: when it's snowing in Tasmania, it will likely be warm and dry in Queensland. You'll need to match the season with the location to get it right. In the southeast of the country, in Victoria, Tasmania, southern New South Wales and coastal South Australia, winter months can be cold and wet.

North from Brisbane and winter (June to August) is a fine time for riding: days are dry and mild with cool nights. Spring (September to November) in the north sees temperatures climb a few degrees and the humidity increases to unpleasant levels during summer (December to February), thanks to

Kangaroo, Sunshine Coast (p71)

JON PAUL PHOTO/SHUTTERSTOCK ©

Weather Watch (Sydney)

JANUARY	FEBRUARY	MARCH	APRIL	MAY	JUNE
Avg daytime max: **26°C**	Avg daytime max: **25.8°C**	Avg daytime max: **24.8°C**	Avg daytime max: **22.5°C**	Avg daytime max: **19.5°C**	Avg daytime max: **17°C**
Days of rainfall: **8.6**	Days of rainfall: **9**	Days of rainfall: **9.9**	Days of rainfall: **8.9**	Days of rainfall: **8.6**	Days of rainfall: **8.8**

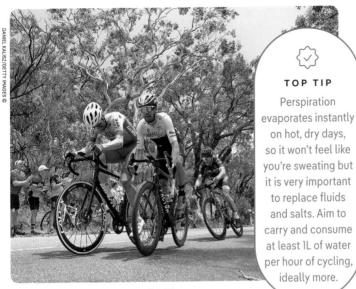

DANIEL KALISZ/GETTY IMAGES ©

TOP TIP

Perspiration evaporates instantly on hot, dry days, so it won't feel like you're sweating but it is very important to replace fluids and salts. Aim to carry and consume at least 1L of water per hour of cycling, ideally more.

Santos Festival of Cycling race, Adelaide

BIG EVENTS

The world's second-largest annual independent arts festival, **Adelaide Fringe**, takes over Adelaide for a month and stages an exciting and unpredictable roster of acts, including comedy, cabaret, theatre and music, in around 300 venues. Plenty of events are free. **February–March**

If you're in Tasmania for some summer cycling, time your trip to coincide with the avant-garde arts festival **MONA FOMA**, hosted by Hobart's Museum of Old and New Art, if you wish to catch some thrilling events and exhibitions. The festival is sometimes staged in Launceston. **February**

LOCAL FESTIVITIES

The **Santos Festival of Cycling** brings not only professional racing cyclists to Adelaide, but also events, parties and a sportive that follows the race route. **January**

Celebrating craft beer and gravel riding, weekend-long **Gears and Beers** takes place in Wagga Wagga. Register for one of the group rides, which cover distances from 40km to 130km, then enjoy some beers in the festival village. **September**

the highest rainfall and temperatures of the year, which also cause thunderstorms. Rainfall and humidity eases in autumn (March to May). Out west, summer is hot in Perth, but dry. Winter brings more rain. Spring is a beautiful time for riding in Western Australia, with wildflowers blooming.

WEATHER

Humidity is more of a problem for cyclists than outright heat. The most humid months vary according to location but generally are in the winter in the south of the country and in the summer in the tropical north.

Take note of the prevailing wind direction and strength when you plan a bike ride as it can make all the difference as you progress (and check bushfire forecasts too). During some seasons, hot winds come off the interior, while in other places icy gales blow in from Antarctica.

JULY	AUGUST	SEPTEMBER	OCTOBER	NOVEMBER	DECEMBER
Avg daytime max: **16.4°C**	Avg daytime max: **17.9°C**	Avg daytime max: **20.1°C**	Avg daytime max: **22.2°C**	Avg daytime max: **23.7°C**	Avg daytime max: **25.2°C**
Days of rainfall: **7.4**	Days of rainfall: **7.1**	Days of rainfall: **7.1**	Days of rainfall: **7.9**	Days of rainfall: **8.3**	Days of rainfall: **7.9**

Get Prepared for Australia

Useful things to load in your bag, your ears and your brain.

Clothing

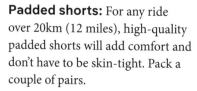

Padded shorts: For any ride over 20km (12 miles), high-quality padded shorts will add comfort and don't have to be skin-tight. Pack a couple of pairs.

Base layer: A light, polypropylene vest layer next to the skin acts to both insulate and cool, and wicks moisture away quickly.

Short-sleeved jersey: Select a top made from either a polyester or merino wool material, but definitely not cotton. Some cycling-specific jerseys have pockets on the back, which can be useful. And a zip allows the jersey to be opened when you're too hot.

WATCH

Two Hands
(*Gregor Jordan; 1999*)
Rose Byrne and a
young Heath Ledger
star in a Sydney-set
gangster caper.

The Block
(*2003–ongoing*) The
Aussie obsession with
real estate collides
with reality TV in this
show about house
renovations.

The Castle
(*Rob Sitch; 1997*) A
classic comedy about
small-town strivers that
put Bonnie Doon on the
map and is the source
of many Australian
catchphrases.

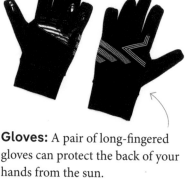

Gloves: A pair of long-fingered gloves can protect the back of your hands from the sun.

Long-sleeved jersey: Again, go for a polyester or merino fabric. Long sleeves can be useful not only in cool conditions, but also to protect skin from the sun – some fabrics have built-in UV protection.

Buff: This is a tube of fabric that is useful for protecting the face, head or neck from the cold or the sun.

Socks: You'll probably want lightweight socks made from a wicking material rather than woollen socks for warmth (possibly only useful in Tasmania and Victoria in the winter).

Jacket: A lightweight, windproof jacket or gilet that can be rolled up and stowed in a pocket.

Cycling in Brisbane (p70)

LISTEN

16 Lovers Lane
(*The Go-Betweens; 1988*) A perfect, jangling pop debut from Brisbane's best storytellers, Grant McLennan and Robert Forster, featuring 'Streets of Your Town'.

Lonerism
(*Tame Impala; 2012*) Perth-based polymath Kevin Parker dives into deep psych-rock and kickstarts Australia's psychedelic scene.

Gurrumul
(*Geoffrey Gurrumul Yunupingu; 2008*) Soulful and absorbing songs, including 'Djarrimirri', from this award-winning Indigenous artist.

Words

You may think you know English, but sometimes speaking 'Australian' is something entirely different. Here's a quick guide to the many 'o's in Aussie slang:

Ambo An ambulance driver

Arvo An afternoon

Avo Are you getting the hang of it? This is an avocado.

Bottle-o A bottle shop. This term is so common that many pubs will label their attached bottle shop a bottle-o.

Defo Definitely!

Garbo No, not the 1930s actress (far from it). This is a shortened form of 'garbage collector'.

Journo A journalist

Muso A musician

Relo A relative or family member

Servo A petrol station (formerly called a 'service station') or sometimes a convenience store

Smoko A quick break from work. Though the word comes from 'smoke break', a smoko no longer requires a cigarette.

READ

True History of the Kelly Gang
(*Peter Carey; 2000*) Not so much a straight story of Ned Kelly's life but a rambunctious, fictionalised ride-along with the bushranger.

The Fatal Shore
(*Robert Hughes; 1986*) Hughes' description of Australia's convict history is written with customary panache.

Welcome to Country
(*Aunty Joy Murphy; 2018*) Aboriginal Elder Aunty Joy Murphy and Indigenous artist Lisa Kennedy craft an introduction to the traditional lands of the Wurundjeri people.

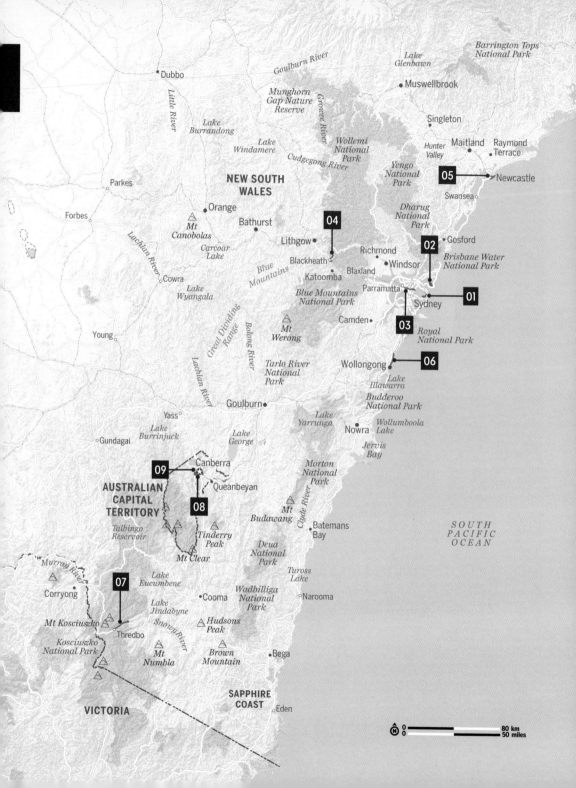

National Arboretum (p62), Canberra

Sydney to the Snowies

Explore

Sydney to the Snowies

The area around Greater Sydney is Australia's biggest, busiest and most populous. Stretching from Wollongong in the south to the Hunter Valley in the north and the Blue Mountains in the west, it offers the cyclist a huge variety of landscapes to explore. With everything from beach to bushland, and city to singletrack, the Sydney region arguably packs more attractions than any other area in Oz. Adventure seekers often flock to the mountains, but there are surprising challenges to be found cityside too. More than anything, it's a region that rewards exploration – there's always another find around the corner to surprise you.

Sydney

The big smoke, and the point of entry for most visitors to the area. Sydney is not only one of the country's largest city, it also boasts one of the world's most jaw-dropping urban settings. With a spectacular harbour and a string of lovely seaside beaches, it's graced by fine weather, and a network of trains and ferries that – while imperfect – makes many outlying areas surprisingly accessible. Any conceivable supplies – from food to clothing to bike parts to camping equipment – are easily available, and if you want to wine, dine or go out on the town, you'll be spoilt for choice.

Many visitors naturally choose to base themselves harbourside in the City of Sydney itself, but the beachside hubs of Bondi and Manly also remain perennially popular.

Katoomba

The large town of Katoomba is the heart of the Blue Mountains. Lying approximately 100km to the west of Sydney, it sits on a plateau at about 1000m, with its high ochre cliffs plunging spectacularly to the Jamison Valley far below. Easily accessible by both train and road, the town is known for its quirky subcultures, including artists, writers, outdoorspeople and environmentalists. As the service town for the Blue Mountains, it has the best assortment of lodging, dining and shopping in the region, including outdoors shops (along with all other provisioning needs).

WHEN TO GO

At its best, the Sydney summer (December–February) is a combination of high heat and humidity far better suited to the beach than bicycling. The Blue Mountains, by contrast, are normally cooler, but temps can drop below freezing in winter (June–August). Spring and autumn in the Sydney area offer moderate temperatures and (in spring) lovely blooming jasmine and jacarandas.

Beautiful, relaxed and friendly, Katoomba is a natural place to base yourself when exploring the region, with heaps of pubs, restaurants and cafes to enjoy when you're done playing in the mountains for the day.

Newcastle

'Newy' is NSW's second city, beloved of locals and visitors alike for its gorgeous beachside setting, relaxed vibe and supreme liveability. At just a tenth the size of Sydney, Newcastle punches above its weight as an important regional centre. With good transit connections, a full range of services and (all-importantly!) no shortage of great places to eat and drink, Newcastle is the natural hub for visiting the Central Coast and Hunter regions of NSW.

Canberra

Set among the backdrop of the stunning Brindabella Ranges, Canberra is also known as the Bush Capital, owing to its easy access to prolific nature reserves.

TRANSPORT

Sydney is home to the region's international airport, though Newcastle also has domestic air connections. The local Sydney train network has frequent good connections to the Blue Mountains, Newcastle and the Central Coast, as well as various destinations on the near south coast. A car, while not necessary, will get you to many spots off the beaten path.

In addition to being the capital city of Australia, it also boasts a vibrant food and coffee scene. Braddon is a top spot for cafes, bars and restaurants, while the Kingston Foreshore offers waterfront dining on the shores of Lake Burley Griffin.

 WHERE TO STAY

Euroka Campground, in the lower Blue Mountains outside of Glenbrook, is a special spot. With its towering trees, steep grassy hills and abundant birdlife, the best word to describe it is 'idyllic'. It's understandably popular with families. Be aware that access over the Glenbrook Causeway closes during and after heavy rain.

When in Newcastle, Noah's on the Beach proves that there is indeed sometimes truth in advertising. The rooms themselves are comfortable, but the real draw is the ocean views, which are worth paying for.

 WHAT'S ON

Annual Gay and Lesbian Mardi Gras

(*mardigras.org.au;* February) The biggest Pride event in Oceania, and arguably Sydney's best party.

Annual Winter Magic Festival

(*wintermagic.org.au;* August) A street festival in Katoomba with music, arts and food, celebrating the best of what's weird and wild about the Blue Mountains.

This is Not Art (TiNA) Festival

(*thisisnotart.org;* October) A new media and arts festival in Newcastle showcasing music, theatre and visual art.

Resources

Time Out Sydney (*timeout. com/sydney*) remains a reliable guide for what's on in the city.

The **NSW National Parks website** (*nationalparks.nsw. gov.au*) is a great source of info, including up-to-date information on what's currently open/closed at the national parks.

The **Transport NSW website** (transportnsw.info) is an excellent resource for getting around Sydney and the region.

01

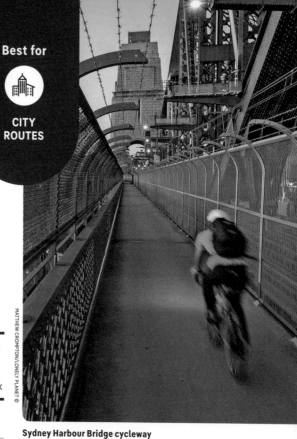

MATTHEW CROMPTON/LONELY PLANET ©

Three Bridges

DURATION	DIFFICULTY	DISTANCE	START/END
1–1½hr	Easy	9km	Glebe fore-shore park/Bradfield Park

TERRAIN	Well-paved and mostly separated cycle path; a few short climbs

Sydney Harbour Bridge cycleway

Sydney's waterfront simply sparkles. The city centre boasts kilometres of stunning foreshore that's perfect for cycling, but for the best views, you have to get up high. Enter the Three Bridges ride: crossing the ANZAC Bridge, Pyrmont Bridge and iconic Sydney Harbour Bridge, this easy, mostly car-free route takes you through the heart of the city, delivering one knockout vista after another. With outstanding cafes, museums, bars and restaurants scattered all along the route, it's a ride that rewards taking it slow and savouring what Sydney has to offer.

Bike Hire

Bonza Bike Tours rents out bicycles complete with locks, helmets and emergency repairs kit for $15 per hour, or $30 for four hours. Book ahead online.

Starting Point

The Glebe foreshore near the Sydney Fish Market, a short cycle from Sydney Central Station. Alternatively, it's possible to do the ride in reverse, starting from Milsons Point Station.

01 The ride starts from the foreshore park on Bridge Rd, near the new Sydney Fish Market. From here, the route follows the shared pedestrian and cycle path curving northwest along the edge of Blackwattle Bay. The shared path can get busy, especially on weekends, so go slowly and use your bell as needed. The route winds along the shoreline through Blackwattle Bay Park past preserved artefacts from bygone times, including a large crane from the area's former shipbreaking yards. As you round the point, you'll get a great view of the Anzac Bridge across the water.

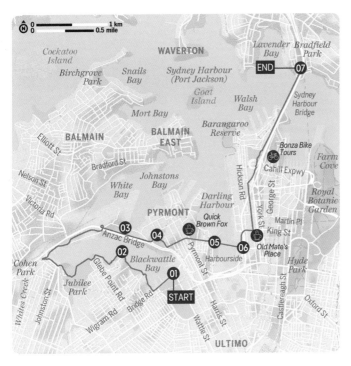

Sydney Harbour Bridge

The Sydney Harbour Bridge is one of the best-known sights in Australia, and it's not hard to see why. Marking the very centre of the city, the steel through arch bridge is a thing of beauty, its soaring web of 58 truss panels held together by six million individually hand-driven rivets. At 134m from its top to the water, it's the tallest steel arch bridge in the world. At the bridge's official opening ceremony in 1932, the Premier of NSW – Jack Lang – was famously upstaged by local man Francis de Groot, who rode in on horseback and cut the ribbon before Lang could do so!

Elevation (m)

02 The path continues west along the foreshore past enormous Moreton Bay fig trees with their sprawling systems of buttress roots. These trees date back to the 19th century, the genteel heyday of Sydney's leafy Glebe neighbourhood. Ahead, other relics from these days await across the heritage-listed Allan Truss Bridge and, just beyond, past the lovely 28-arch redbrick span of the Jubilee Park viaduct, dating from 1892–1922. The path follows the foreshore around the bay past industrial sprawl, then climbs onto the Anzac Bridge.

03 The Anzac Bridge, completed in 1996, is the longest cable-stayed bridge in Australia, and one of the longest in the world. As you pedal across it, you'll get great views of the city and glimpses of the Harbour Bridge (as well as the enormous decommissioned White Bay Power Station precinct; a popular location for film production, it was used as a set for *The Matrix Reloaded*).

04 The bridge ends with a fun swooping descent down a long spiral ramp –

check your brakes! Here the route enters the lovely neighbourhood of Pyrmont. Once a site of sandstone quarries during Sydney's early history, today the Pyrmont peninsula is a leafy oasis dotted with an excellent selection of restaurants and cafes. The cycleway passes through Union Sq, surrounded by several fine colonial-era sandstone buildings harking back to the quarry days, then runs downhill along leafy streets past the gigantic Star casino. At the bottom of the hill, the broad pedestrian zone of Darling Harbour opens, looking like a fairground.

05 Originally a working commercial port, today Darling Harbour has been reinvented as a tourist and nightlife precinct, complete with a Ferris wheel and IMAX theatre. More interesting is the Australian National Maritime Museum, which houses the nation's largest collection of maritime exhibitions. Kids will love climbing aboard the collection of historical floating vessels, which is one of the most extensive in the world. Slowly proceed across the pedestrianised Pyrmont Bridge, which can get crowded at peak times. As you cycle across the heritage-listed swing bridge, take in the views to the north, where Sydney's tallest building, the Crown Tower, rises in a twisting spire of blue glass above the harbour.

06 At the end of the bridge, follow the cycleway as it curves left alongside the highway. Here the route enters the forest of skyscrapers of Sydney's central business district (CBD). The cycleway turns onto Kent St through a canyon of office blocks, which – depending whether it's during a workday or not – can either be buzzing with suits or else eerily quiet. Regardless, it's a good spot to appreciate the variety of the city's architecture of stately sandstone edifices alternating with glass towers. At the top of the hill, follow the signs towards the Harbour Bridge, past the landmark of Observatory Hill and then up the cycleway onto the Sydney Harbour Bridge.

07 The views thus far may have been great, but nothing compares to those from the Harbour Bridge itself. Known as 'the Coathanger', it's one of the key symbols of Sydney, and of Australia itself. To the east lies the iconic Sydney Opera House and to the west the endless labyrinthine sweep of Sydney's inner harbour. Take your time and savour the 1.5km crossing, and when you've reached the far end, roll your bike down the steps and into Bradfield Park below for an underside view of the colossus you've just crossed.

☕ Take a Break

Is OLD MATE'S PLACE Sydney's best insider cocktail bar? Hidden in the heart of the Sydney CBD, both the bar's dark, speakeasy interior and its tiny rooftop are an incredible place for a drink. Staff are great and the ever-changing selection of cocktails is reliably top-notch.

QUICK BROWN FOX in Pyrmont goes some distance to explaining why Sydneysiders are collectively obsessed with brunch. The coffees are amazing, the alfresco setting perfect for a sunny day, and dishes like the truffle mushroom toastie are endlessly yum-inspiring.

RONALD SUMNERS/SHUTTERSTOCK ©

Sydney Harbour Bridge

Observatory Hill

With its commanding outlook over the Harbour, Observatory Hill was the original site of Fort Phillip, the first defensive fortification for the newly founded penal colony of New South Wales, built in 1803. By the 1850s the fort had been partially dismantled, the Hill becoming a signalling station, meteorological station and, in 1859, the site of Australia's first astronomical observatory – giving it the name we use today. Located just to the southwest of the present-day Harbour Bridge, the old observatory and signal station are now a museum, and the park surrounding them remains one of the finest places in Sydney to perch yourself for a BYO sunset drink.

02

Manly Dam MTB

DURATION	DIFFICULTY	DISTANCE	START/END
1½–2½hr	Difficult	11km (main circuit)	King St, Manly Vale

TERRAIN	A mix of firetrail and technical singletrack, with plenty of rocks, roots and steep climbs and descents. A few quiet on-road sections

ROGERSGLASSES/SHUTTERSTOCK ©

Manly Dam

The circuit around Manly Dam is the city's best mountain bike (MTB) adventure. You'll want to have some trail experience before coming here: there are enough roots, rocks, drops and other technical features to challenge expert riders, but also lots of milder terrain for intermediate skill levels. Individual segments of the ride each have their own character – from the lovely singletrack of the Trig Trail to the grinding forested climb of Heartbreak Hill. Bring a GPS, take it slow and remember: you can always walk the tricky sections!

Bike Hire

At a minimum, you'll need fat, knobby tyres, and ideally some suspension for the rocky bits. Manly Bikes (near Manly Wharf) rents out full-suspension MTBs for $72 for two hours.

Starting Point

A car is the easiest way to get to the trailhead near Manly Vale Public School. Using public transport, the ride is about 6.5km from Manly Wharf on quiet back streets.

01 Turn left off King St onto Gibbs St and follow it two blocks past Manly Vale Public School, past the wooden bollards and onto the Manly Dam trailhead. The trail bends right and then left, and you'll get your first taste of what's ahead with a section of bone-shaking roots and a short, sharp climb.

02 The early part of the route has several suburban interludes – the first of these takes you clockwise on quiet streets along the border of the reserve. If you want to warm up before

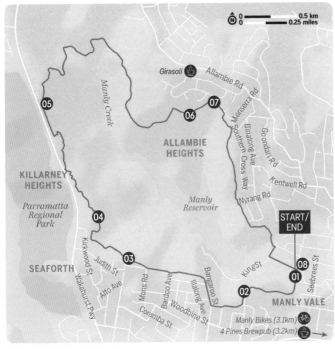

Manly

Sydney's Northern Beaches – the so-called 'insular peninsula' stretching from the harbour north to the Hawkesbury River – are not renowned for their accessibility. The happy exception to this rule is the beachside suburb of Manly, situated between the harbour and the ocean a 30-minute ferry ride from Circular Quay. Improbably named by the first Governor of NSW after the 'manly' bearing of its original inhabitants (they speared him), it became a popular seaside resort in the 19th century. Today, the tradition continues, with surfers flocking to Manly Beach, snorkellers to Shelly Beach, and beautiful people to its many bars and restaurants.

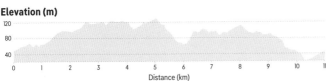

hitting gnarlier terrain further on, you can test yourself on the dirt track winding behind the houses, which is peppered with small jumps and kickers built by local kids. Catch a tiny bit of air as you plough ahead, then dip right onto the bush track through the trees.

03 Limber up your arms as the singletrack climbs over chunky terrain through the trees, getting used to lifting the front end of your bike over obstacles and maintaining momentum as you do so. Up ahead the track crosses a car park

and heads onto a gravel path. Be sure to follow the singletrack uphill to the left when it appears – if you go straight ahead, you will end up on the golf course, and you won't be the first! You've now officially cleared the intro to the route, and are coming to the serious riding, so get ready.

04 This is the beginning of the Trig Track, a 1.5km-long section of lovely twisty singletrack with some great views. The trail gets muddy when it rains, and mixes chunky rock-garden descents

with technical sandstone climbs, which can be slippery when wet. Be sure to keep your weight back on the descents, and don't hook your handlebars on the trees! The track ends up joining a firetrail near Wakehurst Pkwy.

05 Turn right onto the firetrail and begin a fun, fast and rocky descent all the way down to the creek – splash! If it's been wet, this section will feature big sections of sticky clay mud. Shortly after the creek, you'll start climbing, and soon you'll hit the circuit's toughest climb. This is the aptly named 'Heartbreak Hill', a short but brutal slog up a grade that regularly tops 15%. If you can make it without walking, you're a hero! Continue to climb as the trail winds around through the forest and up into a section of more open scrub.

06 At the top of the climb, turn right onto the short section of descent known as the '19th Hole'. With some big rock rollovers to negotiate, this is one of the more technical sections of the entire trail – signs are posted to indicate the difficulty of different lines. Exercise caution and be sure to look before you leap! At the bottom, you'll pop out behind some houses once again. Turn right and follow a short section of path alongside Cootamundra Dr, then turn right onto the East Trail.

07 If the climbs along the rest of the trail have worn you out, consider the East Trail – which runs along the eastern edge of the reserve beside some suburban sprawl – your reward. This final 1.5km of the circuit is a fast, flowy single-track descent with plenty of fun features and obstacles, including small drops, rock ledges and rollovers. Have fun, but watch out for walkers.

08 At the bottom of the trail, you'll pop out onto a short paved path beside some industrial-looking buildings. The path almost immediately joins King St, only a few hundred metres from where you started the ride, but take a short detour down the track to the left before you go. Here, you'll find the lovely secluded waterfall of Mermaid Pool – a quiet spot to relax for a few minutes after your romp around the dam.

☕ Take a Break

If you need a break before tackling the final descent of the East Trail, try CAFÉ GIRASOLI, a short detour off the track in Allambie Heights. It features breakfast favourites like toasties and acai bowls, but the real star here is the coffee, with a cracking house blend and a great selection of single-origins. Once you've smashed the circuit, head back to Manly and the 4 PINES BREWPUB – the perfect place to wrap a paw around a cold one and recount your exploits on the trail.

Mermaid Pool

Mermaid Pool

A natural oasis in the heart of the suburbs, Mermaid Pool is a conservation triumph with a surprisingly rich backstory. The spot got its current name during the Great Depression, when local girls would supposedly skinny-dip in the cool, creek-fed waters. As Sydney's sprawl expanded, however, the site gradually became what so many natural places do in the face of relentless growth: a dumping ground. After being filled for decades with rubbish, junk and discarded shopping trolleys, in 2002 the community mobilised, pulling 4 tonnes of rubbish from the pool in a single day, and kickstarting its remarkable rehabilitation.

03

Parramatta Valley Cycleway

DURATION	DIFFICULTY	DISTANCE	START/END
1–1½hr	Easy	14km (18km with Newington Armory detour)	Kissing Point, Ryde/ Parramatta Station
TERRAIN		Flat, well-paved cycle path; a few quiet back streets and sections of boardwalk	

Newington Armory

The beauty and history of the Parramatta River are often overlooked by visitors to Sydney. This vast tidal estuary forms the western half of Sydney Harbour and connects Australia's first two European settlements. Once given over to heavy industry, today its shores have been rehabbed into lovely green parkland that's ideal for cycling. An easy spin along the Parramatta Valley Cycleway, which winds through endangered coastal saltmarsh and past the odd industrial relic, is the perfect way to appreciate what the area has to offer.

Bike Hire

Bonza Bike Tours in Sydney rents out bicycles complete with locks, helmets and emergency repairs kit for $15 per hour, or $30 for four hours. Book ahead online.

Starting Point

Kissing Point Wharf on the Parramatta River, 45 minutes by ferry from Sydney's Circular Quay. The ride is also accessible from Meadowbank train station, a 10-minute cycle away from the start.

 01 After a short ferry journey upriver, hop off at Kissing Point Wharf. In 1798, Australia's first brewer, James Squire, operated a pub here called 'The Malting Shovel', though today it's just quiet parkland. Across the river stands the stately heritage-listed Rivendell hospital, which was used as a set for Baz Luhrmann's 2013 film *The Great Gatsby*. Turn left and head northwest alongside the bank of the river.

 02 The track continues on a shared cycleway following the river, occasionally joining for short sections with quiet back streets. After

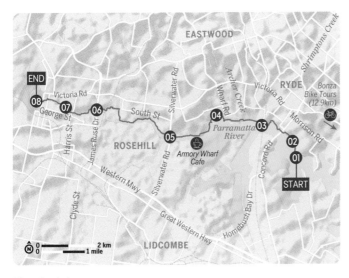

Elevation (m)

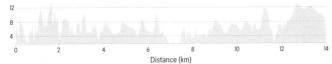

Distance (km)

approximately 2.5km, the cycle-way passes under the historical landmark John Whitton rail bridge. Dating to 1886, the beautifully rusted lattice truss bridge has been decommissioned and today carries only foot traffic.

03 Continue west along the foreshore on a mixture of shared paths and quiet back streets; as you do, you'll begin to pass stands of mangroves. After several hundred more metres you'll hit the elevated steel boardwalk of the Ermington Bay Nature Trail, which curves through the river's coastal saltmarsh ecosystem. Stop off at the bike racks along the way and take the short side walkway through the mangroves leading out to a viewpoint over the river and tidal flats. It's a great place

to spot birdlife, with white-faced herons, eastern great egrets and Sydney's world-famous 'bin chicken' (the white ibis) in frequent attendance.

04 The cycleway now winds past a long stretch of athletic fields, then closely follows the river foreshore alongside the buildings of the suburb of Ermington. Lying roughly halfway along the route, this is a good spot to stop for a coffee or pick-me-up snack. A short distance ahead, the Silverwater Bridge leads to a potential 2km detour to the heritage-listed Newington Armory, a parklands and former munitions depot for the Royal Australian Navy that's popular with families. There's also a waterfront cafe. To reach the Armory, cross the bridge and

Colony of Parramatta

When the British 'First Fleet' landed at Sydney Cove in January of 1788 with more than 1000 convicts in tow, they soon realised they had a problem: feeding themselves. Soils around the harbour were poor, and not viable to feed a colony of the size just founded. With the settlement facing a food crisis, Governor Arthur Phillip sent ships up the Parramatta River to its furthest navigable point, founding a farm at Parramatta in November 1788 and ensuring the survival of the fledgling colony in the process.

Today Parramatta is the metropolitan heart of western Sydney, boasting a fantastically diverse mix of cultures.

backtrack east for 10 minutes along the paved cycle path.

05 From the Silverwater Bridge, continue west on the north side of the river. The track winds along the foreshore through lush parkland, with frequent good views of the river to the left. After 1km, the track passes Rydalmere Wharf. From here, the route passes along the rear of an industrial park past many warehouses, then turns right along Subiaco Creek, jogging through a series of well-signposted turns back west along the riverside. You'll ride beside the campus of the University of Western Sydney, passing a historic cottage at the edge of the grounds.

06 The river continues to narrow as you draw nearer to the city of Parramatta. Continue west through the lovely Baludarri Wetland nature preserve, passing beneath the old lattice girder Gasworks Bridge, which was completed in 1885 and carries two large gas pipelines. A short distance ahead, you'll pass onto the lovely curving Parramatta River Escarpment Boardwalk, with great views of the tall buildings of the city of Parramatta. Just past the boardwalk, you'll see the small waterfall of the Charles St Weir – the borderline between the freshwater river upstream and the estuarial river below. Across the river lies Parramatta Wharf, the last stop for river ferries to and from Sydney.

07 From here, the cycleway follows the Parramatta River Walk upstream through the heart of Parramatta; signage about the area's Aboriginal history and culture is scattered along the way. A tunnel passes beneath the sandstone-arch Lennox Bridge; completed in 1839 using convict labour, it's one of the longest-surviving artefacts of the early colonial settlement of Parramatta.

08 The route continues on for another 600m, passing CommBank Stadium on the right, then enters the lovely green expanse of Parramatta Park. Spreading for 85 hectares around the horseshoe bend of the Parramatta River, the park contains a host of cool historical sites from the early days of colonial settlement, including the UNESCO-listed Old Government House. When you're ready, head into Parramatta to explore the restaurant scene, or catch a train or ferry back to the city.

☕ Take a Break

Located on the south bank of the river, the NEWINGTON ARMORY and its accompanying ARMORY WHARF CAFE make a good midway detour. Service at the waterfront cafe can be hit and miss, but the coffees are good and the location can't be beat. Kids will love exploring among the old military-industrial buildings, cranes and machinery, and the history of the place – where explosive shells, torpedoes and rockets were once stored – is fascinating. The nearby playground at Blaxland Riverside Park is worth a visit while you're here.

Cycling path along the Parramatta River

Coastal Saltmarsh

Much of the riverside cycleway passes through the endangered ecological community known as coastal saltmarsh. Normally found behind stands of mangrove forest in estuarine areas like the Parramatta River, the ecosystem is home to communities of rare salt-tolerant plants like samphire and Austral seablite, which are regularly flooded and exposed by the tides. The marsh serves as a home or food source for a wide variety of animals, including fish and crabs, numerous waterbirds, and kangaroos and swamp wallabies. After long being destroyed for waterfront development, coastal saltmarsh in the Sydney area is now protected, and is bouncing back.

04

Hanging Rock Firetrail

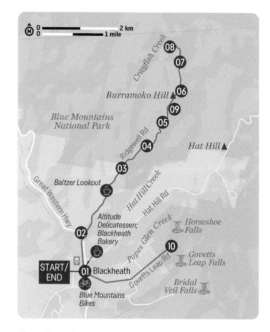

DURATION	DIFFICULTY	DISTANCE	START/END
2hr	Intermediate	14km	Blackheath Station

TERRAIN	Dirt road and rough firetrail; a short section of highway riding

Elevation (m)

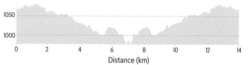

The ride out to Hanging Rock, overlooking the magnificent Grose Valley, is a beginner-friendly introduction to what's so special about the Blue Mountains. Quickly leaving the pavement behind, the route follows a dirt road to the Burramoko Ridge Trail, which runs through the gum forests of Blue Mountains National Park. After a few kilometres of rough firetrail riding (with some short, sharp descents and climbs), the trail ends at a lookout with views over the Grose Valley. Hike down the cliffs for a close-up view of Hanging Rock.

Bike Hire

Blue Mountains Bikes runs a mobile bike rental service starting at $88 per day. Bikes are booked online and picked up at the train station or trailhead.

Starting Point

Blackheath Railway Station on the Blue Mountains Line is the best starting point. It's approximately 15 minutes from Katoomba, or 2¼ hours from Sydney's Central Station. Bikes are allowed on the trains.

01 From Blackheath Station, head north along the Great Western Hwy for approximately 650m to the turnoff to Ridgewell Rd. The Great Western is the main highway across the Blue Mountains and can be very busy, so exercise caution, keep left and utilise the shoulder where you can. If you need food, water, coffee or a toilet before your ride, the shops and cafes of Blackheath Village are just south of the station. Ride approximately 250m south and turn left onto the main drag of Govetts Leap Rd.

Hanging Rock

The Blue Mountains aren't actually true mountains at all, but instead a high sandstone plateau that's been eroded into dramatic cliffs, canyons and valleys over millions of years of geologic time. The escarpments of the plateau have eroded into a wide variety of distinctive rock formations, and none is lovelier or more dramatic than the Hanging Rock. This thin, overhanging sliver of sandstone is separated from the bulk of cliffs around it by a gap that's just under a metre wide, but hundreds of metres deep. It might be the best photo opportunity in the Blue Mountains, but isn't for the faint of heart.

02 Turn right off the Great Western Hwy onto the well-graded dirt of Ridgewell Road, and follow it approximately 2.5km northeast. It runs through forest past a series of turnoffs on the left and right, following signs towards the Burramoko Ridge Trail.

03 Approximately 3km into the ride, you'll reach a small parking area, and the locked gate that marks the entrance to Blue Mountains National Park. Weave past the gate, and onto the firetrail beyond.

04 You'll encounter no more vehicles from this point, but the trail gets its fair share of walkers and mountain bikers, especially on weekends. Always be on the lookout, and use your bell when necessary to warn others as you approach. The firetrail that leads out to the end of the ridge is often rough and rocky, so be wary of pinch flats. The track loses elevation gradually, with some short sharp dips and climbs along the way.

05 As you ride, the trail passes through both heathland and gum forest, with gaps in the trees offering glimpses of undulating valleys and ridges stretching into the far distance to the north and south. The area is scattered with numerous grass trees, and distinctive tall red waratahs – the state flower and emblem of NSW – can be spotted in bloom throughout spring.

06 Approximately 4.5km into the ride, you'll hit a moderate climb followed by a descent that marks the approach to the end of the trail. At the trail's end, approximately 6km in, the ridge narrows, the firetrail terminates in a wide dirt turnaround. Ditch your bike here and grab your camera.

07 It's just a short walk from here to the unfenced bluff at Baltzer Lookout, and the views – some of the finest in all of Blue Mountains National Park – do not disappoint. Sheer red sandstone cliffs fall off precipitously into the enormous canyon of the Grose Valley, which none other than Charles Darwin described as 'stupendous' when he visited in 1836. At the valley's bottom, hundreds of metres below, lies the Grose River. Over millions of years it has carved out the grand vista before you, stretching as far as the eye can see from southeast to northwest.

08 If you're feeling adventurous, carefully scramble 250m down the steep footpath for a view of Hanging Rock below. The distinctive rock formation is a soaring, knife-edge point of sandstone that's partly separated from the rest of the cliffs. It's possible to walk 100m further down and onto Hanging Rock itself, though the rock is exposed and can be very dangerous, especially on windy days.

Take a Break

BALTZER'S LOOKOUT is unquestionably the pick of picnic spots – grab something in Blackheath before you go to nosh on while you take in the view. The MRT (mushroom, rocket and tomato) sandwich on Turkish bread from ALTITUDE DELICATESSEN is a great choice, as is the brown rice vegetarian pasty from BLACKHEATH BAKERY. If you're visiting on the weekend and looking for an altogether more luxe experience, the HYDRO MAJESTIC HOTEL one stop down the line at Medlow Bath does an outstanding high tea – book ahead.

Baltzer Lookout

09 When you're ready, climb back up the cliffs and head back to where you left your bike. The ride back retraces your steps up the firetrail, but regaining the roughly 100 vertical metres of altitude you've lost. The hills that had you whooping with delight on the way down will now have you sweating and panting on the way up. Steep and rocky as they are, don't be surprised if you have to walk a few of them!

Grose Wilderness

The Greater Blue Mountains are a UNESCO World Heritage Site in recognition of their outstanding natural value and heritage. Of the Blue Mountains, only a small percentage is classified as true 'wilderness' – the largest, most pristine areas of the natural environment. One of these is the Grose Wilderness, through which a part of the Burramoko Trail passes, and over which Baltzer Lookout gazes. The 37,000 hectares of the wilderness were one of the early sites of the NSW environmental movement, which in 1932 successfully lobbied to have the Blue Gum Forest at its heart declared a permanent reserve.

10 Back out on the Great Western Hwy, head back 1km south back to Blackheath Village for a celebratory coffee, meal or beer. If you're not done with blockbuster views, cycle 3km down the road to the lookout at Govetts Leap, one of the Blue Mountains' most celebrated viewpoints.

05

FOOD & DRINK

Shores of Newcastle

DURATION	DIFFICULTY	DISTANCE	START/END
1½–2½hr	Intermediate	12km	Newcastle Interchange/ Merewether Beach

TERRAIN	Flat, well-paved bike path with moderate climbs and on-road sections

MATTHEW CROMPTON/LONELY PLANET ©

View of Newcastle

Newcastle isn't Sydney, and lots of locals like it that way. The two cities share more than you might imagine – both, after all, are built around a lovely working harbour and world-class beaches, and both are full of superb spots to eat and drink. But where Sydney can be hectic and impersonal, Newy is friendly and relaxed. The city has done a wonderful job of making its endlessly photogenic foreshore cycle-friendly and you can easily turn this short ride into a full day with stop-offs to nosh, swim and explore.

Bike Hire

Metro Cycle in Newcastle rents out bikes starting at $30 for the day. Reserve online ahead of time.

Starting Point

Newcastle Interchange is the endpoint for regular train services from Sydney (about 2¾ hours). Bikes are allowed on the train, though be aware that it can get crowded at weekends.

01 From Newcastle Interchange, exit the station and turn left onto Hannell St, then immediately turn right onto Honeysuckle Dr. A short distance ahead, turn left onto the path through the parking lot, then right onto the shared cycleway that runs alongside the Hunter River. Across the water you'll see industrial cranes and huge ships moored at the port of Newcastle. The inland Hunter region has enormous coal deposits, and Newcastle is the one of the largest coal-exporting ports in the world. A short distance ahead on your right you'll find the excellent Newcastle Museum, which is pop-

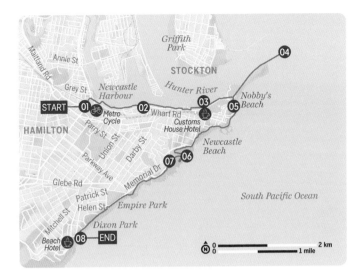

Elevation (m)

Distance (km)

ular with families and features exhibits on science and local history.

02 The path continues along the harbour as it widens, passing a variety of restaurants and watering holes. A short distance ahead you'll pass Queens Wharf, from which regular ferries run across the harbour to the town of Stockton. The clock tower of Customs House rises to your right as you continue along the foreshore towards Nobby's Head at the mouth of the harbour.

03 Passing the open green space of Foreshore Park on your right, turn left onto the peninsula running out towards the lighthouse on the hill. To your right you'll see

bathers and surfers on Nobby's Beach – the city's safest and most sheltered beach. Past some dunes, a short, steep climb leads up to Nobby's Lighthouse, which is open to the public on Saturday and Sunday only, and has great views out over the sea and breakwater to the north.

04 Dating to 1858, Nobby's is still a working lighthouse, broadcasting a beacon that's visible more than 20 nautical miles away. From the turnoff to the top off the hill, a flat path to the left leads approximately 1km out to the end of the wind-whipped Newcastle breakwater. To the north, the long sweep of Stockton Beach and its sand dunes stretches endlessly into the distance.

The Hunter Valley

Newcastle is the major city and main port for the region locals simply call 'the Hunter'. Named for the Hunter River at whose mouth the city lies, it was home to the Wonnarua people for tens of thousands of years before the British stumbled upon it (predictably, while searching for escaped convicts). Today, the region is chiefly known for three things: its massive coal deposits, its equine culture (most of the country's best racehorses are bred here) and its wine. Famous for its Sémillon, viticulture here dates to the early 19th century, and it's been drawing dipsomaniacal visitors from Sydney ever since.

05 Head back down to the road and follow Shortland Esplanade as it bends south around the hill of Fort Scratchley and past the newly restored Newcastle Ocean Baths. Shortland Esplanade passes the Surf Lifesaving Club at Newcastle Beach, then joins the famous Bathers Way running south along the shore. At the base of the cliffs 1km ahead lies the rock pool known as the Bogey Hole – an adventurous spot to swim among the crashing waves, provided the surf isn't too high.

06 From the Bogey Hole, backtrack a short distance and climb the road into King Edward Park past its glorious rose garden. Follow York Rd as it curves through the park, gradually climbing to Shepherds Hill. The one-time military artillery battery has some interesting ruins to explore and great views out over the coast.

07 From Shepherds Hill, there are two possible paths to follow: you can join Memorial Dr as it curves down the hill behind the cliffs, or else dismount and walk your bike (riding not allowed) along the Memorial Walk atop the cliffs themselves. The clifftop boardwalk is dedicated to the Anzac soldiers who lost their lives in WWI, and offers glorious panoramic views of Bar Beach to the south. Be warned that you'll have to carry your bike down a long-ish flight of stairs at the end if you choose this route.

08 Both routes join up again approximately 600m further on, where the Yuelarbah Track runs beside Memorial Dr as it descends for 2km past Bar Beach, Dixon Park Beach and finally Merewether Beach. The path is often chockers with pedestrians, so go slow and use your bell. Any spot along this stretch of sand makes a great stop-off to chill and soak in the vibes, but remember to only swim between the flags. If you'd prefer a more sheltered swimming experience, the lovely Merewether Ocean Baths mark the terminus of the route.

☕ Take a Break

With its lovely architecture and location just a stone's throw from the harbour, it's hard not to like the CUSTOMS HOUSE HOTEL. Built in 1877, the building's iconic clock tower is a Newcastle landmark, and its lively beer garden makes an ideal stop-off. At the other end of the ride, the BEACH HOTEL stands a block back from Merewether Beach, with great views of the waves. The pub grub is reliably good and the enormous seafood platter is perfect to share at the conclusion of a ride.

BELINDA MORDUE/SHUTTERSTOCK ©

Bogey Hole

The Bogey Hole

One of the great lessons of Australia's early colonial period is that the British were positively mad for free labour. Famous for building impractical things in impractical places, the one-time penal colony's long dalliance with convict labour nevertheless managed to produce some hits, including Newcastle's beloved cliffside pool, the Bogey Hole. Also known as the Commandant's Baths, this rock pool at the foot of Shepherds Hill was hewn out of the cliff in 1819 at the behest of Newcastle Commandant James Morriset, a renowned disciplinarian and apparent lover of alfresco bathing. Under public ownership since 1863, today it's the city's wildest spot for a swim.

06

South Coast Cycleway

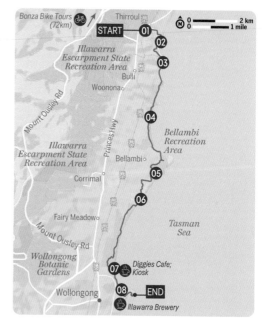

DURATION	DIFFICULTY	DISTANCE	START/END
1–1½hr	Easy	16km	Thirroul Station/ Flagstaff Point Lighthouse

TERRAIN	
	Flat, well-paved cycle path; a short smooth section of dirt track

Elevation (m)

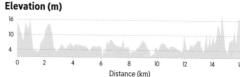

Every section of the NSW coast has its own particular flavour. The near south coast, which stretches down to the port city of Wollongong, is the epitome of chill. A lazy ride down the south coast cycleway, which meanders past beaches, bushland, ocean baths and lagoons, is an ideal introduction with plenty of opportunities to take photographs, swim or stop for a cheeky drink. The route ends at the beautiful and historic Wollongong foreshore and harbour, where it's well worth giving yourself time to explore.

Bike Hire

Bonza Bike Tours in Sydney rents out bicycles complete with locks, helmets and emergency repairs kit for $15 per hour or $30 for four hours. Book ahead online.

Starting Point

Thirroul Station on the South Coast train line is about one hour from Sydney. It's also possible to do the route in reverse starting at Wollongong Station.

01 You can already smell the sea and feel the salt air of the south coast when you hop off the train at Thirroul Station. As you wheel your bike off the platform and onto Station St, though, you'll catch a whiff of something else: the vibe. Peaceful, quiet and – above all – chilled out. Head east towards the beach and you'll start to see signs for the coast cycleway, which you can follow from here on out.

02 About 1km from the station, you'll pass onto the separated cycleway itself as it hugs the coast along McCauley's Beach and

Track through Puckey's Estate Reserve (p48)

The Illawarra

The region that the cycleway transits – bounded by the Tasman Sea to the east and the looming mountain escarpment to the west – is known as the Illawarra. Inhabited by the Dharawal people for millennia, the Illawarra is a grassy coastal plain that is at its narrowest in the northern section that the cycleway passes through, ensuring a dramatic backdrop of wooded peaks and cliffs. It's well known for the brilliant Illawarra flame tree, whose blaze-red blossoms are at their peak over the summer season. Wollongong is the heart of the region and a centre of heavy industry, supported by the deepwater harbour at Port Kembla.

then Sandon Point Beach. Both are pretty, uncrowded stretches of sand with generally gentle surf. The coast around Sandon Point is a significant Aboriginal heritage site, including a burial site more than 6000 years old. Signage along this stretch of the route gives information about the history, culture and significance of the place.

03 The route continues south on winding, mellow track, occasionally bridging small lagoons. A short way down the coast you'll pass the Bulli Rockpool, the first of the route's many ocean baths. These baths are a Sydney institution, and a great place to stop for a sheltered dip on a hot day. There's a cafe nearby if you need a pick-me-up.

04 The track winds onward through parkland past Bulli and Woonona beaches and then past Bellambi Beach, where there's another excellent rock pool. About 7km into the ride the path suddenly detours near a set of athletics fields – jog quickly right onto the road and then immediately left onto the path, following the signs painted on the pavement. Here, the track bends inland behind the large tree-fringed lagoon of Bellambi Lake, where you might spot waterbirds like the striated mangrove heron.

05 The path winds alongside a suburban street, past a caravan park and across another large bridge spanning a lagoon, then joins the beach once again. Cruise past the Towradgi ocean pool and Towradgi Beach, then dip inland beside housing developments and a small creek. About 12km in you'll hit the parking lot for Fairy Meadow Beach. It's possible to continue on the cycleway here as it bends right following Elliots Rd, but a more rewarding route heads up the dirt path into the trees directly off the corner of the parking lot.

06 Follow the wide dirt track through the trees for 1.3km as it tunnels through the lovely swamp oak floodplain forest of Puckey's Estate Reserve, with the lagoon wetlands intermittently visible just to your right. The track ends at a T-junction, where you turn right, following a pretty section of elevated boardwalk beside the water of Fairy Creek. Here, the track rejoins the road; turn left and cross the bridge, then bend left on the cycle path as it enters Stuart Park.

07 At the edge of the park the cycleway crosses the street and leads onto the seaside promenade at North Wollongong Beach. This stretch of pathway heading into Wollongong is buzzing, and is a great place to stop off for a beachside coffee or some fish and chips. The shared promenade follows the route of the old Mount Pleasant Coal Mine tramway; signage along the way gives its history. A few hundred

🍵 Take a Break

There are good spots for a drink or quick nosh spread all along the route, but the greatest concentration of them is undoubtedly clustered in and around Wollongong itself. Cliché as it might be, it's tough to beat fish and chips on the beach, and both DIGGIES CAFÉ and the KIOSK at North Wollongong Beach do a roaring trade in that seaside staple. If your post-ride interests extend more to libations, the ILLAWARRA BREWERY a few hundred metres south of Flagstaff Point has a great selection of beers on tap.

ALF MANCIAGLI/SHUTTERSTOCK ©

Wollongong Harbour Lighthouse

metres ahead lies the superb rock pool of the Gentlemen's Baths, where the scandalous activity of men swimming was once hidden from the fairer sex as Victorian propriety demanded.

08 Continue along the path as it skirts the small harbour behind the breakwall, following the relevant signage. Pass by the restaurants and bars clustered along the

The Blue Mile

The Blue Mile, which stretches from the beach at North Wollongong south to Flagstaff Point, is rightly a source of local pride. More than a decade of work has gone into developing the foreshore promenade, and the resulting mix of scenery, dining, leisure and historical interest is hard to argue with. Ocean baths like the Lighthouse Rockpool are about as gorgeous a spot for swimming as you'll find on the NSW coast, and colonial relics like the Old Courthouse and the coastal defence batteries of Smith's Hill Fort are deservedly popular with kids.

shore, and head up towards the lighthouse atop the hill at Flagstaff Point. There are various points of interest here, including a Vietnam War Memorial, old coastal gun battery emplacement and, of course, the lighthouse itself, which was built in 1936 and is still in use today. From here, you can explore Wollongong or just head up to the train station for the trip back to Sydney.

Best for

MOUNTAIN
ROUTES

Thredbo Valley Track

DURATION	DIFFICULTY	DISTANCE	START/END
2½–3hr	Difficult	19.2km	Thredbo Village Centre/ Lake Crackenback Resort

TERRAIN	Dirt trail, rocky, tree roots. Suitable for mountain bikes

Thredbo Valley Track suspension bridge

The Thredbo Valley Track has fast become one of the premier summer activities in the NSW Snowy Mountains. The cycling route takes users from Thredbo, tracking the Thredbo River as it winds its way down the valley. The trail, open from October to May, provides visitors with a great opportunity to explore the unique landscape in this alpine region. Riders can choose to ride the track in either direction, however, a shuttle service operates regularly throughout the day, making it easier to enjoy a mainly downhill ride from Thredbo.

Bike Hire

A wide variety of mountain bikes are available for rental from Thredbo Retail and Rental. Rentals start from $55 for a half-day rental; e-mountain bikes are also available.

Starting Point

The trailhead is located at Friday Flat, Thredbo Resort. Alternatively, multiple shuttle buses operate daily from Jindabyne and Lake Crackenback, including some that can be reserved by private customers.

01 Setting off from Mowamba Pl at the centre of Thredbo Village, head downhill from the supermarket and then turn right at the T-junction. Go straight through the roundabout before joining the trailhead located 100m on your left. Once on the trail, begin cycling in a northerly direction towards Lake Crackenback. This initial section of the trail runs parallel to the car park for the first few hundred metres, before being diverted off to the grassy woodland. It doesn't take too long at all to leave the resort behind and be fully immersed in the beauty of the Snowy Mountains.

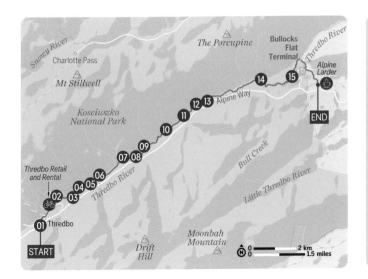

TOP TIP:

Morning Run

The Thredbo Valley Track is an extremely popular outdoor activity in the Snowy Mountains. To enjoy a clearer run down the trail, set off on your bike early in the morning. You will feel you have most of the trail to yourself.

Elevation (m)

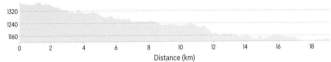

Local Wildlife

Cycling along the Thredbo Valley Track is a fully immersive outdoor experience. As you make your way down the trail, be sure to keep an eye out for some of the local animals that call this alpine landscape home. It is not uncommon to come across kangaroos, echidnas, blue-tongue lizards, and occasionally even emus trailside. When you are enjoying a stop by the Thredbo River you may also spot some rainbow or brown trout swimming in the clear water. If you are really lucky you may even spot a platypus.

02 At the 1.6km mark you will see signage for the Bridle Trail Loop, a short and technical trail. The Thredbo Valley Track is clearly signposted, so if in doubt, follow the direction of the track marked in green. Alternatively, if you are an experienced mountain biker, you can choose to ride the Bridle singletrack which rejoins the main Thredbo Valley Track further down.

03 After a mainly downhill start to the trail you will reach the first of five suspension bridges at the 2.3km mark. The bridges provide a great vantage spot to view the river below and they act as a natural viewing platform on the trail. If you feel like a longer rest, then take advantage of the historic

chairlift seat which is located at the far end of the bridge.

04 Cross the bridge and the trail continues to wind its way gently downhill. While there are some rocks and tree roots in places, all in all, the track provides a ride that always feels flowing. It is worth remembering that the Thredbo Valley Track is rideable in both directions and you will see hikers as well as other cyclists enjoying the trail. Signage along the trail will remind you to be vigilant of people coming in the other direction and cyclists must always give way to hikers on the track.

05 At the 3.3km mark you will reach the second bridge, which is very

☕ Take a Break

One of the highlights of cycling the Thredbo Valley Track is there is no shortage of fantastic spots for you to stop and enjoy a longer break. Before leaving for your ride, make sure to pack some lunch so you can enjoy a picnic while you relax by the Thredbo River and take in the alpine surroundings. For an added experience, do as the locals do and pack your bathers so you can take a dip in the cooling waters of the river itself.

closely followed by the third bridge. Indeed, these two bridges are only separated by a short 200m. As with the first bridge, the large steel structures make traversing the Thredbo River feel so easy. They also act as a reminder that you are never tracking too far away from this beautiful river.

06 From the third bridge the trail continues to flow in a downhill direction. At the 4km mark, you will ride over a raised platform to take you over Bullock Yard Creek. This small creek feeds into the larger Thredbo River and, compared to the three larger bridges you have crossed already, this one will feel more low-key. While the track here is predominantly downhill, you will encounter a couple of short sharp pinches to pedal up and over. These aren't technical parts of the trail but they do require some extra effort, so be aware of this.

07 Keep pedalling downhill through tall snow gums in the thick woodland. The infrastructure on the trail continues to impress and there are large sections of raised platforms to cycle over which have been incorporated into the track. At the 5.7km mark, you will encounter a section containing two banked berms where the track turns in on itself. Take care here,

before continuing to descend downhill.

08 This next section of the trail once again opens out as you leave the thicker woods behind. The Thredbo River is right next to the trail and on a warm day will be appealing. As you cycle over a long, raised platform, large power lines stretch overhead. There's a short uphill section here once more, before a descent to the rangers station. If necessary, you can access the Alpine Way road from this point to leave the trail.

09 At 6.8km you will approach the fourth bridge on the trail. This bridge is a totally different shape to the three before, rising up sharply in an arch. Be sure to select an easier gear to cycle up onto the bridge. The vantage point at the top of the bridge is quite spectacular and worthy of a pause before cycling back onto the track.

10 This part of the Thredbo Valley Track closely follows the river initially, before once again heading slightly inland. Here you will be right in the midst of the trees. The track continues to flow in a downhill direction, with only some brief uphill sections for you to negotiate. Be mindful of tree roots and rocks as you make your way.

FILEDIMAGE/SHUTTERSTOCK ©

Trails at Lake Crackenback (p55)

For Advanced Riders

This write-up of the Thredbo Valley Track only incorporates the section from Thredbo to Lake Crackenback. The upper section of the Thredbo Valley Track is more suited to the occasional rider and is extremely popular with riders of all ages as well as young families. If you are a confident rider with a more advanced skill level then you can continue on from Lake Crackenback, cycling all the way to the Thredbo River picnic area. This will extend your ride to a total distance of 37km. Shuttle services are available at all points along the track.

11 At the 9.5km mark you will reach the fifth and final bridge on this ride. As you take the right turn to cross the bridge, again make sure to select a low gear. The bridge is the same shape as the one before it, and rises up steeply to traverse the river, before dropping back down the other side just as quickly. Shortly after, you will cycle over two larger raised platforms to cross over Number One Creek. On crossing the second platform you will reach the Ngarigo camping ground.

12 Coming at 10.2km into the ride, the Ngarigo camping ground is a good place to take a longer pit stop. On a hot day, it is always pleasant to roll up next to the river and put your feet in the cooling water. There is a toilet block here, as well as tables and chairs where you can stop to enjoy a picnic lunch. In the summer months, this camping ground is quite popular and it is very common to find the area filled with campers and tents. Be aware: there is no fresh water located at the camp site so you will not be able to top up water bottles here.

13 Follow the trailhead signs to leave the camping ground and continue riding towards the Thredbo Diggings. It is worth noting this next 3.5km section of the trail does become slightly more technical.

While the trail is predominantly downhill, there are a number of short, steep climbs to negotiate along the way. This section is still achievable for beginners, but it is prudent to be cautious. At the 11.5km mark, you will encounter a set of six downhill berms to negotiate. These are some of the more challenging trail features you will encounter on this ride.

14 Having arrived at the Thredbo Diggings camping ground, you again have the choice of taking a longer stop. The camping ground is well situated right on the banks of the Thredbo River, and you can also make use of the toilets, picnic spots and barbecues. However, be aware there is no access to fresh water here. On leaving the camping ground you have the choice of sticking to the easier Thredbo Valley Track or taking the Muzzlewood MTB trail, which is graded as intermediate. Both trails will again connect at Bullocks Flat.

15 At 17.7km you will reach the intersection to Bullocks Hut. The hut itself was built in 1935 and was primarily used for fishing by its owner, Dr Bullock. From here, it's just a short 600m before reaching your final destination of Lake Crackenback Resort. Once at the resort, you have the choice of taking the main resort roads or cycling along the MTB trails

☕ Take a Break

The ALPINE LARDER cafe is located at Lake Crackenback Resort and is a very popular place to grab a bite to eat at the end of your ride. Open from brunch to late in the evening, you can choose to refuel with smaller snacks both sweet and savoury – you'll find something for everyone on the menu. If you are after a heartier meal, be sure to try their wood-fired pizzas or burgers.

Thredbo Valley Track

08

Lake Burley Griffin

DURATION	DIFFICULTY	DISTANCE	START/END
2½hr	Intermediate	21.5km	Regatta Point

TERRAIN	Fully sealed asphalt path, shared with walkers. Suitable for all types of bikes

Lake Burley Griffin and the Captain Cook Memorial Jet (p61)

Lake Burley Griffin is one of Canberra's major attractions and is centrally located in the heart of the city. The human-made lake was constructed in 1963 and is an extremely popular spot for locals and visitors alike who are seeking to enjoy the best of the Canberra outdoors. The shared path is fully sealed and loops around the circumference of the lake. It is 100% separated from motorised traffic, making it a safe option for families and enthusiasts to explore during a bike ride.

Bike Hire

The Canberra and Region Visitor Information Centre offers bicycles for hire with prices starting at $20 for 2 hours. The centre is located at Regatta Point on the Lake Burley Griffin waterfront.

Starting Point

This circuit is accessible from multiple starting points. Buses 2, 4 and 7 regularly stop on Commonwealth Ave, just a two-minute walk from the lake path at Regatta Point.

01 Starting directly below the Canberra and Region Visitor Information Centre at Regatta Point, begin cycling in an easterly direction towards the Kings Ave Bridge. Keep straight on the path to cross over a small red bridge. Alternatively, you can take the left turn to explore Commonwealth Park before rejoining the main lake path.

02 A statue of Sir Robert Menzies on your right indicates you are in the area known as the Menzies Walk. From here you can spot the flags of 110 Nations flying proudly on the other side of

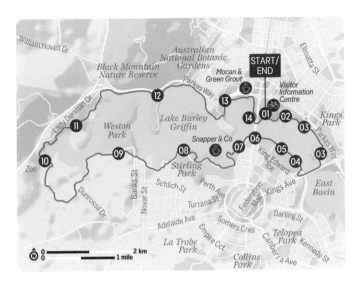

TOP TIP:

Cycle Early

For a quintessential Canberra experience, cycle around Lake Burley Griffin early in the morning. Not only will the path be quieter, but you'll also spot rowers and kayakers gliding across the water, and if you're lucky a hot-air balloon floating overhead.

Elevation (m)

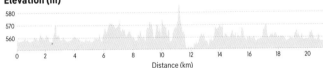

the lake, as well as both New and Old Parliament House, further off in the distance. There's another landmark ahead as you continue on the path across the red asphalt section. On rejoining the wider concrete path you will see Blundell's Cottage, a remnant of the city's farming heritage from 1860.

03 Turn left at the National Carillion and cycle onto the ramp leading to Kings Avenue Bridge, then cross the bridge, taking care to stick left and give way to pedestrians on the congested path. Once you've come down the wide ramp off the bridge, take a left turn and continue cycling west. Many of Canberra's popular attractions are located nearby, including the National Gallery, National Library, Old Parliament House and National Portrait Gallery.

04 Directly off the path to your left is the Sculpture Garden, which is home to 26 large sculptures belonging to the National Gallery of Australia. You may notice the *Angel of the North* sculpture by Antony Gormley, which is a life-size replica of the same sculpture located in Gateshead in the north of England.

05 Two cafes operate along the central lakefront, right next to a wooden jetty. This isn't just a good place to stop for some refreshments; it also provides a panoramic view of the central basin, the city and beyond. From the wooden jetty,

you can also look across the water to spot the Australian War Memorial. It's also a popular spot to stop for a few minutes and watch some of Canberra's black swans glide across the water. From here, take the central path which leads through the trees and continues towards the Commonwealth Ave Bridge.

06 Once you come to the Commonwealth Ave Bridge, you have reached the beginning of the 16km section of the lake known as the Western Basin. Take the path which leads directly under the bridge and continues along the lakefront. This first section of the lake weaves in behind Lennox Gardens, taking you through two parks. The first is the Japanese Gardens that

☕ Take a Break

The NEWACTON cultural precinct is conveniently located close to the Lake Burley Griffin shared pathway. This makes it a perfect place to refuel. You'll often spot bicycles parked outside the MOCAN & GREEN GROUT cafe, a popular pitstop for cyclists. The owners pride themselves on using the best products and seasonal ingredients. With an all-day breakfast menu their bacon and egg rolls are extremely popular, but if you want something different try the baked eggs instead.

were established as part of the Canberra Nara Peace Park. Across the water, you will also have a perfect view of the National Museum. As the path continues, the Nara Peace Park gives way to the Beijing Gardens. To your left you will see concrete sculptures and a traditional Chinese gate, designed in the Chinese imperial style of the Qing dynasty.

07 Take a right turn when you reach the T-junction to remain on the shared pathway and continue cycling clockwise around the lake. After 100m, you will reach a road crossing and the section of the lake where the Southern Cross Yacht Club is based. Keep an eye out for traffic as you cross, then enjoy the brief and gentle climb as the cycle path bears around to the right. From here you have a magnificent view over Black Mountain and the Telstra Tower, which, standing at a height of 195m, is Canberra's most prominent landmark. A short downhill section follows before you reach the road crossing at Alexandrina Dr.

08 Cycle straight across the road, following the cycle path as it winds its way through Stirling Park. At the end of the pathway, you will need to cycle straight across Brown St. At the next T-intersection, continue

straight to cross Weston Park Rd and remain on the lake path. Alternatively, you have the option of taking a right turn here to reach the cycle path, which incorporates a tour around Weston Park itself. Taking this side route will add 3.6km to your ride before linking back with the main cycle route around the lake.

09 Follow the path as it meanders through the Westbourne Woods, a plantation of trees dating back to 1913. Leaving the woods behind, you will cross over a wooden bridge. To its left you can see the Royal Canberra Golf Club and over to the right you will have sweeping views looking across to the National Arboretum. Once across the bridge, the path heads uphill and leads you across Dunrossil Dr where you will see the entrance to the Governor General's House. On the other side of the road, there is a water station where you can refill bottles if needed. A short incline and descent follow before you pass through two tunnels and cycle across the Lady Denman Dr Bridge.

10 A brief climb ensues here as you pedal through open grassland. Stop briefly at the top of the climb to take advantage of the bench seat and views across the lake.

PHILLIP MINNIS/SHUTTERSTOCK ©

National Carillion

Basin & Bell

The Central Basin is the area of Lake Burley Griffin located between the Kings Ave and Commonwealth Ave bridges. This 5km stretch is also the most popular part of the shared pathway and it is a hive of activity. Several Canberra landmarks, art galleries and museums are also located within easy walking distance. These include the National Carillion, the large bell tower that is situated on Queen Elizabeth II Island, adjacent to the Kings Ave Bridge. There are 57 bells housed in the tower and you can hear them being played every Wednesday and Sunday from 12.30pm to 1.20pm.

Weston Park

Located on the southern side of the Western Basin, Weston Park is a popular spot to enjoy the great outdoors. Its tranquil location makes it an ideal place for a leisurely barbecue or picnic. There are several outdoor playgrounds to keep smaller children amused, as well as a 27-basket disc golf course. In recent years an extension was added to the Lake Burley Griffin cycle path, which now includes a 4.2km circuit that allows you to cycle around the entire perimeter of the park. This is a great way to explore the sights of the park and also find your own perfect picnic spot.

Black Mountain view from Lake Burley Griffin

From here, you can look across at the route you cycled just a short while earlier before enjoying the short descent through an old cork forest plantation. As you emerge from the cork forest the path opens up. There is a fork in the track which leads to the National Rock Garden, a collection of large rocks from all over Australia. Information signs detail the type and origin of each rock on display.

11 Remain on the path heading eastwards and enjoy the open lake views to your right. As you reach the base of Black Mountain Peninsula you have the option to either continue straight on the lake path or take a right turn and explore the peninsula with a brief 2km detour. This track weaves right around the peninsula before joining back up with the main path. The stretch here is a very popular spot on the lake where you can take a swim or enjoy a picnic. If you do take the diversion, be sure to stop at the lookout and take advantage of the impressive views across the lake towards the central basin.

12 A pleasant downhill now follows, leading you towards the section of the lake approaching the Australian National University. You can choose between continuing to cycle straight ahead or following the path to the right. The latter will take you on a short excursion around the Acton Peninsula before rejoining the main path. It's only a brief diversion, but cycling in this direction also means you skip a short and sharp climb.

13 Leaving the Acton Peninsula behind, you will notice the city centre fast approaching on your left. The shared pathway curves around to the right leading you through Henry Rolland Park. This section of the lake precinct was created from reclaimed land and the area directly in front of the lake has benefited from the redevelopment.

14 Continue cycling on the path leading you underneath Commonwealth Ave Bridge. If you are cycling between 11am and 2pm, you'll see the Captain Cook Memorial Jet in full action before arriving back at your starting point.

☕ Take a Break

SNAPPER & CO is a real local favourite where you can enjoy some of the best fish and chips Canberra has to offer. Located on the grounds of the Southern Cross Yacht Club in Yarralumla, getting there from the lake path couldn't be easier.

On a sunny day, there is no better place to enjoy a relaxed lunch or dinner while soaking up the waterfront views.If fish and chips don't take your fancy then you may be interested in some of their charcuterie and cheese boards.

09

National Arboretum

DURATION	DIFFICULTY	DISTANCE	START/END
1½hr	Intermediate	11.5km	Trailhead left of the main gates at the entrance to the National Arboretum
TERRAIN	Dirt trails suitable for a mountain bike		

Dairy Farmers Hill

Located on the slopes of Black Mountain, the National Arboretum in Canberra is fast becoming one of the top attractions in the nation's capital. Spread across 101 hectares, there are 94 different forests that contain rare and endangered tree species from around the world. The arboretum also benefits from a prime location, making it perfect for a picturesque view of Lake Burley Griffin, the Molonglo Valley and the Brindabella Ranges. A mountain bike is the perfect mode of transport to explore the series of trails.

Bike Hire

Cycle Canberra offers a range of bicycles for hire with prices starting at $40 for a half-day (four-hour) rental, including delivery to Canberra hotels and Lake Burley Griffin.

Starting Point

If arriving by car, take Lady Denman Dr and utilise the free parking at the National Rock Garden. From there, follow the marked cycle path, which is signposted to the National Arboretum just 500m away.

01 Enter the arboretum via the cycle paths from the main gate and follow the signage for the Explorer Track. This is marked in pink as Track 6 on the signage posts. Head straight across Forest Drive to enter the dirt singletrack.

02 After 650m you will once again cross Forest Dr. Continue on the Explorer Track by taking the dirt path to the left of the car park and begin to cycle through the beech forest. This lower section of trails is gentle and flowing On reaching the intersection at Deeks Dr, you will notice a dirt

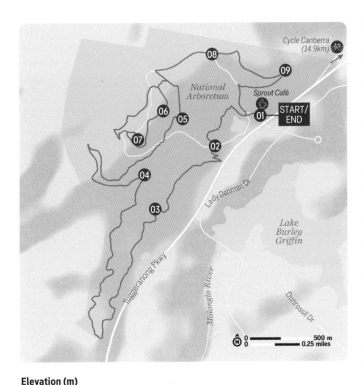

Bird's-eye View

When you arrive at the top of Dairy Farmers Hill, be sure to take some time to divert to the lookout and take in the magnificent views from the summit. This vantage point gives you a great sense of perspective, not only of all the different forestry plantations you've cycled through but also of Canberra itself. The Telstra Tower is ever present, as are Lake Burley Griffin and many other landmarks, such as Parliament House and Red Hill. The steel handrail has been engraved with the outlines of 94 leaves – signifying each of the forestry plantations currently growing at the National Arboretum.

Elevation (m)

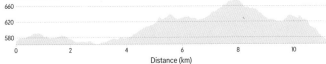

fire road. Head left towards it and then re-enter the single trail to remain on the Explorer Track.

03 The track takes you up to a large art installation designed to represent a bird in flight on a windy day. From here, you will continue to roll gently downhill along the Explorer Track. The distinct shape of the bottle tree is quite striking as you make your way from one plantation to the next on the lower slopes of the arboretum.

04 At the 4.6km mark you will reach a fork in the track. Take a left turn here to utilise the link road which will guide you onto the Mountain View Track. This is marked as Track 4 and indicated in green on the map signage. As the name suggests, you will now be climbing for the next kilometre. The gradients get up to 5%, but are never too steep for a sustained period of time. You will once again reach a fork in the track, this time following the trail marked out on the right, leading you uphill and through a pine forest.

05 Once through the shady forest, you'll ride out onto a clearing, where you can enjoy magnificent views towards Lake Burley Griffin. The trail flattens out here and you'll now follow the signage to the Village Centre. Head left, taking the road towards the car park, before once again joining the singletrack on the left. You will now be on the Dairy Farmers Hill Track, which is signposted as Track 5 and indicated in red on the official signage.

06 This track once again rises gently uphill, but your efforts will be all worthwhile as you continue to be afforded spectacular views. In 900m you will be at the summit of Dairy Farmers Hill, where you will be treated to a stunning 360-degree vista. It really is evident why Canberra is known as the Bush Capital, a city surrounded by mountain peaks and rolling, country landscapes.

07 Cycle straight across Forest Dr to rejoin the Dairy Farmers Hill Track as it begins winding downhill. From this side of the National Arboretum, the views are equally spectacular looking out towards the Molonglo Valley. After descending for 1km you will once again arrive at the Village Centre. You can choose to take a break here and enjoy a refreshment at the Sprout Cafe. Otherwise, turn right onto Forest Dr and continue downhill for 500m before turning left onto Himalayan Cedar Rd.

08 Continue on Himalayan Cedar Rd for 200m before taking a right turn onto the Himalayan Cedar Track. This is signposted as Track 2 on the official signage and indicated by the colour lime green. The great thing about riding in the arboretum is that at various points you get to see the trails from a different perspective. As you begin cycling uphill through the Californian fan palm plantation, you can look over your right shoulder and see the landscape you've been riding through.

09 As you enter the Himalayan cedar forest that the trail takes its name from, you will take a sharp turn to your right before beginning the final downhill descent back to Forest Rd. Once here, take a left turn, and after a few hundred metres you will arrive back at your starting point.

☕ Take a break

SPROUT CAFE is located within the visitor centre at the National Arboretum. The cafe has an extensive menu with a variety of options catering for all dietary requirements, whether you're in the mood for a warm meal or a refreshing salad. It is also a great spot to enjoy a mid-ride coffee and cake, while looking out at arguably the best views in Canberra. Those travelling with younger children can also take advantage of the Pod Playground, which is conveniently located next to the cafe.

BELLA MOLLOY/LONELY PLANET ©

Nest III **by Richard Moffatt**

Art in the Arboretum

There are six large-scale sculptures and art installations located within the grounds of the National Arboretum. These have been created by renowned artists from Australia and around the world. The sculpture *Wide Brown Land* by Marcus Tatton spans 35m in length and stands 3m tall. It dominates a prominent position on the eastern edge of the arboretum and was inspired by Dorothea Mackellar's poem 'My Country'.

Another prominent sculpture is *Nest III* by Richard Moffatt, which is located next to the main lookout at Dairy Farmers Hill. This depicts a wedge-tail eagle perched on a nest, seemingly surveying the Canberra landscape below.

Also Try...

Narrow Neck plateau

Narrow Neck

DURATION	DIFFICULTY	DISTANCE
3hr	Difficult	31km

The ride out to the end of the Narrow Neck plateau is a much harder slog than the trip out to Hanging Rock, but the payoff is well worth it.

A thin, high, isolated clifftop stretching between the Jameson and Megalong Valleys, Narrow Neck boasts the best views of any ride in the Blue Mountains, with a bit of adrenaline thrown in for good measure. The firetrail is in good condition, but alternates between steep climbs and descents that are tough enough that you're sure to walk some of them. After some stunning vistas, and a few hair-raising downhills, the trail ends at the far edge of the plateau, where chains and ladders bolted into the rock descend to the valley floor.

The Fernleigh Track

DURATION	DIFFICULTY	DISTANCE
1hr	Easy	15km

This converted rail trail on the outskirts of Newcastle has won awards for infrastructure and urban design, and it's not hard to see why.

Running 15km from Adamstown to Belmont, the shared cycle and walking route passes through a lovely mix of shady forest and lush wetland interspersed with rail relics from Newcastle's industrial past. Heritage highlights along the popular, well-paved path include old sleepers and rails, decommissioned railway platforms and a very cool old train tunnel, all accompanied by interpretive signage. Wildlife frequently spotted along the route includes lizards and bush turkeys. If you've got the time, take a short detour from the southern end of the route to the coast at Nine Mile Beach with its expanse of lovely undeveloped dunes.

Centennial Park

The Bay Run

DURATION	DIFFICULTY	DISTANCE
30min–1hr	Easy	7km

This 7km circuit around the Iron Cove in Sydney's inner west is a classic.

Hugging the foreshore through five harbourside suburbs, the mostly flat route is eminently lappable, but it's worth going slow to savour the views, including the Sydney skyline. The separated pathway crosses no roads, winding through long expanses of parkland, past moored sailboats and through lovely neighbourhoods with eye-watering property values. The heritage-listed Iron Cove Bridge, spanning the mouth of the bay, is a highlight, but so are the potential stops for brunch or coffee along the way. The track is popular with runners, walkers and cyclists, and can be chock-a-block on the weekend, so get there early or go during the week.

Centennial Parklands

DURATION	DIFFICULTY	DISTANCE
1hr	Easy	3.5–7km

There's likely no ride in NSW more accessible than the classic ramble around Sydney's sprawling Centennial Parklands.

The main paved road loop around Grand Dr is an easy 3.5km and takes in a lovely swathe of ponds, gardens and bushland, but there are a dozen other paths and tracks to discover, each with unique features. It's worth hopping off the bike from time to time to explore. Less visited, but equally rewarding, is Queens Park just next door, with its high rolling grassy hills, stands of massive trees and views of the Sydney skyline. New cycleway has recently been added around the park's margins, but it's also great fun to leave the path behind and strike out cross-country.

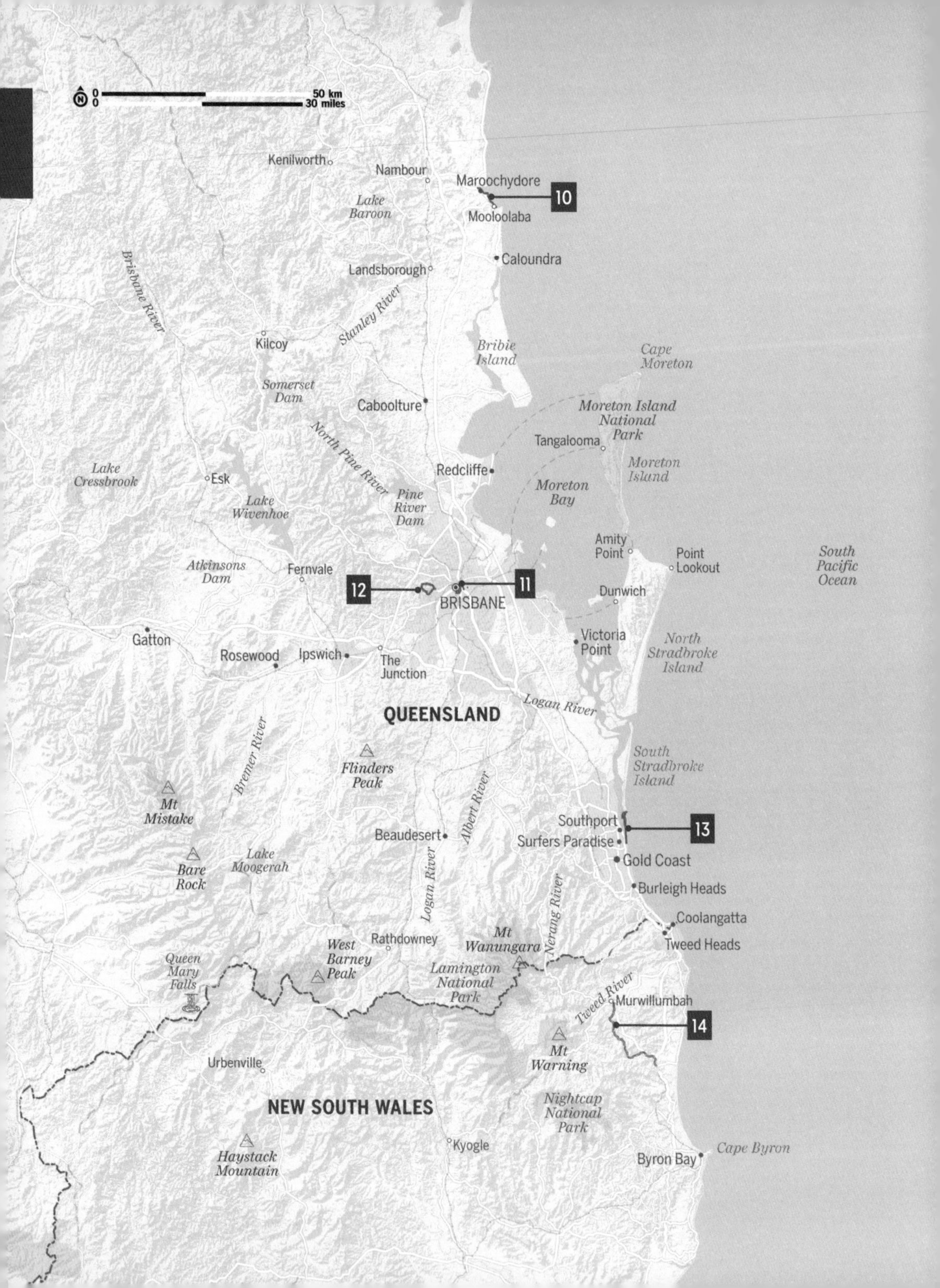

0
0
50 km
30 miles

Kenilworth
Nambour
Maroochydore
Mooloolaba

10

Lake Baroon

Caloundra

Landsborough

Stanley River

Kilcoy

Bribie Island

Cape Moreton

Somerset Dam

Caboolture

Brisbane River

North Pine River

Esk

Lake Cressbrook

Lake Wivenhoe

Pine River Dam

Redcliffe

Tangalooma

Moreton Island National Park

Moreton Island

Moreton Bay

Amity Point

Point Lookout

South Pacific Ocean

Atkinsons Dam

Fernvale

Dunwich

Victoria Point

North Stradbroke Island

12

BRISBANE

11

Gatton

Rosewood

Ipswich

The Junction

QUEENSLAND

Logan River

Bremer River

Flinders Peak

Mt Mistake

Albert River

South Stradbroke Island

Beaudesert

Southport

Surfers Paradise

13

Lake Moogerah

Logan River

Bare Rock

Gold Coast

Burleigh Heads

Coolangatta

Tweed Heads

West Barney Peak

Rathdowney

Mt Wanungara

Nerang River

Queen Mary Falls

Lamington National Park

Tweed River

Murwillumbah

14

Urbenville

Mt Warning

NEW SOUTH WALES

Nightcap National Park

Haystack Mountain

Kyogle

Byron Bay

Cape Byron

POC/SHUTTERSTOCK ©

South Bank Parklands (p77), Brisbane

Byron Bay to Sunshine Coast

Explore

Byron Bay to Sunshine Coast

From the beaches of Byron Bay in the south to the beaches of the Sunshine Coast in the north, this region is all about – you guessed it – beaches. The councils of South East Queensland and the Northern Rivers region of New South Wales are keen to show off their best assets, as evident from the well-developed and maintained oceanside cycleways that can be found here. But don't just stick to the coast; head further inland, and you'll be rewarded with fun inner-city circuits, challenging mountaintop rides and family-friendly hinterland adventures that are rich in Aboriginal and colonial history.

Brisbane

Brisbane is known for its urban sprawl, so to easily reach its cycleways, make sure you're centrally situated along a public transport route. However, that doesn't have to mean booking into a hotel in the central business district. Some areas to consider include the West End (a spot that's consistently and accurately described as 'eclectic'), New Farm (a leafy green suburb near the river) and the Fortitude Valley (renowned for both its shopping and nightlife). All three neighbourhoods are situated beside the water, serviced by the city's ferries and offer quick access to riverside pathways, including the Brisbane River Loop.

Gold Coast

Famed for its endless golden beaches, the Gold Coast, for most, is synonymous with the glittering skyscrapers of Surfers Paradise. This is where you'll find luxurious hotels, busy cafes, bike hire shops and plenty of tourists. But the stretch between Burleigh Head and Broadbeach (including the suburbs of Mermaid Beach and Miami) is where some of the country's top chefs are now setting up shop. Accommodation in this area (mainly beachside motels) also tends to be more affordable, with good cycling paths connecting it to the rest of the region.

The Tweed

At the heart of the Tweed Shire's hinterland is the Murwillumbah, a community that attracts the alternative, artistic and sustainably minded. Though smaller in size, it has everything you need

WHEN TO GO

NSW's Northern Rivers region and South East Queensland are popular year-round destinations for domestic and international visitors. If you're planning to visit during the busy school holidays – including the scorching summer months of December and January – make sure to book accommodation in advance. For beachside bike rides, time your visit for the cooler period, between June and November, when migrating humpback whales can be seen.

to set out on your bike ride, including bike hire shops and plenty of bakeries and delis to stock up on picnic supplies. It's also where you'll find the official start of the Tweed Rail Trail. However, if you're after true hippie heaven, book a rainforest stay in Uki, where the post office doubles as a coffee roastery and the park boasts public pianos. For those who prefer a beachside locale, Kingscliff is where you'll find resort-style accommodation.

Sunshine Coast

The Sunshine Coast stretches for more than 60km along the Queensland coastline, with suburbs ranging from beachside developments to historic towns situated high in the hinterlands. At its northern edges, Noosa is perhaps the Sunshine Coast's most famous spot, but Mooloolaba, Maroochydore and Alexandra Headlands all offer plenty of amenities for tourists, including streets lined with self-contained holiday rentals and restaurants.

TRANSPORT

The region is serviced by four major airports: Ballina Byron Gateway Airport, the Gold Coast Airport, Brisbane International Airport and the Sunshine Coast Airport. There is good public transport all along the coast, including bus and train lines. However, to explore the hinterland areas, you will need to hire a car.

They also are located directly on the Sunshine Coastal Pathway. Head up into the Blackall Ranges, and you'll find the cute mountain villages of Maleny, Montville and Mapleton. Of the three, Maleny offers the most restaurants and accommodation for visitors.

 WHERE TO STAY

Featuring a pool, kitchen, four bedrooms and a curated collection of furniture, Uki's luxurious Chesson Lodge in Tweed is perfectly equipped for groups of friends cycling together.

In a sea of midrange motels, family-owned Blue Heron on the Gold Coast stands out. Affordably priced and minutes from surf and sand, the rooms are clean and bright, and the courtyard features a pool and barbecue.

In the hinterlands of the Sunshine Coast, the boutique Mapleton Springs has three units with kitchenettes and an infinity pool. It's also the home of a wildlife rescue-facility. On a guided tour available to guests, you can feed orphaned wallabies and koalas.

 WHAT'S ON

Blues on Broadbeach

(*bluesonbroadbeach.com;* May) During this Gold Coast music festival, international, national and local artists play the blues.

Lismore Lantern Parade

(*lismorelanternparade.com.au;* June) For just one night, giant glowing effigies are carried through Lismore's streets in northern NSW by costumed revellers.

The Curated Plate

(*thecuratedplate.com.au;* July and August) This 10-day culinary festival celebrates the Sunshine Coast's top producers and chefs, with tastings, farm tours and long-table lunches.

Resources

Bike Queensland (*bq.org.au*) is an advocacy organisation, but its website is a treasure trove for visiting cyclists. Under 'Where to Ride', you'll find trails categorised by skill level and bike type.

Need a soundtrack for adventures in the Tweed? Visit the **Northern Rivers Rail Trail** (*northernriversrailtrail.com.au*) website, which contains everything from track maps and historic information to curated Spotify playlists.

10

Sunshine Coastal Pathway

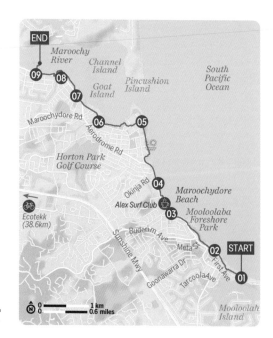

DURATION	DIFFICULTY	DISTANCE	START/END
45min	Easy	7km	Mooloolaba Beach/Chambers Island

TERRAIN	Paved paths with gentle inclines

Elevation (m)

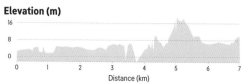

Running alongside the ocean from Mooloolaba Beach to the mouth of Maroochydore River, the Sunshine Coastal Pathway offers up a slice of Sunshine Coast lifestyle in under an hour. Every morning, walkers, runners and cyclists can be found huffing and puffing their way along this coastal track, while surfers catch breaks just out to sea. Ideal for young families and casual cyclists, this route comprises a safe paved path that's best savoured over a couple of hours, with plenty of restaurants, shops, beaches and playgrounds along the way.

Bike Hire

EcoTekk offers e-bike rentals from $39 per half day and will deliver bike rentals to you throughout the Sunshine Coast. Have Fun Tours has cruiser bikes from $30 per day, with delivery available around Mooloolaba.

Starting Point

Although the Translink bus doesn't permit bikes, it will get you to the starting point at Mooloolaba, where you can arrange to have a bike delivered. If driving, there's free two-hour parking at the Beach Tce car park.

 As a point of orientation, this route never strays far from the water. The Sunshine Coast's glistening surf and white-sand beaches should always be on your right. Set out from the Mooloolaba Beach car park and head north on the path beside the beach. This section will likely be quite busy with locals making the most of their enviable coastal lifestyle.

 You'll soon approach a boardwalk that slopes uphill. Cyclists are required to dismount, so you'll need to walk your bike for about 250m

Best for

COASTAL RIDES

Mt Coolum

The volcanic dome of Mt Coolum has presided over the Sunshine Coast for some 25 million years. For those who have extra energy, the 208m climb offers 360-degree views. Situated on the traditional land of the Gubbi Gubbi people, there's an oft-told story about the mountain's formation: Coolum, a warrior, was in love with Maroochy. But Ninderry, a warrior from another tribe, kidnapped her. A fight ensued, and Ninderry beheaded Coolum. Flung out to sea, his head became Mudjimba Island. His body turned to stone and formed Mt Coolum, while Ninderry was immortalised as nearby Mt Ninderry. As for Maroochy? Her tears created the Maroochy River.

to its end. The rest of the trail has gentle undulations, with a nice mix of small inclines and flat areas to coast along.

03 You'll know you've arrived at Alexandra Headland when you see the surf lifesaving club. This is a perfect place for a small breather, as the beach here is great for a swim and will provide ample opportunity to soak up that cruisey Sunshine Coast lifestyle. Leave your bike at the surf club's beachside cafe and grab a coffee to sip while keeping an eye out for humpback whales – you can see them migrating offshore in the cooler months.

04 Once back on your bike, the path departs slightly from the ocean. The water will be obscured from view as you cycle alongside Alexandra Pde. After Parker St, the path curves to the right, where you'll see a lovely park with sculptures carved from Chillagoe white marble. Just past this park, head across Alexandra Pde towards those breathtaking ocean views. You'll see a small beachside car park for Maroochydore Beach. The path resumes through the car park.

05 Up ahe ad, you'll see a holiday park. Hang a left before the entrance, and

you'll pass the busy shops and restaurants of Cotton Tree. In addition to a handful of trendy cafes selling sandwiches, snacks and smoothies – the perfect place to pick up some picnic supplies – you'll find a thriving market here on Sundays. Follow the path as it curves right and back towards the water and into Cotton Tree Park, at the mouth of the tranquil Maroochy River. Take a breather here and stop to admire the conical Mt Coolum and the wave-shaped Mt Ninderry in the distance.

06 At the western edge of Cotton Tree Park, you'll reach a small car bridge at Duporth Ave, which crosses one of the tributaries of the Maroochy River. This denotes the spot where Cotton Tree ends and Maroochydore – the final suburb of your bike ride – begins. Past the bridge, you'll have to join cars on the road, so if you're not a confident cyclist, you may want to use the footpath for the next few blocks.

07 Turn right and follow the signs for Maroochydore. After Gibson St, hang a right at Picnic Point Esplanade. This will take you to a shady and quiet waterfront park, which – as the name implies – is a serene spot for a picnic. You can unpack and enjoy those picnic supplies now!

08 At the end of Picnic Point, continue north by turning left under the Ken Neil Bridge. Follow the path over the bridge, then left to head back down to the water. The water will still be on your right, but it's no longer the ocean – now, you're officially riding alongside the Maroochy River.

☕ Take a Break

Surf clubs are serious institutions on the Sunshine Coast. They provide vital lifesaving services to swimmers, and they're also the social heart of the community, often boasting restaurants, bars and cafes. ALEXANDRA HEADLAND SURF LIFESAVING CLUB (fondly known as the 'Alex Surf Club') is no exception. With beachfront views and a location right next to the cycleway, their Beach Kiosk is open every day from 6.30am to 2pm, serving smoothies, coffee, fish and chips, and breakfast wraps. It also has a great menu for kids.

Alexandra Headland

09 Look for the narrow pedestrian bridge stretching over the river on your right. Follow it across the water to Chambers Island – one of the area's best-kept secrets. There's a good chance you'll have the 16-hectare park all to yourself. Here, you'll find shaded picnic tables, barbecues, public

Whale Watching

The Sunshine Coast is a major migratory route for humpback whales. Every year, tens of thousands of whales travel from their feeding grounds in Antarctica to the warmer waters of the Coral Sea to breed and birth their young. If you bike along the Sunshine Coastal Pathway between the months of June and November, keep your eyes on the horizon – you may be lucky enough to spot their telltale blow. Alexandra Headland is considered one of the best places in the area to spot them from afar, while several operators in the region offer guided boat tours.

restrooms and a playground. The river is better suited to fishing than swimming, however, thanks to the bull sharks that frequent the area. To finish the route, return the same way you came, this time always ensuring the water is on your left.

11

Brisbane Mini River Loop

DURATION	DIFFICULTY	DISTANCE	START/END
1hr	Easy	10.5km	Kangaroo Point Cliffs
TERRAIN	Paved paths and cycleways with gentle inclines		

JESSICA WYNNE LOCKHART/LONELY PLANET ©

Cycling track, Brisbane

Everyone has their own version of the Brisbane River Loop. On most days of the week, you'll find the Lycra-clad pedalling furiously from South Bank to Indooroopilly and back again. But for those not interested in elevation gain, complex navigation or battling with traffic, this abbreviated version sticks to relatively flat paths and showcases the best of Brissie. Following the Brisbane River, you'll cycle beside the Kangaroo Point Cliffs, through the South Bank Parklands, Queen's Wharf Precinct and the Howard Smith Wharves.

Bike Hire

Situated at the base of the Kangaroo Point Cliffs, directly beside the cycleway, Riverlife Adventure Centre offers half-day (from $25) and full-day (from $39) bike hire.

Starting Point

Kangaroo Point Cliffs can be reached by the free CityHopper ferry, which runs every 30 minutes. From the ferry terminal, it's a 15-minute walk to the Riverlife Adventure Centre to pick up your bike rental.

01 First things first: this bike ride follows the Brisbane River for its entirety, which means it's difficult to get lost – just keep the river on your right at all times. Set off from Kangaroo Point Cliffs and head down the cycleway, taking in the sheer pink-hued cliff faces on your left. Formed of volcanic rock, they were chipped away in the early 1800s by convicts quarrying stone for the Moreton Bay Penal Settlement. Today, they're a popular spot for rock climbers and abseilers, who you may spot hanging above as you pedal along. This is also a

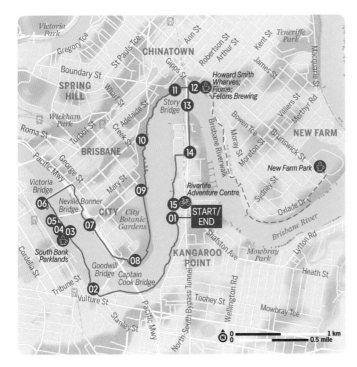

Elevation (m)

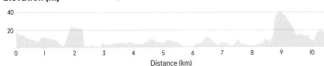

Distance (km)

(or 'Streets Beach') on your left. This public pool is a good vantage point from which to look across the water and admire the new Queen's Wharf Precinct. It's also where you'll find the South Bank ferry terminal, one of the stops for the Brisbane CityHopper – a free transport service that travels to nearly every site included on this route. So if you decide at the last minute that a boat ride is more your speed, you can get back to Kangaroo Point Cliffs or travel onwards to Howard Smith Wharves with minimal effort.

04 You might be surprised to encounter a traditional Nepalese pagoda on your left. Intricately carved, this three-storey attraction pays homage to South Bank's history as the home of the World Expo '88. Following the event, the site was entirely cleared, save for three heritage buildings and the boardwalk. The government planned to sell the site to commercial developers, but the public lobbied that it be transformed into parkland for all. As for the pagoda? It took more than 160 families two years to hand-carve it, and it was brought to Brisbane by the Kingdom of Nepal for the World Expo. Its lower level is still open to visitors, where you can admire the expert craftsmanship from within.

05 Pass under the Neville Bridge and you'll see the Wheel of Brisbane on your left. While the 60m-tall Ferris wheel now feels like a fixture of the Brisbane skyline, it's actually a relatively new addition. It was built in 2008 as part of the State of Queensland's sesquicentennial. Continue onwards until you see

good place to look for eastern water dragons – small lizards resembling iguanas – who have healthy populations throughout Brisbane's parklands.

02 After about 1.5km, the path will depart slightly from the river, and you'll see the Queensland Maritime Museum on your right. Cross Stanley St at the pedestrian crossing, and you'll now have the South Brisbane Memorial Park on your left. The arbour, covered in vibrant purple bougainvillea, is beautiful but diminutive in comparison with the

much-photographed one you'll see next, which is made of 443 steel tendrils and announces your arrival at the South Bank Parklands. The path through this arbour is narrow, so it's best to either dismount to go through it or continue riding on the path alongside it.

03 You have your choice of paths through South Bank, as they all run parallel to the river, but the widest one is directly next to the water. This is also where you'll find restaurants, cafes and bars with waterfront views, and the South Bank Lagoon

☕ Take a Break

With 17 hectares of parkland to explore, the SOUTH BANK PARKLANDS is the ideal spot to rest your legs – whether it's to grab a cocktail at one of the waterside restaurants, take a spin on the Wheel of Brisbane or lounge in the grass beside the river. It's also where you can take a dip in Australia's only inner-city artificial beach, STREETS BEACH (more commonly known as the South Bank Lagoon), which is a free public pool surrounded by white sand and subtropical plants.

Victoria Bridge ahead, but don't go under it. Instead, just before the bridge, turn left up the ramp and follow it around and away from the water. Get your camera ready: at the top is where you'll find the large-scale 'Brisbane' sign, silhouetted against the city's backdrop.

06 It's time for your first river crossing. Follow Stanley St as it curves around to the right, past the Queensland Performing Arts Centre and onto Victoria Bridge. You have two options here: take the painted bike lanes, which share the road with cars, or cycle with care across the shared-used path.

07 Now you are in Brisbane's CBD. Directly after the bridge, you'll need to travel down to water level again via the Bicentennial Bikeway. Due to construction at the time of writing, this was done via the elevator, but in the future, you can go down via a ramp. Once riverside, you'll be cycling beneath the Pacific Motorway for a portion, which is less than ideal – but it's only about 1.3km until you reach the lush green calm of the botanic gardens.

08 Brisbane's expansive City Botanic Gardens are not to be confused with their counterpart at Mt Coot-tha (p82). These are Brisbane's original bo-

tanic gardens, established in 1828 to provide food for the Moreton Bay Penal Settlement. It's also where many of the state's now-famous crops were first trialled, including mangoes, pineapples, sugarcane and ginger. You'll know you've arrived when you see majestic giant fig trees at the gates. To enter the gardens, take the path to your right, which winds behind Riverstage, the outdoor entertainment venue. From here, the path will run north beside the water.

09 Before you pass the Carron Canyon, an 11kg cannon that was cast in iron in 1803 in Scotland, hang a right at the bridge. If you look directly across the river here, you'll see Kangaroo Point Cliffs, where you began and will end your journey.

10 Exiting the gardens, the path turns onto Eagle St Pier. This will be the narrowest section of your journey, with the added obstacle of dodging office workers on their breaks. The restaurants of Eagle St Pier and Riparian Plaza – including local favourite Madame Wu – can be found to your left. Take it slow through this section, and yield to pedestrians.

11 After roughly 1.5km, you'll arrive at Howard Smith Wharves, below

JESSICA WYNNE LOCKHART/LONELY PLANET ©

Brisbane CBD from Kangaroo Point Cliffs

Queen's Wharf

The multi-billion-dollar Queen's Wharf Precinct – which houses a casino, four hotels, and 50 restaurants, bars and cafes – transformed the Brisbane skyline when it opened in 2023. But while its buildings are shiny and new, the site itself is steeped in history. Home to Aboriginal people for thousands of years, it's also the site of the first wharf built on the Brisbane River in 1827, where boats carrying convicts and their overseers first docked. Throughout the 19th century, it remained pivotal to the city, when it served as an entry point for immigrants. Today, about 11 heritage buildings remain, all of which have been preserved by the new development.

Side Trip to New Farm Park

If you've finished the Brisbane River Loop and want to explore further, extend your ride with a 3km trip to New Farm Park, known for its rose garden and as the home of the Brisbane Powerhouse, a cultural and performing arts centre. To get there from Howard Smith Wharves, cycle along the River Walk path, keeping the river to your right. Just past Merthyr Park, the separated path ends, but the route to New Farm Park is well-signed. Head past the bowls clubs and turn right on Oxlade Dr. After about two blocks, the quiet residential street will deliver you to your destination.

Story Bridge. First built in the 1930s, the area fell into disuse and disrepair until 2018, when Felons Brewing opened here, turning it into one of the city's coolest precincts. It's packed at night-time and on weekends, but during weekdays, it's easy for cyclists to roll up and savour a cold beer and well-deserved lunch on one of the riverside beanbags.

12 From this point, you can extend your journey with a side trip to New Farm Park. Otherwise, if you're ready to wrap up your ride, look for a lift on your left, just past the Crystalbrook Hotel and across from Felons Brewing. Hop on and take it to the top of the clifftops. Don't worry about turning your bike around inside the elevator – the doors will open on the opposite side.

13 Exit the elevator and turn left, following the signs for the Eastern Walkway. Don't worry about the name, as bikes are permitted! This path uses the Story Bridge to cross the river and is separate to traffic. Zoom across the bridge and revel at the views below.

14 At the end of the Eastern Walkway, you'll see an underground pedestrian crossing on your right. You'll need

TOP TIP:
Flat Tyre?

If there's not quite enough air in your tyres, keep an eye out for the community bike station just past the Neville Bonner Bridge on South Bank. Here, you'll find a bike pump and Allen keys for quick tune-ups on the go.

to use this to get to the western side of the motorway. There are a couple of small sets of steps, so you'll have to dismount. Fortunately, you won't have to lift your bike, as you can wheel it down the ramps adjacent to the steps.

15 Exiting the pedestrian tunnel, continue straight towards the water. You'll hit a set of steps, from which you can see the river below. Look for a ramp on your right and follow it down, where you can turn left back onto the cycleway. As always, keep the river to your right until you're back at Kangaroo Point Cliffs.

☕ Take a Break

Set under Story Bridge, the heritage-listed HOWARD SMITH WHARVES is one of Brisbane's buzziest precincts. This is where you'll find lots of restaurants, with the massive FELONS BREWING topping the list. Here, enjoy a craft beer and a wood-fired pizza while sitting at a barstool overlooking the river. For something more upscale, FIUME – located on the Crystalbrook Vincent rooftop – has an infinity pool and daybeds, and offers sharing dishes heavy on local seafood, including Moreton Bay bugs (a type of crustacean), oysters and cuttlefish.

New Farm Riverwalk

12

Mt Coot-
tha Loop

DURATION	DIFFICULTY	DISTANCE	START/END
1hr	Difficult	10km	Mt Coot-tha car park

TERRAIN	Steep and winding roads

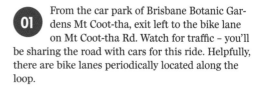

ROB D THE PASTRY CHEF/SHUTTERSTOCK ©

JC Slaughter Falls

Don't be surprised if you're passed by a pro with bulging calf muscles. This scenic loop – which encircles Mt Coot-tha – is the unofficial training ground for the city's competitive cyclists. The challenge isn't the length, but rather the 286m elevation gain. The good news? What goes up must come down. Your reward for slogging uphill is an adrenaline-pumping downhill. That's why we recommend first-timers tackle it counterclockwise. Although you'll have a steep climb up the 'back', the 'front' offers a safer descent – fun guaranteed.

Bike Hire

Located on Elizabeth St, 99 Bikes offers daily road-bike hire, starting from $69. Rentals include a helmet, lock, pump, saddlebag and spare tubes. It's a 30-minute bike ride from here to the trailhead.

Starting Point

The car park for the Brisbane Botanic Gardens Mt Coot-tha (not to be confused with the City Botanic Gardens) is located at Mt Coot-tha's base. You'll have to ride the 7km from 99 Bikes, or take a car there.

01 From the car park of Brisbane Botanic Gardens Mt Coot-tha, exit left to the bike lane on Mt Coot-tha Rd. Watch for traffic – you'll be sharing the road with cars for this ride. Helpfully, there are bike lanes periodically located along the loop.

02 After 500m, Mt Coot-tha Rd turns into Sir Samuel Griffith Dr, named for the early-20th-century Australian judge and politician. Enjoy the reasonably level ride – it won't last long! You'll first pass the picnic area for JC Slaughter Falls

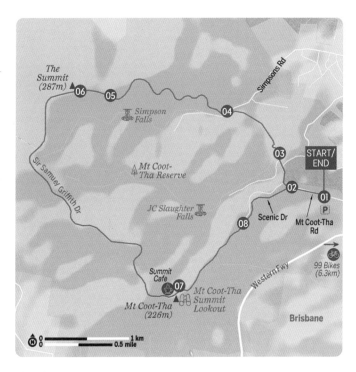

One Tree Hill

Mt Coot-tha is currently a woodland oasis, but in the last 200 years, it's been logged, mined for gold and used as a depot for wartime explosives. In the early 19th century, its summit was cleared of trees, save for one gum tree. European settlers, who frequented the spot for picnics, took to calling it 'One Tree Hill'. That changed in 1883 when it was declared a park and renamed. Its current name is a derivation of *ku-ta* – the word given by the Turrbal people in this area to the honey they traditionally collected from the native stingless honeybees.

Elevation (m)

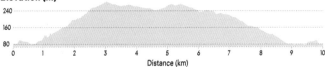

on your left. The falls are only a 600m walk away, but unless there's been rain, don't bother stopping, as they will be dry.

03 In quick succession, you'll pass the Hoop Pine and Silky Oaks picnic areas. The latter is a good spot to use the restrooms and catch your breath, because it's about to get a lot hairier. You're only at about 90m above sea level right now, and you've got to reach the summit at 287m. It's time to start climbing up the 'back'. You'll pass Simpson Falls, but again,

we recommend giving this one a miss, as it's a 5km round-trip hike with an elevation gain of 245m. You'll need all the energy you can muster for the bike ride ahead.

04 The next 2km is the bulk of your climb. Be careful on this section, as the road is steep, curving and narrow. Although it's a scenic drive – and as a result, doesn't attract heavy traffic – there's little room for error. Use the bike lanes when they appear to allow drivers to pass safely.

05 When you see a transmission tower appearing on your right-hand side, feel free to celebrate – you've nearly reached the top! For around 60 years, Mt Coot-tha has been the main broadcasting site for many of Brisbane's television networks and FM radio stations. Stay strong, as it won't be long until you're at the top. For the best view, you'll have to continue along the road to the Mt Coot-tha Lookout, sitting at just 226m.

06 Look out for the 'Crest' road sign. It signals reprieve in the way of a short descent. (The sign is such a popular sight that its location has even been marked on Google Maps.) From here on out, it gets easier, but be forewarned: it's not all downhill. Instead, the road undulates for the next 3.5km until you reach the car park for the Mt Coot-tha Lookout. Ride to the top of the Mt Coot-tha Lookout car park. Here, you'll be rewarded with sweeping views of Brisbane and its suburbs – and the knowledge that the climbing is behind you. A cafe (the only food stop on this route), restrooms and a gift shop are also available at the lookout, as well as some hiking trails, if you've got any energy left!

07 Once you're ready to head downhill, follow the one-way road south of the lookout and turn right at the yield sign, back onto Sir Samuel Griffith Dr. It's a steep 2km descent, but with wider curves and more generous shoulders than you experienced on the way up. If you're uncomfortable going fast (you could potentially clock up to 80km/h), rest assured there are plenty of areas to slow down and pull over.

08 After 1km, you'll see a car park with two picnic shelters on your left. Here, the road splits into Sir Samuel Griffith Dr on the left and Scenic Dr on the right. Most cyclists find that taking the less-trafficked one-way road to the left makes it easier to turn onto Mt Coot-tha Rd. At the bottom of the road, turn right at the stop sign to get to the bike lane, which will deliver you back to the start – almost no pedalling necessary.

☕ **Take a Break**

This ride isn't just about the bragging rights of ascending Mt Coot-tha – it's also about the views. From the Mt Coot-tha Lookout, you can see as far as the Glass House Mountains of the Sunshine Coast to the north, the Gold Coast hinterland to the south, the sand islands of Stradbroke and Moreton to the east and the city of Brisbane sprawling beneath you. For some well-deserved sustenance, the SUMMIT CAFE is open daily, serving breakfast, hot meals, ice cream, coffee and refreshing drinks.

ALEX CHBAL/SHUTTERSTOCK ©

Brisbane Botanic Gardens Mt Coot-tha

Mountain Biking

Brisbane's largest conservation reserve isn't just a popular destination for road cyclists – it's also a mountain biking mecca, with 31km of shared-use tracks and an additional 25km of dedicated mountain bike (MTB) trails. With grades to suit most skill levels, trails range from the family-friendly 2.2km Rocket Frog Trail to the more technical 850m Pipeline Trail, which includes a 180-degree wooden wall-ride berm (a banked corner, in normal parlance), log rollovers and large drop-offs. Most of the trails are located on Mt Coot-tha's western side, with many starting from the Gap Creek Reserve Picnic Area.

13

Surfers Paradise to the Spit

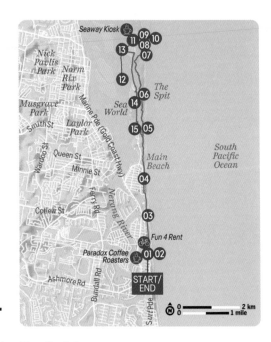

DURATION	DIFFICULTY	DISTANCE	START/END
2hr	Intermediate	20km round trip	Surfers Paradise

TERRAIN	A combination of flat paved pathways and some loose gravel tracks with gentle inclines

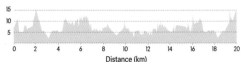

From beach to bush and back again, this ride showcases the best of the Gold Coast. Leaving behind the glitzy resorts that line its golden shores, you'll ride north along paved paths to the sand dunes of the Spit. Home to the 93-hectare Federation Walk Coastal Reserve, this is where the adventure starts as trails turn to sandy gravel and traffic is replaced by birdsong. There are opportunities for swimming and snorkelling along the way, but the true highlights of this ride are the sweeping views of the Gold Coast's skyline and a close-up look at a modern engineering marvel, the sand pumping jetty.

Bike Hire

The shared e-bike service, Lime, is widely available. Using Lime's app, find and unlock your chosen ride for $1 plus $0.54 per minute. For mountain bikes, visit Fun 4 Rent in Surfers Paradise.

Starting Point

It's hard to miss the beachside banner welcoming visitors to Surfers Paradise at the end of Cavill Ave. This iconic location is relatively easy to reach by either Translink or Greyhound bus.

 01 Mount your ride beneath the metal sign welcoming visitors to Surfers Paradise, a 2km stretch of golden sand and rolling crystal-blue surf. Now is a good time to consider if the spot would still have the same cache if it was called 'Elston' – the area's name until 1933, when it was changed to make the destination more marketable. It clearly worked – this touristy suburb is the Gold Coast's most well-known destination, with glistening hotel towers, high-end restaurants and a packed waterfront. It's also the best place to grab a coffee before you start your ride.

ALISTAIR MCLELLAN/SHUTTERSTOCK ©

Surfers Paradise

02 Keeping the ocean to your right, start making your way northward, up the Jubilee Walkway. The path here is smooth and generous but can be busy at all hours of the day. Take care as you ride and use your bell if necessary, as tourists taking photos may be distracted and fail to see you approaching. In addition to tourists, you'll see plenty of locals running, walking, swimming and surfing along this much-loved strip. This is one of the best spots along the route to go for a swim, although it won't be the last.

03 It's a relatively flat, easy ride northward to Main Beach, the last major sub-urb before you reach the isthmus and the start of your parkland ride through the sand dunes. After riding through Narrowneck Park, the oceanside path will curve west towards Main Beach Pde, where it temporarily ends.

04 Turn right to stay on the footpath. It's just a four-block ride north from here to John Kemp St, from where you turn right onto a leafy paved trail in Hollindale Park. You're roughly at the base of the Spit – a good place to look for nocturnal bush stone-curlews, especially in the early evening hours. The eerie wails of the endemic bird – identifiable by its large yellow eyes and gangly legs – are most often heard at night.

05 On your left, you'll see the flashy Sheraton Grand Mirage Resort, the last bit of civilisation for a while. Just past this hotel, the path comes to a fork in Philip Park. Take the trail furthest to the right and continue heading north. You'll be surrounded by green bush on both sides, and all signs of the city will start to fade away, providing an entirely different perspective on the Gold Coast.

06 When the trail turns from paved pathways to a gravel track that can

☕ Take a Break

Close to the starting point and just off Beach Rd, the flagship location of
PARADOX COFFEE ROASTERS is your caffeination station. With an emphasis on
local ingredients, you can rely on the huge breakfasts and acai bowls to fuel you
for the big bike ride ahead.

get a bit sandy, it's a sign that you've arrived at the Federation Walk Coastal Reserve. Although it's technically beginner-friendly, you're likely to find the cycling more challenging because of the small hills and loose sand. The 3km stretch winds northward through the vegetation – every year, volunteers plant over 10,000 native plants to rejuvenate and preserve the reserve. To your right, you'll see side trails that will take you to hidden beaches (they may not be patrolled by lifeguards).

07 The coastal reserve is a popular spot for bird-watching, where dozens of species can be seen, including red-back fairywrens, black-shouldered kites and azure kingfishers. Try to spot them as you continue riding on the trail until you see the yellow roof of the lifeguard station ahead – one of the Gold Coast's 40 specially designed surveillance towers – then follow the trail around to the left. You're now riding parallel to the ocean.

08 After riding through what feels like a true wilderness area, it might be a bit jarring to see the fenced industrial plant on your left. This massive 1.5km pipeline is connected to the sand pumping jetty. Continue under this pipe, but take care – the sand underneath is particularly loose, so you may need to dismount and walk. The bush beyond this is home to a fair number of

brush turkeys, who maintain their mounds of brush and leaf litter in the area with meticulous care.

09 From this point, it's not long before you'll emerge from the woods at top of the Spit. The northbound dirt trail you're on will truncate at a paved waterside path known as the Gold Coast Seaway, which was constructed from one million tonnes of rocks. You'll also likely discover that you're no longer alone on the pathway, as cars can access this point. The channel you're looking at is where the Pacific Ocean meets Broadwater Estuary, which feeds the Nerang River.

10 Turn right on the paved path and head east towards the lighthouse at its end. Once you reach it, turn back to admire the sweeping views of the Gold Coast skyline behind you, including the glittering crystal-like towers of the Langham Hotel. Just north of this is where you started the ride.

11 To explore further, turn around and bike west along the seawall. You'll see the Seaway Kiosk, one of the few places to get a bite to eat and a cold drink on the route. Nearby is the colourfully painted water tower emblazoned with the words 'Bright Skies, Water Clear'. It was painted by Brisbane-based sign-writer Rick Hayward and visual artist Emily Devers (known collectively

JESSICA WYNNE LOCKHART/LONELY PLANET ©

The lighthouse at the Spit

The Spit

Although riding up the Spit (sometimes called the South-port Spit) can feel like travelling back to a time before the Gold Coast's rapid development, it's actually a relatively recent landform, created by storms and the migration of sand over the last 100 years. It wasn't until the 1970s that work began to stabilise the shifting sand dunes, including extensive revegetation programs. Then, in 1986, the Gold Coast Seaway was constructed, establishing a permanent channel between the ocean and the mouth of the Nerang River. In addition to the Federation Walk Coastal Reserve, the Spit is also home to several major resorts.

The Sand Pumping Jetty

The presence of the sand pumping jetty (open to the public between 8am and 8pm daily) is one of the most intriguing features of the Spit. A marvel of engineering, the 1.5km pipe intercepts the natural northward drift of sand on the south end of the Seaway channel. It then deposits it across the channel onto South Stradbroke Island, where it can continue its drift northward. Each year, over 500,000 cubic metres of sand are transferred using this method – and soon, a new 8km underground pipe will pump sand southward to replenish the beaches of Surfers Paradise.

Sand pumping jetty

as Frank & Mimi) in 2018 as part of an urban art project to beautify utilitarian infrastructure.

12 From here, the path will curve back south. On your right are the sheltered waters of the Broadwater Estuary, a popular fishing and snorkelling area, with sandy spots providing access to the water. This isn't the Gold Coast's best swimming spot, but if you have brought your snorkelling mask and fins, jump in! Don't expect coral, but do expect hundreds of fish milling about. You'll also find plenty of public restrooms and picnic areas. This is a great spot to take a break, as you're at the midway point of the route.

13 Once you're ready to return to Surfers Paradise, turn around. Follow the path until you see a trail to your right, just past the roundabout. Take this path through Doug Jennings Park, then turn right. You're now headed south on Sea World Dr. There are bike lanes on the two-lane road, and while it's not particularly busy with traffic, it's best to stay on the wide and smooth footpath next to the road, which is also an official cycle path.

14 After roughly 1km, you'll see the entrance to Sea World Resort, followed by the roller-coasters and amusement-park rides at Sea World Marine Park. (Although it bears a similar name and

TOP TIP:

Keep Cool

The ecosystems of the Spit include littoral rainforest, native grasslands and wetlands. Unfortunately, none offer much coverage from the sun. To stay cool, it's best to head out on this ride early in the morning or later in the afternoon.

attractions to the American theme parks, the two are not affiliated.) This is just one of the many theme parks that has made the Gold Coast such a beloved destination for families. The footpath here is rough, so it's best to ride the remaining 1km on the road, where there's a bike lane and little traffic.

15 At Sea World's main entrance, you'll reach a roundabout. Take your first exit into the parking lot for the Federation Walk and Philip Park. Ride east through the car park towards the ocean, and you'll find a paved path. Follow this path south past the outdoor exercise area. After 500m, it will rejoin the path that you arrived on, where you can safely cycle back to the starting point.

Take a Break

At the midway point of your ride, you'll find the SEAWAY KIOSK (p89), right at the tip of the Spit. While the waterfront views are spectacular, the delicious crab sandwiches will also provide lots of necessary fuel.

14

Tweed Rail Trail

DURATION	DIFFICULTY	DISTANCE	START/END
3hr	Intermediate	24km	Murwillumbah Railway Station/Crabbes Creek

TERRAIN	Paved and packed gravel paths with gentle hill climbs

Murwillumbah Railway Station

From 1894 to 2004, the North Coast Railway Line carried freight and passengers throughout NSW's Northern Rivers region. It then fell into disuse until 2023, when it was transformed into a cycling trail. Featuring seven railway station sites and 26 bridges, the Tweed Rail Trail is an easy half-day pleasure ride. Although the route can be biked in either direction and is relatively flat, if you start in Murwillumbah and wind your way southward to Crabbes Creek, you'll ensure that the 184m of elevation gain works in your favour.

Bike Hire

Murwillumbah Cycles is located at the trail's starting point at Murwillumbah Station, and near the trail's end in Mooball. Shuttles go between the two stops, with bike hire starting from $30 for a half day.

Starting Point

Murwillumbah Railway Station can be accessed using the TransLink public service, or from Tweed Heads via Transport NSW's service. Murwillumbah's centre is a five-minute walk away.

01 A lot of investment has gone into the Tweed section of the Northern Rivers Rail Trail (colloquially known as the 'Tweed Rail Trail'), and it shows. Signage along the route is frequent, there are clear start and end points, and wide pathways make it easy to pass oncoming cyclists. Simply start your ride at the heritage-listed Murwillumbah Railway Station, where the green sign marks the beginning of the trail. As you ride, keep an eye out for information signs, which both signal your location on the trail and provide context to the

03 After just 2.2km, you'll see a set of steps leading up to the Tweed Regional Gallery on your right. You'll need to lock your bike at the bottom, but it's worth the hassle. The art gallery is also home to the Margaret Olley Art Centre, which celebrates the work of Margaret Olley, the late still-life artist who attended primary school in Murwillumbah. It features a recreation of her home studio, which includes the original windows and doors, as well as the more than 20,000 items she collected over the years as subjects for her paintings. Meanwhile, the on-site cafe has sweeping views of the region and serves excellent coffee.

04 Back on the trail, you'll come to your first road crossing at Dunbible, which is less of a place and more of an intersection. Stokers Rd is a fair indication of the road crossing you can expect on the rest of the trail. It's indicated well in advance by yellow barriers that will require you to slow down, and the road itself isn't highly trafficked. After crossing this road, you'll reach the 65m-long Dunbible Creek Bridge. Although the Tweed Rail Trail features 26 bridges (16 of which you cross), this is one of the most distinctive. At a time when most bridges were wooden, it was constructed with steel trusses and has been fully refurbished.

05 From this point, it's only about 10 minutes until Stokers Siding, where you'll find a covered picnic table for a well-deserved break. The first major settlement along the rail trail, Stokers Siding is home

Elevation (m)

sites you're visiting. The brown and green signs contain historic community and railway information, while the accompanying red signs are dedicated to the region's Aboriginal history. Designed by local Bundjalung artist and graphic designer Christine Slabb, each sign incorporates elements from the surroundings, including native bush tucker and flora.

02 As you leave the outskirts of Murwillumbah behind, swaths of green sugarcane fields flank the pathway. Sugarcane has been growing in the Tweed region since the late 1860s, and it continues to be one of the biggest industries here. (Husk Farm Distilleries, a popular tourist destination in the region, even makes its rum with the sugarcane grown exclusively on its farm.) Although this section of the rail trail is exposed, don't worry; the train stopped running 20 years ago, which means the vegetation has had a chance to grow high around the former tracks. Thankfully, you'll be in the shade for most of this ride. You will also have a great vantage point for the iconic peak of Wollumbin (Mt Warning) in the distance.

☕ Take a Break

Situated just south of Stokers Siding, you'll find HOSANNA FARMSTAY. Kids love this family-friendly campground because they get to feed the animals (daily feeding times are at 9am, noon and 5pm), and cyclists love it because they get to be fed. This is the place to stop for a mid-morning coffee, smoothie or toastie. It's also an ideal place to pick up some picnic supplies, with the small general store stocking plenty of locally made goods, including corn totopos and salsa, and sourdough crumpets with lemon-myrtle curd.

to a thriving arts community, but once upon a time, this was where cream, sugarcane and logs were loaded onto trains to be sent for processing at nearby factories and mills.

06 If your stomach is starting to growl or you're feeling a bit parched, you're in luck. Just past Stokers Siding, you can take a slight deviation from the trail to Hosanna Farmstay. Ignore the first large sign you see for Hosanna along the road – that's for cars, and you're on a bike! Instead, continue riding for another 100m along the trail and you'll see a dedicated bike turnoff, with chalkboards indicating Hosanna is ahead. If you see a wooden train trestle on your right, you've gone too far.

07 After returning to the trail at Stokers Siding, you will start a gradual uphill climb until you reach the trail's highlight: Burringbar Tunnel. Originally built in 1894, the 524m archway is the longest of the nine tunnels along the Casino to Murwillumbah line. Take care as you head through the tunnel: some cyclists insist on lights here, as it's difficult to see without some illumination. However, others eschew lights so as to be

mindful of the tunnel's population of bats and glow worms. If you don't have a light or choose not to use one, be sure to use your bike bell or call out (quietly, so as not to disrupt the bats and glow worms) to alert other cyclists to your presence and avoid a collision. It may also be advisable to consider dismounting for safety.

08 Directly after the tunnel, the trail starts to gently decline and will continue to do so until the end. The hard parts are behind you. Now's a good time to rest your legs as you slowly coast towards the site of the Upper Barringbar Station. This is followed by Burringbar, which was historically used by the coaches of Cobb & Co – who brought mail and supplies to the community – as an overnight stop. It used to have one of the most beautiful railways stations in the state (it even won an award for its garden in 1968), but it was dismantled in the 1990s after the train stopped running. Fortunately, the community here is still thriving, and this is one of the largest villages on your ride, with a population of about 1100. Today, it remains an ideal stopping point to grab a cool drink or refill your water bottle (there's a trailside water bubbler here).

JESSICA WYNNE LOCKHART/LONELY PLANET ©

Burringbar Tunnel

Glow Worm City

The Burringbar Tunnel's length isn't just an ideal roosting spot for microbats (including the eastern horseshoe bat, the southern myotis and the little bent-winged bat) – it's also home to glow worms. Endemic to Australia and New Zealand, these bioluminescent creatures are the larvae of gnats, which use sticky, silky threads to trap their prey. To see them, visit during the warm, wet months of summer and take care to avoid making excessive noise and shining lights, particularly on the roof of the tunnel.

Northern Rivers Rail Trail

The Tweed Rail Trail is only the first section of what will become known as the Northern Rivers Rail Trail. To be completed in four stages, the 132km rail trail will eventually stretch from Murwillumbah to Byron Bay before taking visitors inland and ending in Casino. Work is already underway on the other sections of the track, with a 13km trail at the western end between Bentley and Casino scheduled to open later in 2023. Until then, you can extend your stay in the region by trying the tracks at the Uki Mountain Bike Park.

Hosanna Farmstay (p94)

09 After exploring Burringbar, cycle on towards Mooball Station, which is hard to miss with its cow-patterned light poles and 1930s-era pub. Although it's the penultimate stop on the trail, if you've hired a bicycle from Murwillumbah Cycles, this is where you'll return it and catch the shuttle back to Murwillumbah Railway Station. You can either choose to end your journey here (at a very respectable 20km) or continue to the trail's end at Crabbes Creek, just 4km away. However, doing so will mean doubling back to Mooball to return your bike, thus bringing your ride distance to 28km.

10 If you choose to continue onwards, you'll pass through the second tunnel of the trail between Mooball Station and Crabbes Creek Station. The Hulls Road Tunnel is only 50m in length, so it's not quite as impressive as the Burringbar Tunnel – but it does make for a good photo opportunity. Shortly afterwards, you'll reach the Crabbes Creek area. Running from Yelgun Ridge down to Wooyung, it's a significant area for the Bundjalung people, who acknowledge it as the path of the sun.

TOP TIP:

Elevation

Owing to its historical origins as a train line, you won't find any steep gradients on this trail. You will, however, find a gradual hill climb of about 95m, starting after Stokers Siding. Although we've rated this trail as intermediate owing to its length and slight incline, hiring an e-bike turns it into an easy ride.

11 If you see signage mirroring the kind you saw at the start of the trail, don't think you're at the end. Yes, this is the southern terminus for the Tweed Rail Trail, but it's not its true end – that's about 100m further down the path. You'll know you've reached the end of the line (so to speak) when it ends abruptly with an 'End of Trail' sign. Well, at least for now. Soon, the Tweed Rail Trail will form part of the Northern Rivers Rail Trail, a multiday ride.

☕ Take a Break

Burringbar is one of the largest villages on the trail and is easily accessible from the path. For sweet treats, fresh-made sandwiches, salads and drinks (including organic wines, the perfect reward for finishing the trail), stop in at the BARN: its blue facade is visible from the trail. Be sure to budget enough time to wander through the vast aisles of HEATH'S OLD WARES, just down the street. This industrial-sized antique shop displays all manner of yesteryear on its shelves, including bicycles.

Also Try...

Brisbane Valley Rail Trail sign

Brisbane Valley Rail Trail: Blackbutt to Moore

DURATION	DIFFICULTY	DISTANCE
3½hr	Intermediate	30km one way

The Brisbane Valley Rail Trail is a 161km adventure that carries riders through the rural regions of Somerset and South Burnett. The trail can also be explored in bite-sized portions. The Blackbutt to Moore section is one of the most scenic.

Only suitable for gravel or mountain bikes, start this ride at Blackbutt. The route starts out easy, with the first 5km to Benarkin running along compact gravel with some steep banks. From Benarkin, the challenge is turned up a notch, with the next 18km presenting rougher gravel, grass, hill climbs and rocky sections, but the views of the Brisbane Valley make up for it. At Linville, break for lunch and admire the restored railway station. The last 7km is on packed gravel.

Brunswick Heads to Byron Bay

DURATION	DIFFICULTY	DISTANCE
1½hr	Easy	13km one way

This is one of the region's best beach rides (in the literal sense), as you get to ride directly on the beach. However, remember to carefully check the tide times before setting out, because it's only at low tide that you can ride along the packed sand.

Starting from the Brunswick Heads South Wall (near the main beach), head south on the sand, keeping the ocean to your left. Just north of your destination, cross Belongil Creek, which will likely require you to dismount before continuing the remaining 3km to Byron. Try to avoid disturbing any resting shorebirds – and be sure to take advantage of your location by taking a dip along the way.

Bird in the Boondall Wetlands

Boondall Wetlands Trail

DURATION	DIFFICULTY	DISTANCE
40min	Easy	6.5km one way

Birdwatchers, this bike ride is for you. Situated on the eastern edges of Brisbane, this 1150-hectare wetland is home to migratory shorebirds, who land here in high numbers from September through to March, while other species can be seen year-round. A flat and easy ride, this one is great for families.

To fully appreciate the tidal flats, mangroves, salt marshes, melaleuca wetlands and open forest, start at the Boondall Wetlands Environment Centre, where you can learn more about the unique surroundings. Then, head south on the path, which slowly winds east. At the Transfer Centre, hang a left and start heading north. Your end point is the Nudgee Beach Reserve, a tidal flat that you can swim in at low tide.

Ewen Maddock Mountain Bike Trail

DURATION	DIFFICULTY	DISTANCE
1½hr	Easy	10km

Situated in Beerwah State Forest on the Sunshine Coast, this trail is perfect for beginners. The circuit track follows the banks of the Ewen Maddock Dam, and through blackbutt forests, fern gullies and melaleuca wetlands, with views of Mt Beerwah, significant to the Jinibara and Gubbi Gubbi people.

The starting point for this trail is the Ewen Maddock Dam car park, situated just off Steve Irwin Way. While the first part of the trail is two-directional, it's not long before it turns into a one-way circuit, which can only be followed clockwise. It's mainly a flat gravel path with plenty of turns and few technical features, making it very family-friendly.

PAUL HARDING00/SHUTTERSTOCK ©

Polly Woodside (p105)

Victoria

15 **Capital City Trail**

Looping inner-city Melbourne, this urban jaunt traverses a diversity of landscapes, from cosmopolitan riverfront promenades to bucolic bushland belts. **p104**

16 **St Kilda to Half Moon Bay**

A family-friendly pedal along Melbourne's Port Phillip Bay, flanked by beaches, gallery-famous views and some of the city's most iconic heritage landmarks. **p110**

17 **Lilydale to Warburton Rail Trail**

Billabongs, bush and cinematic floodplains set an evocative scene on this ride from Melbourne's outer east to mountain-shadowed Warburton. **p114**

18 **Great Southern Rail Trail**

Rolling Gippsland farmland and food-loving villages mark this leisurely cycle to tiny, artistic Fish Creek. **p120**

19 **Bellarine Rail Trail**

Wildlife, wineries and railroad tales await as you pedal from burgeoning Geelong to pretty seaside Queenscliff. **p124**

20 **Murray to Mountains Rail Trail**

Gold-rush streetscapes, sweeping vineyards and alpine peaks lift the spirit on this two-day, family-friendly adventure through Victoria's High Country. **p128**

Explore

Victoria

Cosmopolitan and relatively compact, Victoria is Valhalla for cyclists of all abilities. Its dynamic, bike-loving capital Melbourne has an abundance of user-friendly bike trails traversing hip neighbourhoods, preserved bushland and landscapes depicted by Australia's greatest painters. Venture beyond the city and trails lead past prized vineyards, richly historic towns and a suite of backdrops ranging from damp, cool rainforest to wide, dusty plains peppered with kangaroos, cattle and riotously colourful rosellas. Best of all, many of Victoria's most memorable trails follow old rail routes, making for safe, relaxing adventures far from four-wheeled hazards.

Melbourne

Known for its ferocious cultural scene, blockbuster sporting events and notoriously fickle weather, Melbourne is a global city and major Australian gateway. Melburnians are avid cyclists (especially in the inner north) and bike equipment is readily available across the city. Victoria's capital also hosts a large number of dedicated bike trails throughout the metro area, many easily reached on the city's extensive suburban train network. While many visitors rightly base themselves in the vibrant central business district (CBD) – home to world-class shopping, dining and cultural behemoths that include the National Gallery of Victoria – many of the coolest eateries, bars and arts venues lie in inner-city suburbs like Fitzroy and Collingwood.

Geelong

Melburnians once mocked G-Town as a hoon-riddled backwater. Today, they're eating their words as Victoria's second-largest city evolves into a vibrant dining, culture and tourism hub. Restored heritage buildings mingle with striking contemporary additions – among them the spherical Geelong Library and Heritage Centre and the $140 million Geelong Arts Centre – while strips like Little Malop St and Pakington St buzz with on-point cafes, restaurants and bars. A 70-minute train trip or drive southwest of Melbourne, Geelong is a gateway to the Bellarine Peninsula, Surf Coast

WHEN TO GO

While cycling is popular year-round in Victoria, autumn (March–May) is especially appealing, with mild, relatively stable temperatures and colour-popping foliage. Icy southerlies and single-digit temperatures can make winter (June–August) less ideal. Book coastal and High Country accommodation well in advance during school holiday periods, including mid-December to late January and Easter.

and Great Ocean Road. It's also a gateway to Tasmania thanks to daily *Spirit of Tasmania* ferry crossings. Cycling shops and a wide range of retailers make pre-ride preparations a breeze.

Beechworth

Snugly set in the foothills of the Victorian Alps, 286km northeast of Melbourne, Beechworth is one of Australia's best-preserved gold-rush towns and an atmospheric base for exploring Victoria's High Country. Museums and historical sites recount the town's action-packed backstory, one of which features infamous Australian bushranger Ned Kelly. Ford, Albert and Camp Sts are lined with boutiques, cafes, restaurants, pubs and wine bars, with bakeries, provedores and a well-stocked IGA supermarket handy for self-caterers. Bike hire and a laundromat add to the convenience. V/Line coaches run to nearby Wangaratta, from where trains reach both Melbourne and Sydney.

 WHERE TO STAY

Hotels and Airbnb properties are the main options in Melbourne, with B&Bs and farmhouses excellent choices in regional Victoria. Special places include Warburton guesthouse Buttercup Hill (buttercuphill.com), complete with three coaxing guest rooms, homemade breakfasts and mountain valley views. In South Gippsland's Koonwarra, The Wine Farm (thewinefarm.com.au) sleeps six people in a self-contained cottage on a working winery and farm. Further north in Victoria's High Country, The Kilnhouses (kilnhouse.com.au) has transformed traditional tobacco kilns into luxurious, self-contained abodes sleeping between four and six people. The designer digs are set on a Porepunkah cattle farm with magnificent mountain views.

TRANSPORT

Melbourne Airport serves both interstate and international flights, while Avalon Airport (located between Melbourne and Geelong) serves mainly low-cost flights to Sydney, the Gold Coast and the Sunshine Coast. V/Line trains and coaches connect Melbourne to regional towns across the state, though most coaches will only carry folding bikes. While not essential, a car is handy for getting off the beaten path.

 WHAT'S ON

Melbourne International Comedy Festival
(*comedyfestival.com.au*) The world's second largest comedy festival, featuring big-name and emerging talent over three weeks in March and April.

Bright Autumn Festival
(*brightautumnfestival.org.au*) A 10-day celebration from late April to early May, with markets, music, tours, open gardens, a parade and Bright's famous autumn colours.

Queenscliff Music Festival
(*qmf.net.au*) A three-day shindig in late November showcasing local and international singer-songwriters, plus Bellarine Peninsula wine and produce.

Resources

Public Transport Victoria (*ptv.vic.gov.au*) Victoria's official public transport website, with a helpful journey planner covering metropolitan Melbourne and regional Victoria.

Rail Trails Australia (*railtrails. org.au*) Covers rail trails across Victoria and Australia, including facilities and nearby atrractions.

Visit Victoria (*visitvictoria. com*) Victoria's official tourism website has information on sightseeing, food, bike trails and more.

15

Best for

CITY
ROUTES

Capital City Trail

DURATION	DIFFICULTY	DISTANCE	START/END
3–5hr	Intermediate	30km	Princes Bridge
TERRAIN		Paved paths	

YMGERMAN/SHUTTERSTOCK ©

Webb Bridge

Grandaddy of Melbourne's urban cycling routes, the Capital City Trail is a manageable yet epic loop around the inner city that takes in some of its quirkier landmarks. Following the Yarra River, its tributaries and a dismantled suburban train line, the journey leads through contrasting landscapes, from cosmopolitan promenades, industrial wilds and picturesque neighbourhoods, to soothing swathes of bushland and a much-loved children's farm. Paved, relatively flat and separated from traffic, it's safe for inexperienced cyclists, with easy access to excellent cafes and bucolic picnic spots along the way.

Bike Hire

Blue Tongue Bikes offers all-day rental starting from $35 for standard bikes and $60 for e-bikes. Lime has dock-less e-bikes scattered across the city, accessible via the Lime app.

Starting Point

Metro trains run to Flinders St Station, located beside the Capital City Trail. V/Line regional trains terminate at Southern Cross Station, a few blocks from the trail. Bikes are allowed on trains.

01 From the base of Princes Bridge, head west along leafy, riverfront Southbank Promenade. Squint and you could be in Paris or Barcelona, especially with Deborah Harepin's Picasso-esque sculpture *Ophelia* looking right at you. That said, don't squint: the promenade is a popular spot for a stroll, so ride carefully.

02 It's only 600m from Princes Bridge to pedestrianised Sandridge Bridge, the oldest steel bridge over the Yarra. While the current

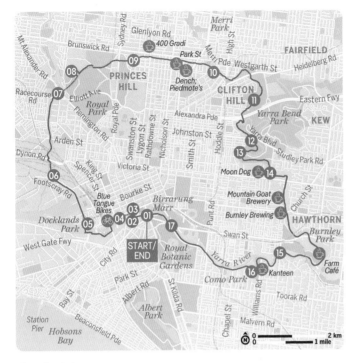

Elevation (m)

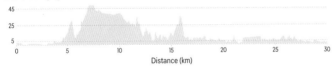

Distance (km)

Jeff Kennett) and Melbourne's endearingly daggy landmark *Polly Woodside*, a 19th-century barque that once carried goods between British and South American ports. Swing left once you rejoin the riverfront to reach Webb Bridge, its striking lattice design inspired by Aboriginal eel traps.

05 Waiting across the bridge is Docklands, a former swamp turned port turned high-rise neighbourhood. Trail signs lead you north along Harbour Esplanade, passing Marvel Stadium, Central Pier and a giant cow stuck in a tree; the latter is the work of artist John Kelly. Ignore the misleading Capital City Trail sign pointing towards La Trobe St and continue straight, where the cycleway skirts a short stretch of Docklands Hwy. To your left is Melbourne's ill-fated, 40-storey-high observation wheel, shut for good during the Covid-19 pandemic.

06 At the traffic lights, cross Docklands Hwy to slip onto the Moonee Ponds Creek Trail. From here, it's a 2.7km ride to Flemington Bridge Train Station alongside Moonee Ponds Creek, a once pristine waterway teeming with tuber daisy yams and eels. Recent conservation efforts have seen its creek beds replanted, a rebirth that inspired artist Tom Civil's giant murals beneath the CityLink overpass. Once you spot them, you're moments away from Flemington Bridge station.

07 Dismount and head up the station ramp to join the Upfield Shared Path, leaving behind the industrial grit of Melbourne's inner west for expansive native parkland. Note

bridge dates from 1888, its original iteration carried Australia's first steam train service on its maiden journey from Flinders St to Port Melbourne in 1853. An installation on the bridge now pays homage to multicultural Melbourne; apt given that Port Melbourne was once a major gateway for immigrants to Australia.

03 Take in the view of the Melbourne skyline as you cross the bridge, turning left to access cobblestoned Banana Alley and cross Queens Bridge St. You're now in Enter-

prize Park, named for the topsail schooner that docked here on 30 August 1835 with Melbourne's first European settlers aboard. Reflection is offered in the form of *Scar – A Stolen Vision,* an installation of 30 carved poles evoking the Aboriginal cultural tradition of tree scarring.

04 Roll on through Enterprize Park and recross the Yarra at Spencer St. Turn right to continue alongside the Melbourne Convention and Exhibition Centre (nicknamed 'Jeff's Shed' for former Victorian premier

☕ Take a Break

A handful of excellent cafes flank the trail. You could have morning coffee and pastries at PARK ST in Carlton North, lunch at FARM CAFÉ at Collingwood Children's Farm and enjoy an afternoon pick-me-up at KANTEEN in South Yarra. Off trail, detour north onto Lygon St for award-winning pizza at 400 GRADI or south onto Brunswick St for artisanal bread from DENCH and deli goods from PIEDIMONTE'S supermarket.

the ancient lava flows and marine sands as you zip through the Royal Park Railway Cutting, after which a signposted detour leads to Trin Warren Tam-Boore, a beautiful urban wetland 400m off the trail. Look out for tiny fairy wrens, one of several native bird species you're likely to spot.

08 Back on the trail, swing right when you reach Poplar Rd to cross the railway tracks, then cross the road and follow the trail alongside Royal Park Train Station. It's a short push up to affluent Parkville, where you'll switch from the Upfield Shared Path to the Inner Circle Rail Trail, a flat 3km stretch tracing the route of a long-gone train line through the inner north.

09 What was the line's North Carlton station is now North Carlton Railway Community House, where locals meet for tai chi or to pick produce in the community garden. The scene sets the tone as you cycle through North Carlton and Fitzroy North, two of Melbourne's most socially progressive neighbourhoods. Expect hipsters, cargo bikes and prohibitively expensive Victorian and Federation-era abodes.

10 At Rushall Train Station, dismount and take the station underpass to join the Merri Creek Trail, where you'll be coasting breezily

through inner-city bushland. Some historians believe that it was on the banks of the Merri Creek that Melbourne's founder, John Batman, negotiated his 'treaty' with local Wurundjeri Elders to purchase 240,000 hectares of their land in 1835. Up ahead is the Merri Creek Labyrinth and Wishing Tree, where scribbled hopes flutter in the breeze.

11 You might wish you'd hired an e-bike on the 280m-long slog up to Ramsden St Oval. Straight after it, take the trail to your left to cross Merri Creek and turn right onto the Main Yarra Trail. Ahead, the Merri Creek joins the Yarra River before its waters leap off Dight Falls. The weir once powered Melbourne's first (and only) water-powered flour mill, built in the 1840s. For millennia beforehand, the falls were an important fishing, hunting and gathering place for the Wurundjeri people, a fact honoured in Tom Civil's 90m-long trailside mural.

12 You can almost touch the Yarra's tea-hued waters as you continue southeast towards fruit trees and a bend in the trail. When you see them, you've reached not-for-profit Collingwood Children's Farm, where urbanites head to milk cows and feed animals. Its garden-like cafe makes for a blissful lunchspot, beside which lie toilets and a water refill station.

Convent Bakery

Creative Convent

Dating from 1863, austere Abbotsford Convent was once home to the Catholic Sisters of the Good Shepherd. Today it's Australia's largest multi-arts precinct, home to galleries, studios, a radio station and performance spaces hosting painters, ceramicists, musicians, choreographers, writers and more. Scroll its website to see what's on (anything from exhibitions to art classes and live music) and to access an Indigenous Sound Trail that uncovers the site's Aboriginal history. You'll find numerous places to chow or imbibe on-site, including Convent Bakery – where bread is baked in century-old ovens – and Cam's Kiosk, a laid-back cafe-bar where creatives graze, sip and chat under a neogothic portico.

Birrarung

The original name of Melbourne's Yarra River is Birrarung, roughly translating to 'river of mists and shadows'. Its current name stems from a meeting between 19th-century surveyor John Hedler Wedge and a Wathawurrung speaker from the Geelong area. When Wedge asked for the name of the cascading waters on a lower section of the river, the speaker replied 'Yanna Yanna' (It flows). Not only did Wedge misunderstand his answer, he misheard him too, leading to the river's current name. From central Melbourne, Kayak Melbourne runs guided tours along the river, including an evocative Moonlight Kayak Tour that includes a fish-and-chip dinner on the water.

13 Continuing along, it's a carefree coast past paddocks and the austere Gothic buildings of Abbotsford Convent, a nunnery turned community arts centre. Penance awaits at the next bend in the river, where you'll need to lug your bike up a steep set of stairs to reach narrow Collins Bridge. Cross it and follow the trail alongside tranquil Yarra Blvd. When you reach the self-service bike repair station, take the downhill trail towards Walmer St Bridge, scanning the view over Abbotsford's rooftops for Melbourne's beloved Skipping Girl, a 1936 neon sign that once advertised vinegar.

14 Across Walmer St Bridge, the trail rejoins the Yarra, heading east momentarily before swinging south (and eventually west) in a leafy, 4.8km stretch to MacRobertson Bridge. Across the river lie the multi-million-dollar mansions of Hawthorn and Toorak, home to business magnates, celebrities and no shortage of Toorak tractors (luxury 4WDS that never go off-road). You'll need to detour onto Yarra Blvd just before Mac-Robertson Bridge to cross it. Once over, a U-turn leads you back onto the trail and down to the river.

15 Heading under the bridge, the trail twists left and passes Grange Rd Wetlands, a handy spot to stretch your pins while looking out for Australian birds. If you're hankering for a coffee, riverside cafe Kanteen is a short 1.2km ahead. The little bushland oasis facing the cafe is Herring Island. Home to an environmental sculpture trail, the island is accessible via a free punt from January to Easter.

16 It's time for the final 4km stretch as the trail leads under Church St Bridge before revealing another of Melbourne's beloved neon relics, the Nylex Clock. Perched atop silos, the famous 1960s timekeeper even gets a mention in singer-songwriter Paul Kelly's classic tune 'Leaps and Bounds'. So too does the Melbourne Cricket Ground (MCG), whose soaring light towers are visible after elegant, drag-on-motif Morell Bridge.

17 After passing under Swan St Bridge, ignore the Capital City Trail sign directing you off the trail and continue along the Yarra, soaking up the prime-time skyline view. The fantastical, four-legged creature across the water is Angel, another sculpture by Deborah Halpern. Once the trail narrows, head up the riverbank and keep cycling along Boathouse Dr, passing the row of heritage-listed boathouses to reach Princes Bridge, from where a riverside beer or cocktail await at nearby Arbory, Riverland or Ponyfish Island.

☕ Take a Break

Once you've crossed the Walmer St Bridge, consider taking a detour to one of the excellent craft breweries in Abbotsford and Richmond. The closest to the bridge is award-winning MOON DOG, hidden down an industrial street and well known for its out-of-the-box creations. Further south in Richmond lie MOUNTAIN GOAT BREWERY (closed Monday to Wednesday), one of Victoria's first craft breweries, and BURNLEY BREWING, the latter also offering a substantial, Italo-centric food menu.

Southbank and the Yarra River

16

St Kilda to Half Moon Bay

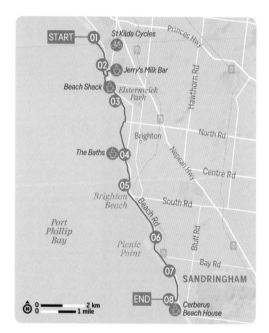

DURATION	DIFFICULTY	DISTANCE	START/END
1–1½hr	Easy	13.6km	St Kilda Pier/ Half Moon Bay

TERRAIN		Paved path

Elevation (m)

Fill your lungs with sea air on this relaxing cycle beside Melbourne's docile Port Phillip Bay. Part of the longer, 50km Bay Trail connecting Port Melbourne to Seaford, it's an easy route that takes in some of the city's best-loved heritage relics, from St Kilda's Edwardian kiosk and roller-coaster to Brighton's Victorian-era bathing boxes. Along the way, learn about the area's Indigenous history, take in views that have inspired generations of artists, sip a latte by the beach and enjoy a swim. Make it a return trip for the impressive skyline views.

Bike Hire

St Kilda Cycles offers all-day rental of road bikes and e-bikes for $69. Alternatively, you'll find Lime dock-less e-bikes across St Kilda and surrounds. Rates are time-based.

Starting Point

Trams 16 and 96 connect central Melbourne to St Kilda; only folding bikes are permitted on trams. The closest train station is Balaclava, 2.2km east of St Kilda Pier.

01 Your starting point is St Kilda Pier, looking curvaceous after a $53 million reconstruction. Its landmark kiosk remains (a faithful replica of the original 1904 building, burnt down in 2003), as does the view of Melbourne's skyline. The breakwater at the end of the pier is home to a colony of little penguins, best fawned over at dusk. From the foot of the pier, head south along St Kilda Foreshore, passing St Kilda Sea Baths and, further along, dining institutions The Stokehouse and Donovan. Rising behind them are the Palais Theatre and Luna Park, the latter home to the world's oldest continually operating roller-coaster.

St Kilda

Seaside resort, postwar Jewish enclave, red-light district, real-estate goldmine: few Melbourne neighbourhoods have a bio as eclectic as St Kilda. Its many layers and strange, mercurial energy have long attracted writers, musicians and actors, and the suburb claims some of Melbourne's most treasured cultural landmarks, including art deco arthouse cinema The Astor, Theatre Works (a long-standing champion of local, independent theatre), and live-music venues Esplanade Hotel (The Espy), The Palais and Memo Music Hall. A more recent addition is the architecturally striking Victorian Pride Centre, home to rotating LGBTIQ+ exhibitions, radio station Joy 94.9 and queer bookstore Hares & Hyenas.

02 At the end of the beach, the cycleway leads around St Kilda Marina before rejoining the shoreline in Elwood. After crossing Elwood Canal – designed by 19th-century Italian engineer Carlo Catani – the trail skirts Point Ormond, a grassy knoll with stunning summit views. This was once a bluff, used for shelter and collecting shellfish by the Yalukut-willam, a clan of the Boon-wurrung people. From here, signs along the trail depict artworks in-spired by this coastline. Toilets and a water refill station are located at the base of Point Ormond, from where it's a quick onward pedal to Elwood's century-old beach kiosk.

03 At Elwood Pier, the trail leaves the waterfront briefly as you weave past a row of blue-ribbon proper-ties. You're now in cashed-up Brighton. Coming up is the Royal Brighton Yacht Club, from where Melbourne's famous Icebergers set out for their early-morning swims. There are only three tem-peratures according to these har-dy local swimmers: warm, cold and #@%! freezing. Neighbouring the Yacht Club is Middle Brighton Baths, one of only two enclosed sea baths left in Victoria.

04 After the baths, the cycleway joins Brighton Esplanade en route to Dendy Beach and its unlikely real-estate goldmines: 82 brightly painted Victorian-era bathing boxes. None have running water or electricity, but this didn't stop number 15 going for a cool $340,000 in 2019. For a classic Melbourne vista, swing right into neighbouring Jim Willis Reserve, where the boxes are juxtaposed against gleaming skyscrapers.

05 It's a downhill race to Brighton Beach Hotel, another water refill station and Brighton Beach Train Station. After it, the trail shoots straight and flat through subur-ban Hampton, foreshore to your right, quarter-acre blocks to your left. As the trail begins to rise, open parkland gives way to na-tive coastal bush. Note the signs offering big cash for information about recent tree poisonings. (Some locals point the finger at Beach Rd residents wanting unobstructed water views.)

06 Ponder what you'd do with the $25,000 reward as you briefly head inland and cross into Sandringham. If you don't fancy cycling all the way back to St Kilda later, you can catch a train back into the city from here. Before long, Port Phillip Bay reappears to your right. Ancient Aboriginal stories recount a time when the bay (Nerm to the Boonwurrung people) was a vast, dry hunting ground through which the Yarra flowed to Port Phillip Heads.

07 Another gentle climb leads past toilets and another self-service bike repair station before you find yourself in Black Rock. Opposite Potter St, dismount and take the

Brighton bathing boxes

☕ Take a Break

You'll find cafes, bars and pubs scattered along the trail. Handy coffee stops include BEACH SHACK in Elwood and THE BATHS in Middle Brighton. The latter is divided into an alfresco kiosk and a restaurant, serving everything from oysters and pasta to fish and chips. You'll find a similar set-up at CERBERUS BEACH HOUSE, located on Half Moon Bay. For an off-trail pit stop, follow the Elwood Canal inland towards JERRY'S MILK BAR, an old-school corner store now serving speciality coffee and high-quality cafe grub.

low steps leading to Red Bluff Lookout for another panoramic beach-and-skyline view. The bluff itself is depicted in *The Red Bluff at Sandrigham,* a watercolour by the great Australian painter Arthur Boyd. On-site art is provided by Glenn Romanis, whose sculpture of six giant emu eggs represents the six clans of the Boonwurrung people.

Aquatic Thrills

If it takes more than a quick dip to get your coastal kicks, Port Phillip Bay offers numerous options. In St Kilda, the Royal Melbourne Yacht Squadron allows non-members to partake in its yacht races, usually held on Wednesdays and on weekends (weather permitting). You'll need to purchase a Sail Pass ($15) via the MemberPoint app. To hone your kiteboarding or stand-up paddleboarding skills, book a lesson at Kite Republic, located at the nearby St Kilda Sea Baths. Alternatively, slip on your snorkel and explore the bay's rich marine life at Ricketts Point Marine Sanctuary, a 3.7km cycle south of Half Moon Bay.

08 Continue along the unsealed bluff trail (or head back to the sealed roadside trail) to reach Cerberus Way, at the bottom of which lies picturesque Half Moon Bay. Waiting for you is Cerberus Beach House, a blissful spot for fish and chips or a drink while looking out at semi-submerged HMVS *Cerberus,* the only surviving breastwork monitor class warship left in the world.

17

Lilydale to Warburton Rail Trail

O'Shannassy Aqueduct Trail (p118)

DURATION	DIFFICULTY	DISTANCE	START/END
3–4hr	Intermediate	30km	Lilydale Railway Station/ Warburton Railway Station site

TERRAIN	Gravel and paved paths

From 1901 to 1965, steam engines puffed dutifully between Lilydale and Warburton, ferrying everything from day-tripping Melburnians to timber. Today, the route is the popular Lilydale to Warburton Rail Trail, an all-day adventure connecting Melbourne's leafy eastern fringe to the Yarra Valley Ranges. It's a magnificent journey, taking you through diverse landscapes, from bushland and farmland to billabongs and mountain valleys. And while there are some sweaty uphill bits, it's generally a laid-back trip, with long, flat stretches. All aboard!

Bike Hire

In Lilydale and Warburton, Ride Time Yarra Valley offers all-day rental from $60 for standard mountain bikes and $100 for e-bikes. You can pick up at one location and drop off at the other.

Starting Point

Metro trains run from central Melbourne to Lilydale, while bus 683 connects Lilydale and Warburton. Bus bike racks only fit two bikes at a time and cannot be reserved in advance.

01 If you're catching the train in from central Melbourne, hop off at Lilydale station. Before hitting the trail, take a moment to appreciate the station's humbler predecessor, now sitting in its shadow. Built in 1915 to replace a smaller building, its heritage-listed refreshment rooms once bustled with the top hats and cloches of Melbourne excursionists. You'll need to push further out for bucolic landscapes these days, so seek the access point from the station car park onto the neighbouring ovals and swing left onto the gravel path, traversing a tiny bridge and cautiously crossing Beresford Rd.

FILEDIMAGE/SHUTTERSTOCK ©

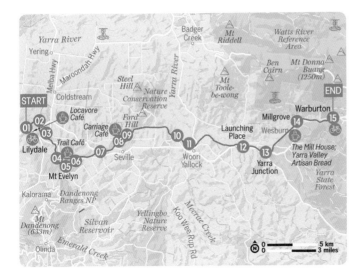

Elevation (m)

Distance (km)

From here, a sign signals the official start of the Lilydale to Warburton Rail Trail; make sure to take the trail on your right.

02 We'll be frank: the first 6km are a slog as you head up to Mt Evelyn. Nelson St brings brief relief with a short, exhilarating descent on a shared footpath, before a trail sign leads you back on gravel and up a short but tough ascent past (the ironically named) Mount Lilydale Mercy College. Veer left to cross the trail bridge over Maroondah Hwy, soon after which you have the option of a detour to Lilydale Lake, 500m down Alfred Rd. If time is on your side, it's worth a visit for its pretty 2.5km lakeside loop.

03 Continuing on, Mt Dandenong reveals itself in the distance. Crowned by TV and radio antennas, the mountain was a summer hunting place for the Bunurong and Woiworung people, who know it as Corhanwarrabul. Take care crossing Old Gippsland Rd, beyond which lies a water refill station. While rooftops are still in view, the trail feels decidedly less suburban now. Pine trees soar skyward and ferns appear by the side of the track.

04 After you shoot through a barrel-shaped tunnel, an information panel marks nearby First Aid Post Reserve, once used by the railways to conduct first-aid competitions. The land had been previously

owned by David Mitchell, father of soprano superstar Dame Nellie Melba. Up next is the entrance to Owl Land Bushland Reserve, an old-growth forest inhabited by Australia's largest nocturnal bird, the possum-hunting powerful owl. You're unlikely to spot these feathered slayers in daylight so forget the FOMO and crunch the last 1.2km to Mt Evelyn.

05 Happy days! Not only does Mt Evelyn mark the highest point (225m) on the trail, it reveals its first solid railway relics: an old station platform and the station master's house. Brightly painted bollards and history panels decorate the former, recounting tales that include a royal visit back in 1954. The station master's house is now a community centre, its cafe one of several in the quiet town. When the train line opened in 1901, this was Olinda Vale station and the town itself was Evelyn – the 'Mount' was added in 1919 as a marketing ploy to lure Melburnians seeking fresh mountain air.

06 Leaving Mt Evelyn behind, you'll relish the wooded downhill run towards Monbulk Rd. Watch out for the odd clump of horse poop – this section is especially popular with horse riders. You might spot a mount or two tied up outside Trail Café, a cosy stop for those on wheels or hooves. The cafe is closed on Mondays and Tuesdays, so get your caffeine fix in Mt Evelyn if riding then. The stringybark trees beside the trail were an important resource for the Wurundjeri people, a fact detailed in an interactive panel after Trail Café. If you're having trouble

☕ Take a Break

Lilydale Train Station is within easy walking distance of numerous cafes on Maroondah Hwy. One standout is LOCAVORE CAFÉ, which bakes its own bread and serves locally roasted coffee. A handful of cafes dot Mt Evelyn's main street, though your best option here is TRAIL CAFÉ, well known for its homemade sausage rolls. One of the trail's most unique pit stops is bucolic CARRIAGE CAFÉ in Seville, its locally focused menu serving anything from breakfast-friendly egg dishes to salads of duck and lychee.

distinguishing your grey shrike-thrush from your bell miner, a second panel soon after plays the calls of 11 local native birds.

07 From the second panel, it's another 2.2km to Warburton Hwy. You're now in Wandin North, long known for its fruit orchards and rich volcanic soils. Take a right onto the highway for a toilet stop in the centre of town or continue across the highway, straight after which is another water refill station and old Wandin station's platform, decorated with local history murals.

TOP TIP:

E-bikes

If your main objective is relaxation, it's worth tackling this trail on an e-bike. While much of the route is easy going, it is relatively long. Most notably, the ascent from Lilydale to Mt Evelyn will be especially strenuous for those with lower fitness levels or for younger kids.

08 No, you're not hallucinating: those really are plush monkeys hanging off the trees ahead. Ponder the randomness of it all as you continue through a pastoral sweep of paddocks and creek beds. If thoughts are turning to lunch, you can nibble inside a vintage train carriage at trailside Carriage Café, 500m after the Howard St crossing.

09 The landscape takes on a European air at Victoria St, where Lombardy poplars announce your arrival at old Seville station. Its surviving platform evokes lost ancient ruins as Mother Nature takes over. Picnic benches make the most of the bucolic backdrop, worth enjoying, if even for a minute.

10 You'll catch a view of the blue-hued Yarra Valley Ranges ahead, where the trail rises gently past a vineyard before racing down into a vast Yarra River floodplain. It's a magnificent sight, made even more special by an interactive panel recounting the river's creation story. A long timber bridge leads over the floodplain and Woori Yallock Creek, the latter gurgling in from the Dandenong Ranges.

11 From the end of the bridge, it's a relaxing 900m to Woori Yallock's

FILEDIMAGE/SHUTTERSTOCK ©

Lilydale to Warburton Rail Trail in Mt Evelyn (p115

Yarra Valley Nocturnal Zoo

Crocodiles may be the last creatures you expect to spot on a Victorian cycling trip, but you're guaranteed a sighting at Mt Evelyn's Yarra Valley Nocturnal Zoo, a community-minded sanctuary run by couple Steven Handy and Loo Scoon. An easy detour down Littlejohn Ave (accessed directly from the trail 1.5km after Trail Café), the zoo hosts a menagerie of native wildlife, including koalas, dingoes, white quolls and critically endangered brush-tailed rock wallabies. Personable 90-minute tours (adult/child $10/5) run daily at 10.30am and 12.30pm, with dusk tours also available (pre-booking essential for dusk tours).

FILEDIMAGE/SHUTTERSTOCK ©

Warburton

From rowdy gold-mining settlement and timber town, to Seventh Day Adventist hub and bohemian magnet, cosy Warburton ('Warby' to locals) has quite an eclectic backstory. Consider staying a night or two for a lo-fi escape, hopping between cafes and wine bars on its time-warped main street, reading a book by an open fire or hitting the beautiful trails in the area. Walk or cycle along the Yarra River on the relaxing Riverside Tracks trail (5.5km) or tackle the forested O'Shannassy Aqueduct Trail. The latter's East Loop section (21km return) skirts ephemeral Cement Creek Redwood Forest, home to tree-art installations by artist David Digapony.

old station platform, where old photographs capture scenes from the area's past. The station yard once bustled with sawmills, turning felled logs from nearby forests into lumber for railways, wharves and fencing across the state. You'll find a rest shelter and water refill station here, as well as toilets across the street.

12 Lily-studded billabongs and the odd artist at their easel greet you on your way to Launching Place, where the Yarra River sneaks up on your left. In the 19th century, boats 'launched' from here carried timber downstream and supplies upstream to gold miners, hence the town's name. Pedestrian lights offer safe passage across Warburton Hwy, from where you'll spot the town's pub, quenching thirsts since 1902. Another water refill station lies 350m away, at what was once the town's station.

13 You'll be travelling alongside Warburton Hwy for the next 1.3km, then crossing it to join the Little Yarra River into Yarra Junction. The township claims the only surviving station on the line, built in 1888. This was Lilydale's first station, moved here in 1915. Today, it houses the Upper Yarra Museum, open on Sundays. Toilets and another water refill station lie ahead, with a major supermarket just across the highway.

14 Bidding Yarra Junction goodbye, the trail crosses gurgling Little Yarra River in a scene charming enough for a storybook. After another gentle curve, the route straightens out as you head northeast towards tiny Millgrove, 3km away. Looming in the distance is Mt Donna Buang (elevation 1245m). The mountain was Australia's busiest ski resort from the 1920s to the early 1950s, after which better roads saw snow-bunnies head for the more reliable snowfalls of Mt Buller and Mt Hotham. If it's the third Saturday (or fifth Sunday of the month), stop by Millgrove's community market, where you can pick up gin, rum or moonshine from local distillery Yarra Valley Whisky.

15 Your buttocks will adore the paved 3km home run from Millgrove to Warburton. To your right, dense, precipitous bushland tumbles down to the track. Looming to your left is Mt Donna Buang, a view that soon includes the Yarra River. As guesthouses pop up, you know you've finally arrived in 'Warby'. Resist the temptation to swing left at the Alpine Hotel (a worthy post-ride destination) and follow through to the site of Warburton's old station, waiting just beyond Station St.

☕ Take a Break

For a culinary detour in Wesburn, swing east from the trail onto Station St to reach Warburton Hwy. Here you'll find YARRA VALLEY ARTISAN BREAD, home to baker Benjamin Griffiths and his naturally fermented sourdough loaves and baguettes. Sweet-tooths will appreciate the rotating selection of pastries, among them canelés and tarts topped with seasonal local fruits. Next door is fromagerie THE MILL HOUSE, where Dutch-born cheesemaker Pieter Tromp and his wife Nicky sell their tasty handmade cheeses, including a cumin-laced gouda.

Rail trail at Launching Place station

18

Great Southern Rail Trail

Map showing the route from Leongatha (START/01) through numbered waypoints 02–08 to Fish Creek (END). Labels include: Loch (32km), Lyon & Bair, Leongatha, Bass Hwy, Ethical Food Store; Milly and Romeo's; Paddlewheel, Koonwarra, Dumbalk, Great Southern Ride, Moo's at Meeniyan, Meeniyan, South Gippsland Hwy, Bridge Creek, Tarwin River, Buffalo, Little Oberon; Gibsons; Long John Pickles, Gurneys Cidery (7.5km), Tarwin Lower, Fish Creek, Fish Creek. Scale: 5 km / 3 miles.

FILEDIMAGE/SHUTTERSTOCK ©

DURATION	DIFFICULTY	DISTANCE	START/END
2½–3½hr	Intermediate	35km	Leongatha Railway Station/Fish Creek

TERRAIN	Gravel and sealed paths

Elevation (m)

Elevation chart showing elevation in metres (30, 60, 90) against distance in km (0, 5, 10, 15, 20, 25, 30, 35).

Traverse fertile farmland, cooling fern gullies and old timber trestle bridges on this upbeat ride through South Gippsland. Starting in the dairy town of Leongatha, it's a manageable half-day trip that forms part of the longer Great Southern Rail Trail, a 103km track that follows what was once the most southerly rail line in mainland Australia. Arty villages punctuate your route, their old timber and brick buildings home to art galleries, providores and quality cafes showcasing Gippsland produce, bread, wines, spirits and beers.

Bike Hire

Opposite the trail, Great Southern Ride in Leongatha rents out e-bikes. All-day hire costs $120, two-day hire is $220. The store is closed Monday to Wednesday. Only half-day rental ($70) is available on Sunday.

Starting Point

V/Line's Melbourne to Yarram coach service stops in Leongatha and Fish Creek, as well as other towns along the Great Southern Rail Trail. Only folding bikes are permitted onboard.

01 The largest centre in South Gippsland, Leongatha is worth a quick wander before setting off. You'll find a cluster of handsome heritage buildings at (and off) the intersection of Blair and McCartin Sts, among them the art nouveau-inspired Leongatha Mechanics' Institute. Both streets have cafes if you need some pre-ride energy. Tiny Loch (p123) is worth a visit, just 28km up the South Gippsland Hwy. Ready to roll, shoot south on the shared bike-and-pedestrian track running beside 19th-century Leongatha Train Station. The sealed track becomes gravel before it dips out

Best for

OFF THE
BEATEN TRACK

Fish Creek

Fish Creek (p123) is a special place. Featured in an episode of *Back Roads* – an ABC TV series showcasing some of Australia's most unique communities – this tiny dairy farming community of around 830 is well known for its resident writers and artists. Among them is celebrated children's author and illustrator Alison Lester, owner of an eponymous gallery and bookshop in the heart of the village. Internationally renowned botanical illustrator Celia Rosser also owns an eponymous gallery in town, open to the public on weekends. For local creativity with a side of sustenance, drop into L ttle Oberon, a cafe-gallery championing regional artists and makers.

of town, eventually flattening out and crossing Simons Lane.

02 Beyond it, the view opens up to sprawling paddocks dotted with cattle, windmills and warbling magpies. You'll find a toilet just before the Gwyther Siding Rd crossing, after which the trail winds its way up a very manageable hill. Your uphill efforts are rewarded with a breezy descent into lowland forest alive with rainbow lorikeets. From here, it's a short 750m pedal into Koonwarra, where a water-refill station, toilets and cafes await.

03 While its headcount may be a modest 366, palaeontologists know all about Koonwarra. In 1966, roadworks on the South Gippsland Hwy unearthed an extraordinary fossil bed. Some 115 million years old, the time capsule held the remains of plants, insects, fish, a rare horseshoe crab and dinosaur feathers. For gluttons, the hamlet is better known for its Slow Food leanings, locavore cafes, produce store and farmers market, the latter held on the first Saturday morning of the month.

04 Depart Koonwarra excited: the next 8.2km to Meeniyan are especially picturesque. Heading downhill and under the South Gippsland Hwy, the trail ascends into another bushland corridor, rolling farmland peeking just behind it. One more highway underpass and you're crossing over lush Black Spur Creek wetland, a haven for platypuses and sacred kingfishers. Just ahead, an old trestle bridge leads you over the Tarwin River and its own bucolic floodplain. The river marks the boundary between the lands of the Bunurong and Gunaikurnai people, the area's traditional owners. It's one of two crossings over the Tarwin here, where the track is briefly sealed.

05 The gradient rises gently after another highway underpass, after which you're back to gravel. The scent of pine and eucalyptus is thick as you edge to another downhill run towards Armstrong Rd. Crossed, you'll feel like you've wheeled yourself into an Australian Impressionist painting as eucalyptus-flecked pastures reveal themselves to your left. Another crossing over the Tarwin sees you pedalling alongside the ramshackle ruins of an old timber trestle bridge. You're now only 2km from mini-sized Meeniyan, where quirky scarecrows and a bike-wheel sculpture welcome you into town.

06 If you didn't lunch in Koonwarra, raise your fork in Meeniyan, where you're as likely to find wood-fired pizzas, speciality coffee, art and trilbies as you are fertiliser pellets. If you're low on water, stock up in town as there are no further refill stations between here and Fish Creek; you'll find a supermarket, bike shop and toilets on the main street too.

DOROTHY CHIRON/SHUTTERSTOCK ©

☕ Take a Break

Leongatha's LYON AND BAIR is a good choice for speciality coffee, baked goods and brunch. In Koonwarra, ETHICAL FOOD STORE and MILLY AND ROMEO'S serve house-made pastries, cakes and lunches, while PADDLEWHEEL stocks artisanal bread and organic produce from local growers. Top lunch choices in Meeniyan include foodie favourite MOO'S AT MEENIYAN, while LITTLE OBERON, GIBSONS and LONG JOHN PICKLES are solid Fish Creek options. On Fish Creek's outskirts, panoramic GURNEYS CIDERY produces excellent small-batch ciders, served alongside locally sourced cheeses and charcuterie.

Loch Station

07 Re-energised, get back on the trail, taking care when crossing South Gippsland Hwy. From this intersection, it's an almost dead-straight 9km to one-horse Buffalo, passing kore paddocks, grassy hills and the odd eastern rosella. When you reach Neals Rd, detour left to admire vintage Buffalo General Store and take a break at the site of Buffalo station across the road, home to picnic benches and a toilet.

Loch

A short detour along the South Gippsland Hwy, 28km north-west of Leongatha, pint-sized Loch is another of Victoria's most endearing hamlets. Restored timber cottages line its Insta-worthy main street, where one-off boutiques and galleries peddle everything from antiques to locally made ceramics and clothing. The village is also home to Loch Brewery & Distillery, set in a 19th-century bank and famous for producing one of Victoria's finest single malt whiskies. On the same V/Line bus service as Leongatha and Fish Creek, Loch is also a stop on the 36km leg of the Great Southern Rail Trail from Nyora to Leongatha.

08 Remind yourself that Fish Creek is less than 7km away as your quads work to get you over another incline. Before long, you'll be heading back downhill as the trail veers southeast. Butterflies rally beside you as another manageable ascent leads to Boys Rd. With less than 3km to go, it's one last, leafy downhill spin into boho-spirited Fish Creek, where an art deco pub and screeching corellas bid you 'G'day'.

19

Best for

FOOD & DRINK

Bellarine Rail Trail

DURATION	DIFFICULTY	DISTANCE	START/END
2½–3½hr	Intermediate	35km	South Geelong railway station/ Queenscliff railway station

TERRAIN	Sealed and gravel paths

K.A WILLIS/SHUTTERSTOCK ©

Steam train, Queenscliff

Easily reached from Melbourne, the Bellarine Rail Trail connects Victoria's flourishing second city to one of its most charming and historic coastal towns. The route traces the old Geelong to Queenscliff railway, opened in 1879 to carry troops from Melbourne to Fort Queenscliff. Before closing in 1976, the line also carried day-trippers, lured by Queenscliff's picture-perfect streets and shore. It's a mind-clearing ride, leading out of suburbia and through farmland, grasslands and wetlands teeming with birdlife and wildflowers.

Bike Hire

In Geelong, Rent My Bike offers all-day rental of mountain bikes from $55 and e-bikes from $85. If you're only riding one way, a bike pick-up service is available ($99).

Starting Point

V/Line trains run between Melbourne and Geelong, while Port Phillip Ferries runs daily services between cities; bikes are permitted on both. Bikes are not allowed on bus 56, running between Queenscliff and Geelong.

01 Jump off the train at South Geelong and follow the signs for Bellarine Rail Trail. At the Breakwater Rd roundabout, the trail leaves the train line and shoots 3.2km through a tranquil reserve flanked by backyards, factories and paddocks.

02 Traffic lights lead you safely across the Bellarine Hwy, where you can pause at the drive-through coffee joint or roll on through an increasingly rural backdrop. Straight after Moolap Station Rd is the site of old Moolap station. Operat

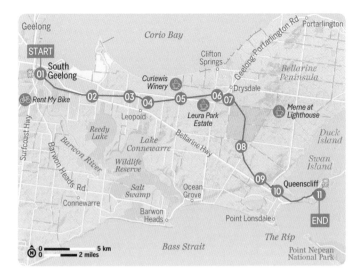

Elevation (m)

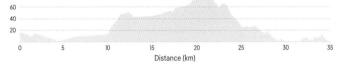

ing from 1881 to 1936, it served workers at the nearby Moolap saltworks. An information board tells its story and that of the area's precious native grasslands.

03 Horses glance as you whizz past their paddocks to cross Melaluka Rd, where a sign marks Leopold station. Its original name – Kensington Flat – was changed to avoid confusion with Kensington station in Melbourne. From here, it's a gentle climb through suburban Leopold, where shiny new homes attest to the Bellarine's booming population.

04 Rainbow lorikeets cheer you on beyond Christies Rd, soon after which the trail leaves suburbia once more to coast downhill towards

Bawtree Rd. Crossed, the trail forms an Avenue of Honour to old Curlewis station, home to a drinking fountain, rest shelter and sole Aleppo pine. The latter is a cutting from the original Lone Pine in Gallipoli.

05 Traffic lights lead across Portarlington Rd and onto an undulating, 3.6km stretch to Lake Lorne. To your right is Curlewis Golf Club, a progressive public course with a hip vibe and good eats. To your left, vast paddocks sprawl north towards Corio Bay and the distinctive peaks of the You Yangs. In the 1960s, the latter inspired painter Fred Williams to produce two series of works that revolutionised the depiction of the Australian landscape.

Rip It Up

The Rip is the stuff of maritime nightmares. Connecting Bass Strait to Port Phillip Bay, this shallow, narrow, reef-riddled passage is considered one of the most dangerous ocean channels in the world, thrashing unpredictably between Point Lonsdale and Point Nepean. Dozens of ships have perished in its waters since the 19th century, tales of which are recounted at the Queenscliffe Maritime Museum. Despite its notoriety, some 4000 vessels safely cross the channel annually to and from the ports of Melbourne and Geelong. If you fancy a sail alongside it, Searoad Ferries operates hourly car-and-passenger ferries between Queenscliff and Sorrento, a fashionable beach town on the Mornington Peninsula.

06 You might just feel an itch to sketch beautiful Lake Lorne, an important wetland harbouring black swans, purple swamphens and threatened blue-billed ducks. Its neighbour is charming Drysdale station, home to a quaint museum and a bike-friendly steam-train service that runs to/from Queenscliff on Sundays.

07 The trail now switches to gravel. Turn left at the T-intersection to follow it over the train tracks. You'll cross the tracks again at Bridge St, after which the trail leads through an especially scenic sweep of farmland and olive trees. Technicolor eastern rosellas flit above as you push gently uphill towards a grove of she-oaks.

08 Relish the solitude before descending gently towards another drinking fountain and Banks Rd. Across it, a pine plantation adds a Nordic touch as you ascend once more, huffing past cattle farms and crossing the railway further ahead. If you're feeling a little fatigued, take solace in the view of Queenscliff and the bay, beckoning in the distance.

09 Around the next corner lies Suma Park station, handy for a toilet break. Take a peek at the vineyard behind the station. It's said that legendary thoroughbred Phar Lap was hidden at this very property before a race in Geelong. A flat 1.2km leads to Queenscliff–Portarlington Rd, where encouragement comes in the form of a sign: '5.7km to Queenscliff Station'.

10 The trail follows the road briefly before a sharp right spills you onto sleepy, sealed Yarram Creek Lane. If it's open, drop into Lonsdale Tomato Farm for local picnic provisions. Alternatively, chug on, passing Lakers Siding and crossing Fellows Rd to slip onto quiet Murray Rd. You'll be sharing the next 1.4km with the odd car as you pedal alongside brackish Swan Bay and Point Lonsdale's beachy abodes.

11 Where Murray Rd intersects the Bellarine Hwy, turn left to rejoin the designated bike path into Queenscliff. After a sweeping view over the bay, the trail farewells the highway for a steep climb up King St before dipping downhill for one last rail crossing, a final short ascent and a breezy dip down to storybook Queenscliff Railway Station.

☕ Take a Break

The trail is within easy cycling distance of cool-climate wineries, including Curlewis' LEURA PARK ESTATE. Open from Thursday to Sunday (book on weekends), bites include grazing platters and pizzas. On Sundays, another option is CURLEWIS WINERY and its own grazing boards, *pizzette* (mini pizzas) and terrines. Both feature on the Bellarine Taste Trail (*thebellarinetastetrail.com.au*), a network of locavore-focused wineries, breweries, distilleries, providores and eateries. Foodies should reserve a table at Drysdale's MERNE AT LIGHTHOUSE, set among olive trees and serving sophisticated, locally sourced dishes.

PAUL FEIKEMA/SHUTTERSTOCK ©

Queenscliff

Buckley & the Wadawurrung

The Bellarine Peninsula lies on the traditional lands of the Wadawurrung people. A unique insight into their lives emerges through the remarkable story of William Buckley. Transported to Australia for theft In 1803, the English convict absconded from his camp in present-day Sorrento. Making his way around Port Phillip Bay, the fugitive befriended the Wadawurrung, with whom he lived for almost 30 years, learning their language and customs, and marrying a Buninyong woman. The period is detailed in his autobiography, *The Life and Adventures of William Buckley*, as well as in *Buckley's Chance*, a well-researched historical fiction account by Garry Linnell.

20

Murray to Mountains Rail Trail

DURATION	DIFFICULTY	DISTANCE	START/END
1½–2 days	Intermediate	74km	Beechworth Railway Station/Railway Ave, Bright

TERRAIN	Paved paths

Views over Victoria's High Country

Traversing Victoria's High Country, the Murray to Mountains Rail Trail is one of Australia's best loved and most spectacular cycling routes, a 116km journey that takes in magnificent heritage architecture, prized vineyards, cattle country and idyllic alpine landscapes. This 74km 'Best of' is bookended by two of Australia's prettiest towns – Beechworth and Bright. Sealed, off-road tracks make this a family-friendly adventure, broken up by an overnight stay in Myrtleford and punctuated by breathtaking vistas, fascinating history, gourmet food and wine, and, in autumn, the region's famous blazing foliage.

Bike Hire

Beechworth's The Bike Hire Company has all-day rental from $45 for hybrid/recreational bikes and $85 for e-bikes. Bike delivery and a shuttle service covering trail towns are also offered.

Starting Point

From Melbourne's Southern Cross Station, V/Line trains run to Wangaratta, from where V/Line coaches continue to Beechworth, Myrtleford and Bright. Bikes (including non-folding bikes) are permitted on both.

01 Squawking cockatoos bid you a bon voyage as you push off from Beechworth's old timber station, in operation from 1876 to 1976. Your exit out of town is a pretty one, accompanied by oak trees and, in the cooler months, the comforting smell of burning firewood. Mellish St crossed, cottages are replaced by grazing cattle as you climb gently towards family-run Pennyweight Winery, 1.3km away.

FILEDIMAGE/SHUTTERSTOCK ©

Elevation (m)

04 You might spot kangaroos in the vineyard to your left as you coast down towards Boundary Rd, where the Beechworth–Everton leg of the Mountains to Murray Rail Trail meets the main Wangaratta–Bright leg. If you need a toilet break, trailside Everton station lies 350m further in the direction of Wangaratta. If not, recross Boundary Rd and continue along the main trail towards Myrtleford, 27km away.

05 You're now in the Ovens Valley, surrounded by sweeping paddocks and low, bare hills. Crows caw languidly as you approach Diffey Rd once more, train rails embedded in the path. If you cheated earlier, it's here that you'll need to turn left off Diffey Rd to join the main trail. Either way, if you need fast food, drinks or a toilet, you'll find them in tiny Everton, 1km further along Diffey Rd. If not, pedal on, flanked by hills the shape of soft, long brushstrokes. Ahead, both the hills and Great Alpine Rd creep up on you as you reach the site of Brookfield station.

06 The trail crosses Great Alpine Rd directly ahead, then follows it southeast in a long, straight line. Red river gum trees speckle the surrounding plains, their branches a perch for dusty-pink galahs. To your left is the Dingle Range, running north–south from Beechworth to Myrtleford. Soaring in the distance: subalpine plateau Mt Buffalo (elevation 1723m). Enjoy the effortless descent towards Burgoigee Creek, after which the trail flattens out on its way to the old Bowman station site, 3.2km away.

02 If it's too early to quaff its organic apera (dry sherry), continue downhill through fragrant, shady bushland, crossing burbling Second Mile Creek and listening out for eastern whipbirds. Dense woods are soon substituted for open paddocks and farmhouses as another short, benign climb leads to Diffey Rd, where a sign marks old Baarmutha station. The station's name means 'land of many creeks' in Pallangan-middang, a now extinct Aboriginal language of this region. Across the road lies Beechworth Wine Estates, open by appointment.

03 Take in the immense sense of space as you cruise past its vineyard, mountains in the distance, epic sky above. Soon after, you're tearing through Murmungee Bushland Reserve on a mainly straight descent towards the Ovens Valley. It's 8km from the winery to a trail sign offering two options: continue straight to Everton station or turn left to join Diffey Rd (back again!) towards Everton township. While the latter shaves 6.3km off your ride, don't cheat – soak up the magnificent panorama and continue straight.

☕ Take a Break

Food lovers slumbering in Beechworth will want to secure a table at PROVENANCE, lauded for its Japanese-inflected tasting menus. AMANDHI'S is one of the town's better cafes, while BEECHWORTH BAKERY is famed for its beestings (custard-filled, almond-sprinkled buns). If it's the first Saturday of the month, stock up on local produce at the BEECHWORTH FARMERS MARKET. En route to Myrtleford, lunch on superb seasonal fare at GAPSTED WINERY before celebrating Myrtleford's Italian heritage with wood-fired pizzas and local vino at BASTONI PIZZERIA.

07 Straight after the Whorouly–Bowmans Rd crossing, whimsy comes in the form of kooky sculptures, cleverly made from upcycled cans and bicycles. Take a pic and perhaps a deep breath: the 2.7km journey from here to Taylor's Gap will be the most exerting on your ride. While not especially steep, it is persistent, with the most arduous part right at the end. No doubt you'll appreciate the rest shelter at Taylor's Gap, the very place where Ned Kelly and his cohort fled through after shooting dead three policemen in 1878.

08 What goes up must come down, including you. Crossing Great Alpine Rd, you now begin an effortless descent into a perceptively lusher, brighter landscape, the Victorian Alps rising in the distance. Blink and you'll miss Gapsted, population 156. Located 2.5km ahead, the farming settlement was once a resting place for diggers bound for the Buckland Valley goldfields. Your own 'Eureka!' moment lies a further 1.2km away, where Gapsted Winery's cool-climate vines meet the sweeping Dingle Range.

09 From the winery, it's a wee 5km to Myrtleford, your overnight base. En route, look out for the old tobacco drying

kilns to your right. Before a nation-wide ban in 2006, Myrtleford was Australia's tobacco farming capital, with many of the plantations run by Italian immigrants who settled in the valley between the 1920s and 1950s. Once harvested, the tobacco leaves would be hung on racks and cured inside the kilns, a common sight across the valley.

10 Oak trees, poplars and a bumpy bridge over Bar-widgee Creek herald your arrival into Myrtleford. Reach the centre via the 4km riverside Loop Trail or via the more direct main trail (1.6km). Taking the latter, Myrtleford's Italian influence is palpable in names like Club Savoy (originally an Italian social club named for the House of Savoy) and Michelini Wines. Just past the latter is the Phoenix Tree, an uprooted river red gum turned sculpture. Beyond it, swing left onto Prince St, then right onto Smith St. On it is 'The Big Tree', standing strong for over 200 years. Ahead is the town centre, with toilets and a water refill station on Myrtleford Piazza.

11 After a sound night's snooze, you're set for the final leg to Bright, a cruisy, mostly flat 30km route through stunning alpine scenery. From Smith St, take the off-road

FILEDIMAGE/SHUTTERSTOCK ©

Beechworth Bakery

Milawa Gourmet Trail

For a delicious detour, side trip it to Milawa, a small town with a big epicurean reputation. It's an easy 16km cycle from Everton to Milawa: head west on Great Alpine Rd, turn left onto Markwood–Everton Rd, right onto Markwood–Tarrawingee Rd, then left onto Milawa–Tarrawingee Rd. After another left onto Oxley Flats Rd, it's a final right onto Milawa–Bobinawarrah Rd, which leads into town. Essential stops include Milawa Cheese Factory, Milawa Bread and historic Brown Brothers winery. From Beechworth, Tour de Vines (tourdevines.com.au) offers a self-guided, day-long cycling tour ($129, including bike hire from $139) to the Milawa Gourmet Region, including lunch and bus transfer back to Beechworth.

Mt Buffalo National Park

Bordering the Ovens Valley, Mt Buffalo National Park is an all-seasons, sub-alpine playground marked by monumental granite tors, vertiginous cliffs and tortuous snow gums. Gentle, cross-country ski trails and tobogganing make it a low-key resort in winter. Come summer, it's a spectacular spot for hiking, with trails including the 11km Big Walk, a five-hour ascent starting from Eurobin Creek picnic area, west of Porepunkah, and finishing at the panoramic Gorge day visitor area. The near-vertical walls of the Gorge provide some of Australia's most challenging rock climbing and abseiling; see Adventure Guides Australia for a range of guided, adrenalin-pumping activities.

Mt Buffalo National Park

trail marked Rail Trail, which skirts the centre of town before rejoining (and eventually crossing) Great Alpine Rd. The deep-green slopes of Myrtleford's pine plantation rise to your left, framing a bucolic scene of paddocks, kilns and hop plantations. Soaring ahead is the unmistakable bulk of Mt Buffalo. Currawongs and magpies serenade you as you cross Happy Valley Creek before a sharp bend left leads you around Happy Valley Hotel, home to a morning coffee van (open Wednesday to Sunday). Watch out for a few bumps after the pub, where the trail resumes its roadside run.

12 An almost imperceptible climb leads you past the 310-hectare Rostrevor Hop Gardens, capable of producing over 650 metric tonnes of hops annually. The plantation was established in the 1890s by William and Ernest Panlook, the sons of a Chinese digger lured to Australia by the gold rush. After another crossing of Great Alpine Rd, it's an easy 3.1km stretch to the site of Eurobin station, where toilets, drinkable rainwater and benches spell 'break time'.

13 If it's nibbles you're after, bag some fresh walnuts or hazelnuts 1.2km ahead at Alpine Nuts. Alternatively, you can go berry picking across the road at Buffalo Berry Farm. Pushing on, another mild incline leads to appointment-only Feathertop Winery and its photogenic sweep of vines and foothills. If you're now craving cheese, charcuterie, vino and mountain views, you'll find all four at Ringer Reef Winery, 2.3km ahead. Straight after it, you'll be recrossing Great Alpine Rd, skirting the Ovens River, then swinging up into the heart of cosy Porepunkah. If you didn't stop at Ringer Reef, you'll find a handful of quality eateries here.

14 It's a leafy exit out of town as you take on the last 6km to Bright. Golf carts whizz past at Bright Country Golf Club, after which a bridge leads you over the cool, clear waters of the Ovens River. You're now 600m from the Bright Information Rotunda, where a retro-esque sign welcomes you to town. Don't jump off your saddle just yet! Cross the road and follow the trail for another 1.3km along a soothing, stream-flanked grove to old Bright Railway Station. Just a few pedals more and and you'll reach Railway Ave, where a trail information board officially wraps up your alpine journey.

☕ Take a Break

A highlight on the ride from Myrtleford to Bright is Porepunkah's RINGER REEF WINERY, where you can quaff wine and graze on generous share platters while overlooking Mt Buffalo. In the centre of town, PUNKAH PANTRY makes fantastic pies and sausage rolls, while super-cute RAIL TRAIL CAFÉ sets a charming scene for sandwiches, burritos, quesadillas, bagels, waffles and excellent coffee. For a post-ride tipple in Bright, hit BRIGHT BREWERY for creative craft beers and REED & CO for award-winning gins, liqueurs and alternative spirits.

Also Try...

Fairfield Boathouse

Fairfield Boathouse to Heide

DURATION	DIFFICULTY	DISTANCE
1–2hr	Intermediate	10km

This journey through Melbourne's northeastern greenbelt weaves among landscapes that inspired the 19th-century painters of the Heidelberg School.

Starting from historic Fairfield Boathouse, a 1.3km ride from Fairfield Railway Station on the Hurstbridge Line, the trail leads up to panoramic Wurundjeri Spur Lookout before joining the Main Yarra Trail below. Cycle past Kew Billabong and wildlife-teeming bushland that was depicted by Australian Impressionist masters. Leave the trail at Manningham Rd to cross the Yarra River and lunch at the renowned Heide Museum of Modern Art, former home of art patrons John and Sunday Reed. If you're not keen on retracing your steps, Heidelberg Railway Station lies 2.6km away via Manningham Rd and Yarra St.

Bass Coast Rail Trail

DURATION	DIFFICULTY	DISTANCE
1½–3hr	Easy	23.4km

Victoria's sole coastal rail trail traces the old Wonthaggi line, a gently undulating journey punctuated by rolling Gippsland farmland, wild beaches, trestle bridges and mining relics.

Starting in tiny Woolamai – a 118km drive southeast of Melbourne – the gravel trail is accessed from McGrath Rd as it heads southwest to miniscule Anderson and its sculpture and glass studio Artfusion. Further ahead, historic Kilcunda is a fine town to stop in for local produce and a glass of local pinot noir. After skirting Kilcunda Beach, the trail crosses heritage-listed Bourne Creek Trestle Bridge before heading inland to the coal-mining town of Wonthaggi. A planned extension of the trail will see it continue from Wonthaggi to Inverloch and from Woolamai to Nyora; check basscoast.vic.gov.au for updates.

GREG BRAVE/SHUTTERSTOCK ©

Tower Hill

Port Fairy to Warrnambool

DURATION	DIFFICULTY	DISTANCE
3–4hr	Intermediate	37.5km

Bordered by two of the most historic towns on Victoria's brooding Shipwreck Coast, this mostly gravel rail trail traverses beautiful landscapes, from big-sky dairy country to wetlands.

Consider spending a night or two in the old whaling town of Port Fairy, famed for its heritage architecture and annual folk music festival. It makes for an atmospheric prelude to your easy 18km ride to cosy Koroit, a farming village with Irish roots and an eclectic, anecdote-filled pub. The town skirts Victoria's largest dormant volcano, Tower Hill, heaving with native wildlife and home to Indigenous-themed walking tours. From Koroit, it's a gentle descent back towards the coast, traversing Kellys Swamp wetlands and reaching Warrnambool, where evocative museums and winter whale watching await.

High Country Rail Trail

DURATION	DIFFICULTY	DISTANCE
2½–3½hr	Easy	34.6km

While it's worth tackling the entire 64km length of the High Country Rail Trail, those not keen on the long, butt-shaping climb from Bullioh to Shelley station will find the Wodonga to Tallangatta section an easy, satisfying ride.

Take a detour to the Bonegilla Migrant Experience to learn about the area's role in Australia's postwar migration program before skirting the deep-blue waters of reservoir Lake Hume. The trail leads past three reserves, each with toilets, before crossing the water via panoramic Sandy Creek Bridge. From the bridge it's a 9.5km home run to lakeside Tallangatta. Relocated here during the reservoir's expansion in the 1950s, its mid-century streetscapes have earned it the title of Notable Town by the National Trust.

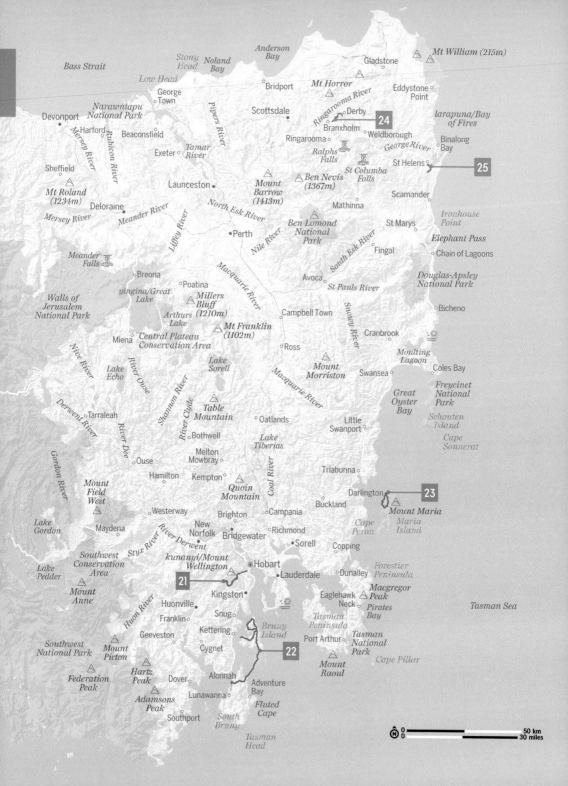

Bass Strait

Low Head
Stony
Head
Noland
Bay
Anderson
Bay
Gladstone
Mt William (215m)
George
Town
Bridport
Mt Horror
Eddystone
Point
Narawntapu
National Park
Scottsdale
Ringarooma River
larapuna/Bay
of Fires
Devonport
Harford
Beaconsfield
Derby
24
Exeter
Branxholm
Weldborough
Sheffield
Ringarooma
George River
Binalong
Bay
Ralphs
Falls
St Helens
25
Mt Roland
(1234m)
Deloraine
Launceston
Mount
Barrow
(1413m)
Ben Nevis
(1367m)
St Columba
Falls
Scamander
Mersey River
North Esk River
Mathinna
Ironhouse
Point
Meander River
Liffey River
Perth
Nile River
Ben Lomond
National
Park
St Marys
Elephant Pass
Meander
Falls
Breona
Poatina
Macquarie River
South Esk River
Fingal
Chain of Lagoons
Walls of
Jerusalem
National Park
yingina/Great
Lake
Millers
Bluff
(1210m)
Campbell Town
St Pauls River
Douglas-Apsley
National Park
Arthurs
Lake
Avoca
Bicheno
Miena
Central Plateau
Conservation Area
Mt Franklin
(1102m)
Ross
Snowy River
Cranbrook
Nive River
Lake
Echo
River Ouse
Lake
Sorell
Mount
Morriston
Swansea
Moulting
Lagoon
Coles Bay
Derwent River
Tarraleah
River Clyde
Table
Mountain
Lake
Tiberias
Little
Swanport
Great
Oyster
Bay
Freycinet
National
Park
Schouten
Island
River Dee
Bothwell
Shannon River
Cape
Sonnerat
Gordon River
Ouse
Melton
Mowbray
Coal River
Triabunna
Hamilton
Kempton
Mount
Field
West
Westerway
Quoin
Mountain
Oatlands
Campania
Buckland
Darlington
23
Lake
Gordon
Maydena
New
Norfolk
Brighton
Bridgewater
Richmond
Sorell
Copping
Cape
Peron
Mount
Maria
Maria
Island
Lake
Pedder
Southwest
Conservation
Area
Styx River
River Derwent
kunanyi/Mount
Wellington
Hobart
Lauderdale
Dunalley
Forestier
Peninsula
Tasman Sea
Mount
Anne
21
Kingston
Eaglehawk
Neck
Macgregor
Peak
Huon River
Huonville
Snug
Pirates
Bay
Southwest
National Park
Mount
Picton
Franklin
Kettering
Cygnet
Bruny
Island
22
Port Arthur
Tasman
National
Park
Cape Pillar
Federation
Peak
Hartz
Peak
Geeveston
Tasman
Peninsula
Adamsons
Peak
Dover
Alonnah
Mount
Raoul
Lunawanna
Adventure
Bay
Southport
South
Bruny
Fluted
Cape

Tasman
Head

N
0
0
50 km
30 miles

TOM JASTRAM/SHUTTERSTOCK ©

Maria Island

Tasmania

Explore

Tasmania

Once considered the end of the earth and isolated from mainland Australia via the Bass Strait, Tasmania (Lutruwita to the local Aboriginal peoples) now boasts a vibrant art culture, a thriving outdoor and adventure scene, and amazing food and wine experiences. The island state is 45% national park and 24% is World Heritage listed. As a result, Tasmania is a destination where you can discover natural beauty barely touched by humans. It is a place to feel at peace with the environment and is perfect for exploration, whether by bike or by foot.

Hobart

The city of Hobart is Tasmania's capital city, with a population just over 200,000. It sits in the island's south on the River Derwent, is full of old sandstone buildings from its convict past, and has the majestic kunanyi/Mt Wellington sitting 1270m above sea level in its backdrop. Hobart is easily reached by plane from the mainland and is the perfect midpoint to explore the Huon Valley, Bruny Island and Derwent Valley or to reach the east coast. You'll find no shortage of accommodation, food and bike shop options in Hobart; make sure you take the opportunity to enjoy some of the surrounding region's excellent produce from coffee roasters Villino and pastries from Pigeon Hole Bakers.

Launceston

Located in northern Tasmania, Launceston is the second-biggest city in the state with a population of just over 70,000, but it still presents an attactive mix of city and country life. As a UNESCO City of Gastronomy, it boasts excellent food options, including the popular Harvest Market showcasing local producers each Saturday. Launceston is a great location to explore the wine regions of the Tamar Valley or the Pipers River, and it also provides access to both the east and northwest coasts. Good accommodation and food options are plentiful, but make sure you head to Bread + Butter and fill up on some of their pastries. We recommend the walnut croissant.

WHEN TO GO

February through June are usually considered the best months to travel to Tasmania. The roads begin to quieten, the weather is more stable and the colours of the autumn season are absolutely magical. Each season has its own pros and cons, so never discount travelling at any time of year.

Devonport

Devonport is the other main hub city in Tasmania and the island's third largest, with a population of just over 26,000; this starts to paint a picture as to how spread out the Tasmanian population is and how isolated certain regions of the state can be. Devonport is the first port of call for travellers arriving via the *Spirit of Tasmania* ferry from Victoria, so it's a great starting location for those coming from the mainland by car. There are a couple of bike shops here, though the facilities become scarcer outside Devonport – make sure you stock up on whatever need for your trip either in Devonport or one of the other hub towns. And if you have the chance, make your way to Pizzirani's, a family-run Italian restaurant boasting delicious, traditional Italian food.

TRANSPORT

Getting around Tasmania without your own vehicle is something that no local would recommend. Make sure you know how you'll get around the state before you arrive and if you need a rental car, book in advance. Bus services will get you to many places around the state in a pinch, but they're not the ideal mode of transportation.

 WHAT'S ON

Tasmanians love a party so the event calendar is often full. Enjoy summer events such as the **Sydney to Hobart Yacht Race** (*rolexsydneyhobart.com*), **Taste of Summer** (*tasteofsummer.com.au*) and **Mona Foma** (*monafoma.net.au*). In autumn, try the **ECHO Festival** (*echofestival.com.au*) and the annual tomato and garlic festival.

Winter highlights include **Dark Mofo** (*darkmofo.net.au*), Festival of Voices (festivalofvoices.com) and the **Huon Valley Mid-Winter Festival** (*williesmiths.com.au/ midwinterfest*). The annual tulip festival and **Junction Arts Festival** (*junctionartsfestival.com.au*) are good options in spring.

Resources

Plan your trip on the **Discover Tasmania** (*discov ertasmania.com.au*) website.

The many **regional informa- tion centres** are the perfect places to ask locals for their recommendations.

Bicycle Network (*bicyclenet work.com.au*), **Dirty Free-hub** (*dirtyfreehub.org*) and **Tasma- nian Cycling Tours** (*tasma niancyclingtours.com*) are ex- cellent websites for learning about cycling in Tassie.

 WHERE TO STAY

Tasmania is filled with wonderfully unique Airbnb's and boutique accommodation options, from cosy cabins and waterfront cottages to beautifully restored barns and outdoor baths. The choices don't stop there, as there is also a whole host of amazing camping grounds located around the state. Whether you want to stay deep in the forest with no humans in sight or relax on a river watching the current move in and out, the hardest part is choosing where to stay. If you do find all the choices dizzying, our special favourite is Thousand Lakes Lodge in the Central Highlands.

21

Foothills of kunanyi

DURATION	DIFFICULTY	DISTANCE	START/END
2–3hr	Intermediate	21km one way	Hamlet Cafe/ Pipeline track
TERRAIN		Road and gravel	

kunanyi/Mt Wellington trail

If you want to learn why Tasmania is fast becoming one of the best cycling destinations in Australia, this is the route for you. Starting from the heart of the city, the trail quickly takes you through the foothills of kunanyi/Mt Wellington and into the forest, providing great views over Hobart as you go. From city centre to secluded bush in just a few minutes, this is a ride that many locals do every week, explaining why Tasmania produces strong cyclists and why locals love riding!

Bike Hire

You can hire a bike through either Roll Cycles or My Ride Hobart. Both are located either in or conveniently close to the city centre.

Starting Point

Start from Hamlet Cafe on the edge of the Hobart Rivulet. This social enterprise serves good food while also providing work for people struggling through disability or misfortune.

01 Starting with a coffee (and maybe even some food) at Hamlet Cafe, head west onto the Hobart Rivulet Track. You will immediately be transported from the cement city landscape onto a gravel path surrounded by trees.

02 Continue following the Hobart Rivulet Track for 2.5km, passing historical sites such as the Cascades Female Factory (p143) before eventually making your way through the car park of the Cascade Gardens and Brewery – the oldest operating brewery in Australia.

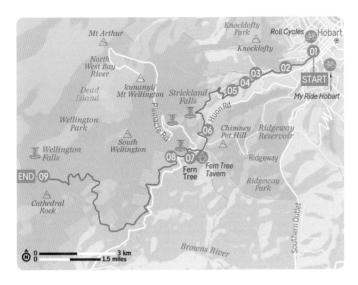

Elevation (m)

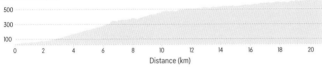

03 The car park provides a perfect opportunity to stop and take an iconic photo of Cascade Brewery with the imposing view of kunanyi/ Mt Wellington in the background. The mountain sits 1270m above sea level and is home to forests, woodlands and alpine environments that provide food and shelter for an incredibly diverse range of native plants and animals. Tasmanian professional cyclists Richie Porte and Nathan Earle have been known to ride to the top of kunanyi five times in one training ride. But if you can make it to the top just once, we would be impressed!

04 From here, continue heading west, taking a right-hand turn onto Cascade Rd. You will make your way back onto the bitumen where you will work your way up through the foothills of kunanyi/Mt Wellington. You will soon begin to feel the many microclimates experienced within Tasmania; the temperature can quickly drop as you worm your way up the top through shaded areas and back into open landscape. You will quickly learn why Tasmanians always carry a jumper around and will be in short sleeves one minute yet rugged up the next.

05 Strickland Ave climbs for approximately 4km through the forest canopy and up to the alpine-like environment above. Here is an opportunity to see some of the houses overlooking the city as you begin to appreciate how quickly the environment can change in Tassie.

Tasmanian Wildlife

You can stand almost anywhere in Hobart and see kunanyi/ Mt Wellington sitting in the background. Rich in wildlife and blanketed in forest, woodlands and alpine environments, it is a natural playground for the people of Hobart. The mountain has an extensive network of walking and mountain bike tracks, taking visitors past waterfalls, through fern glades and gullies, and opening up great views of Hobart. From November to January you can see the mountain lit up with the blooms of the endemic Tasmanian waratah.

06 Once at the top of Strickland Ave, you will hit a T-junction onto Huon Rd. This is the main linking road from the city to the turnoff onto Pinnacle Rd (the only road to the top of kunanyi). Depending on the time of year and the weather, there may be significant car traffic on the road, but there is a cycling shoulder for most of this section and drivers are usually accustomed to seeing bikes. Continue for 2km, passing the turnoff to Pinnacle Rd before riding towards Fern Tree Tavern.

07 The tavern is a good opportunity to take a break, fill up water bottles and maybe even enjoy a pub meal. Opposite Fern Tree Tavern is a park and trailhead which is the main junction for the many trails connecting kunanyi. Head up to this trail and follow the signs to the Pipeline Track.

08 The Pipeline Track runs parallel to the main road for kilometres before diverting deeper into the bushland through a quiet and secluded gravel path. You will be rewarded with views overlooking Hobart and Cathedral Rock, dense bush and, if you're lucky, a little river to go for a dip at the end of the road. If you want to be transported into the bush, then this is the route for you.

09 Once hitting the end of the Pipeline Track, the rest of your adventure is up to you. You can go back the way you came, continue riding some more trails or head to the top of kunanyi to enjoy some stunning views overlooking the city and beyond. The foothills of kunanyi bring a wealth of opportunities for cyclists, so, if you're feeling up to it, take advantage of the roads and trails and go for a big adventure.

TRABANTOS/SHUTTERSTOCK ©

Cascade Female Factory

☕ Take a Break

If you go prepared with a picnic lunch, there is no better place to take a break than at the end of the Pipeline Track. Sit in the river or on its banks and take in the serenity of a spot where you are likely to find no humans but an array of birdlife, wildlife and alpine plants. If, however, you want a bigger stop and more substantial meal, the FERN TREE TAVERN is the place to go.

Convict Past

To the British, Van Diemen's Land, now called Tasmania, seemed like the end of the Earth, an ideal place to send criminals and relieve pressure on an overcrowded prison system. Tasmania was home to some of Australia's largest and most notorious penal settlements as well as the World Heritage–listed Cascades Female Factory. The Cascades Female Factory is a story of the displacement, mistreatment and forced migration of convict women and girls, and their contribution to colonisation throughout the history of colonial Australia to the present day.

22

Bruny Island

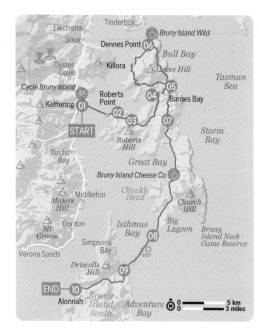

TOM JASTRAM/SHUTTERSTOCK ©

DURATION	DIFFICULTY	DISTANCE	START/END
4–5hr	Intermediate	62km	Kettering/Allonah

TERRAIN	Road and gravel

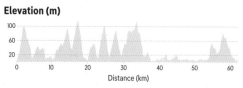

Elevation (m)

Distance (km)

Bruny Island often makes the top of a tourist map...and for good reason. Bruny Island is a small island just south of Hobart. As with much of Tassie, it is home to breathtaking and diverse environments, complemented with some world-class produce. Bruny Island is accessed by a 20-minute ferry trip from Kettering. During the summer months, the line of cars waiting to board can stretch for a kilometre, but as a cyclist you can ride straight to the front to purchase your ticket and jump straight onto the ferry.

Bike Hire

You can hire bikes through Roll Cycles or My Ride in Hobart before taking the ferry. Cycle Bruny Island also has a number of bike options available for hire on the island.

Starting Point

The gateway to Bruny Island, Kettering, is a quiet scenic town located a 30-minute drive south of Hobart. It boasts spectacular views of the D'Entrecasteaux Channel and the adventure that awaits on Bruny Island.

01 You know the adventure is going to be a good one when it starts with a ferry trip! And even better when you know you have at least 20 minutes to enjoy a road with no cars before the arrival of the next ferry. Hang back after getting off the boat and let the vehicles go first.

02 The road quickly works its way uphill – a common theme on Tasmanian roads. As you ascend for 1.5km you can immediately start to appreciate the changing landscapes, from the view of the D'Entrecasteaux Channel and kunanyi in the

Best for

FOOD &
DRINK

The Neck

The Bruny Island Neck is an isthmus of land connecting the island's north and south. The Neck is an important habitat for Bruny Island's native wildlife and gives you a bird's-eye view of the spectacular natural landscape of North and South Bruny. Boardwalks and viewing platforms let you observe short-tailed shearwaters and little penguins (also known as fairy penguins) burrowing in the sand dunes. The best time to see the local seabirds is dusk during the warmer months from September to February.

far distance behind you, to the open paddocks up ahead. It never ceases to amaze just how quickly the scenery and landscape can change in Tasmania.

03 As you're following the main road, ensure you take the time to look out for the many letterboxes decorated by Bruny locals to stand out on the side of the road. Once you have taken a left turn onto Missionary Rd you will quickly be welcomed with the peaceful serenity of the secluded gravel roads that link up to North Bruny. Make sure you keep your eyes high and look out for the many native trees, including native cherry trees which fruit during the summer.

04 Once you hit the T-junction, take a detour left to the sheltered Barnes Bay jetty. This is a great spot to go for a dip if you feel like testing the Tasmanian water temperatures. Otherwise, turn right onto Church Rd and continue on the route.

05 Further along the road is another T-junction where the left turn takes you to Bruny Island's main road, leading up to North Bruny. This is a brilliant opportunity to ride the quieter roads in this often-overlooked part of the island and to snake your way around the nature reserve in the north. You will quickly transition from cattle-grazing farmland to waterside trails overlooking panoramic views of the Tasman in the distance. The North Bruny loop is best completed in an anticlockwise direction; the views and the road just seem to flow better.

06 Once you reach Dennes Point, continue following the undulating road towards Killora, winding your way up and down the coastline while taking in beautiful views of the 'mainland' across the channel. This road will eventually complete its loop at an intersection where you turn to return to the main road.

07 On completing the North Bruny loop you will hit the bitumen again. From here there is only one road in and out, so you can rest assured you will not get lost. Around 15km later, you will reach the 'Neck' and the Truganini Lookout, where you will have ample opportunity to stop and refuel at oyster-seller Get Shucked, the Bruny Island Cheese Co and the Honey Pot.

08 Once you arrive at the Neck on the isthmus of the island, make sure you take the climb up the 279 timber steps to the Truganini Lookout. At the top you will be rewarded with 360-degree views of the island and an opportunity for the iconic Bruny Island shot. At the top of the steps is a monument commemorating Aboriginal woman Truganini. This memorial is dedicated to the Nuenonne tribe and Truganini, who inhabited Lunnawannalonna (Bruny Island) before European settlement.

ANDREW BALCOMBE/SHUTTERSTOCK ©

Bennett's wallaby

☕ Take a Break

There are quite a few secluded spots to stop at on the North Bruny loop. A personal favourite is BARNES BAY, and, if you are on Bruny Island on the weekend, make sure to stop in at BRUNY ISLAND WILD up at Dennes Point. The architecturally designed building overlooks the D'Entrecasteaux Channel and the mountains beyond and houses a cafe as well as a wood-fired oven for pizza nights and lunch specials.

09 Continue south from the Neck, following the main road for another 13km until you reach Allonah. Look out for the fridge sitting on the side of Sheepwash road, where you can find some freshly baked sourdough bread from the Bruny Baker. Trust us when we say it's worth the visit.

Wildlife Conservation

From rainforests in the depths of South Bruny National Park to heathlands by the coast and towering eucalypts on North Bruny, the Bruny Island landscape is rich with diversity. Bruny's vegetation has significant conservation values and is home to a number of endemic species, including the elephant and fur seal, echidnas and short-tailed shearwaters, also known as mutton birds. You may also come across the well known Bennett's wallaby, a wallaby with a rare genetic mutation that gives them their white fur.

10 Once you reach Allonah, be sure to sit and enjoy the view across to Satellite Island while enjoying a locally crafted beer from Bruny Island Cheese Co at Bruny Hotel. This is also a good place to rest your head if you intend to spend a few nights on Bruny, which we absolutely recommend.

23

Maria Island

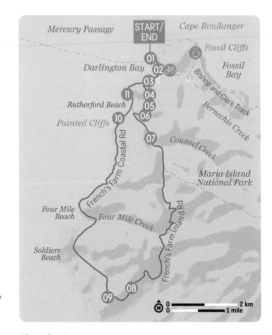

DURATION	DIFFICULTY	DISTANCE	START/END
2–3hr	Intermediate	20km	Darlington/ Maria Island

TERRAIN	Smooth gravel roads, some rocky sections and some sand

Elevation (m)

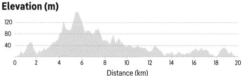

Maria Island is located off Tasmania's east coast and accessed by a 30-minute ferry ride from Triabunna. The island itself has many unique characteristics, from its deep Indigenous and European history to the fact that humans no longer inhabit the island due to its national park status. This makes Maria Island a cyclist's paradise: gentle undulating roads, no cars, abundant wildlife and spectacular views. However, there are absolutely no supplies available, so make sure you take food, plenty of water and anything else you'll need.

Bike Hire

Hire a mountain bike through the Encounter Maria Island website for an additional $33 when booking your ferry ticket. For e-bikes, we suggest visiting Roll Cycles in either Hobart or Launceston.

Starting Point

The ferry leaves from Triabunna, a breezy one-hour drive from Hobart. Once on Maria, you can begin your ride and start exploring the island.

01 While the first part of the 30-minute ferry ride is unspectacular, as you approach Maria Island you are quickly greeted with a spectacle of coastline and convict buildings in the distance, a sign of the adventure to come.

02 Once off the ferry, head 200m southeast towards Darlington, where you will pick up your bike if you are hiring one on Maria. This is a town of rich and varied history, and it's worth exploring either before or after setting out on your adventure. You're sure to see some wombats in

Painted Cliffs (p151)

Evolving Focus

The original inhabitants of
Maria Island were the Puthik-
wilayti people. More recently,
European settlement began in
the 1800s and since that time
the island has seen a whole
host of different intended uses,
from an unsuccessful convict
penitentiary, to an agricultural and tourism hub selling
wine and concrete in the late
1800s, to then being declared
a national park in 1972. Maria
Island is now primarily used as
an animal sanctuary, helping
to counter the spread of the
facial tumour disease afflicting
Tasmanian devils. The presence
of these creatures only adds to
the island's magnetic appeal
for visitors.

Darlington, and a short wander takes you through the old convict buildings and into the museum to learn the island's history.

03 From Darlington, head southeast towards Mt Maria following the inland track. This is the beginning of a route best suited for a mountain bike. If you're on a rigid or gravel bike, you can still do this loop as long as you have confident bike-handling skills; otherwise, you may be better off opting for the manicured gravel paths on the western side of island.

04 Leaving Darlington, head uphill along the gravel track until you reach the left turn towards the Oast House. But don't rush! Make sure you turn around so you don't miss the view of Darlington, the jetty and the silos in the background. This is the first of many beautiful views.

05 Once on the Oast House track, continue heading south. The gravel paths quickly transition as you ride into the eucalyptus tree line, leading to a fairly rocky track for a couple of hundred metres. Mountain bikes will glide straight over, though others may find it harder going.

06 Past the rocks and the track opens up onto grassy plains where you'll

encounter another of the island's landmarks, the Oast House. Stop here to explore the old ruins that remain from the house's days serving its original purpose of drying hops. There are benches scattered among the ruins where you can stop for a break before heading along the track and turning left at the intersection back to the start of the inland track.

07 The 8km inland track can be a bumpy ride with the quality of terrain depending on the season and rainfall; ask the ranger in Triabunna about the condition of trails when you check in at the ferry terminal. The trail leads up and down hills through the eucalyptus forest, with gentle ascents through the first 3km interspersed by a couple of steep sections that less-experienced mountain bikers may choose to walk. After 3km, the path is mostly downhill...with a few ascents thrown in to keep you on your toes!

08 The last kilometre of the inland track is sandy, so expect to take it slow or even walk some sections. Rest assured, before you get too frustrated with the sand and the slow moving you will hit the intersection and smoother, well-maintained tracks with gentle undulations.

09 Turn right at the intersection to head back towards Darlington along gravel tracks where you can take in the scenery, enjoy the coastline and see the many kangaroos, wallabies, pademelons, echidnas and wombats that walk the island. If you're lucky, you may even spot a Tasmanian devil.

TOM JASTRAM/SHUTTERSTOCK ©

Maria Island

☕ Take a Break

While there may not be any food stops to choose from on Maria, on the main track there are several stunning picnic spots to take a break and enjoy the coastline. Whether you want to enjoy a picnic on the hilltop or on the beach, the choice is yours. If you feel energetic enough, there is a perfect open grassy plain set at the top of a cliff near the Bishop and Clerk track just 2km north of Darlington. Sit, take in the view and appreciate the ride just completed.

10 Make sure you stop at the deceptively named Painted Cliffs on the way back into Darlington. The majestic swirling pattern on the sandstone cliff face is the result of erosion. You will only be able to access the cliffs during low tide (the ranger at Triabunna can tell you a good time to see these), but even if you don't get lucky with the timing,

Take Your Time

If you have time, it is well worth spending a night or two on the island to go for some additional rides and walks which you may not be able to complete in a day trip. Bishop and Clerk should be the first walk on your list if you do have the time. Don't let the island's small footprint fool you – like the rest of Tassie, while it may appear small, there is a lot to see. Take advantage of the slow-paced natural environment and take time yourself.

the beach itself is worth stopping at for a swim or a sit-down.

11 Another 2km of smooth gravel road brings you back into Darlington, where you can take advantage of the numerous park benches or beaches to enjoy the scenery and some lunch before catching the ferry back to Triabunna.

24

FILEDIMAGE/SHUTTERSTOCK ©

Valley Ponds Trail

DURATION	DIFFICULTY	DISTANCE	START/END
2hr	Intermediate	16.3km	Derby Park
TERRAIN		Gravel path/beginner MTB track	

Evolution Biking rental shop, Derby

Derby is a small northeast country town surrounded by lush farmlands and dense eucalypt forests teeming with mountain bike trails. The Valley Ponds Trail is the perfect introduction to the labyrinth of world-class trails carved into the countryside; it requires no mountain biking experience yet showcases the unique beauty found in these forests. Keep a lookout for pademelons and the elusive platypus as you ride alongside the Ringarooma River and around Valley Pond on this family-friendly forest trail that connects Derby to Branxholm.

Bike Hire

Derby provides multiple mountain bike rental options. The Derby Bike Shop has the most extensive range of sizes from $119 a day, while Evolution's rentals include e-bikes from $159 a day.

Starting Point

The Valley Ponds Trail begins beside the welcome sign at the western end of Derby. A gravel path following the Ringarooma River provides access to the trailhead from the town centre.

01 Parking at the Blue Derby trailhead on the east side of town, ride west along the gravel path flanking Ringarooma River. The path ends at the Dorset Hotel, so you need to cycle along Main St for 1km until you reach the official Valley Ponds trailhead.

02 Entering the Valley Ponds Trail on the right-hand side of the road, you're immediately transported into a verdant eucalypt forest. The shaded path stretches alongside the river once more, providing a tranquil setting as you leave

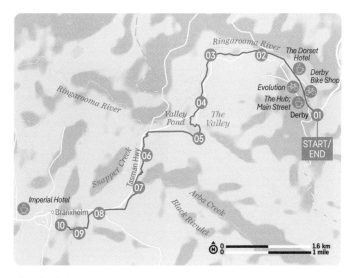

Elevation (m)

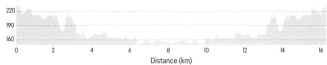

Distance (km)

Derby

Located alongside the Ringarooma River and backed by dense forests of towering swamp gums and tree ferns, Derby is a tiny rural town rich in landscape, history and mountain bike trails. Once a thriving tin-mining town, Derby is now a mountain biking mecca known all over the globe and has hosted multiple international events. Among the world-class mountain biking trails, you'll also find the Floating Sauna on Lake Derby (the first of its kind in the southern hemisphere), plenty of fresh lakes and rivers to swim in and several dining options ranging from quaint cafes to gourmet restaurants.

Derby. As you ride along the wide forest trail, keep an eye out for the furry little pademelons that live in the ferns blanketing the understorey. Pademelons are a smaller relative of wallabies and kangaroos and you'll find them in droves throughout Tasmania.

03 After 1km on the Valley Ponds Trail, you'll emerge from the canopy of eucalypts and briefly enter a clearing before dipping into a pocket of native temperate forest. You'll weave between gnarled tree trunks with enormous tree ferns towering overhead for another kilometre until you reach the road crossing.

04 A sign will warn you 300m before the Tasman Hwy crossing, allowing families to regroup and safely cross together. Then, 200m after crossing the road, you'll arrive at the banks of Valley Pond, a tranquil and secluded spot where native birdsong fills the surrounding forest. A picnic table provides the perfect place for a break and, if you're lucky, you may even witness the elusive platypus swimming by.

05 Continue clockwise around the Valley Pond for 300m before reaching an intersection with a sealed road. Turn right onto the seldom-used road, passing a small cottage before dipping back into the tree line bordering the peaceful pond. You'll pass another picnic table on the southern banks before the trail leads away from the water's edge and into a tall eucalypt forest once again. The gently declining path provides a fun descent into a clearing beside the highway, where you'll turn left and ride alongside a dirt road before veering right and beginning the climb out of the valley.

06 As you gently ascend, the terrain shifts into a dry, boulder-strewn woodland. The path becomes a touch more technical with small rocks scattered across the dual-purpose trail. Long switchbacks assist with the steepest sections and, after 1km, you'll find respite with a short but fun descent full of sweeping corners and an optional rock roll for the mountain bikers.

07 After the descent, the trail passes through open bushland for 300m before crossing a dirt road and dipping back into the tree line. The undulating trail ducks and weaves between tall eucalypts and mossy boulders for 1km until you reach Mt Paris Dam Rd.

08 Crossing Mt Paris Dam Rd, the forest thickens once again as you cycle into a fern-filled gully. A cobbled

path assists in crossing Snapper Creek, which is often barely a trickle. If the creek is running a little higher, it's best to hop off your bike and walk across the stream.

09 A final set of switchbacks lined by giant moss-covered boulders provides a stunning scene for your last 500m. And after a total of 8km, you'll pop out of the forest and onto the Branxholm Public Recreation Grounds. Here, you'll find a toilet block beside the old clubhouse but little else. Ride 1.4km further into town via the Tasman Hwy to purchase lunch, drinks or snacks – but be warned, it's a big hill!

10 Once you've refuelled, and recovered from the climb if you chose to head into town, get ready for a thrilling descent down those switchbacks that you may or may not have been cursing on your way up! With most of the ascending out of the way, you'll find yourself back in Derby in no time, ready for a refreshing Tasmanian craft beer at the Dorset Hotel.

MATT MAKES PHOTOS/SHUTTERSTOCK ©

Mt Paris Dam

☕ Take a Break

The picnic benches at the Valley Pond are the ultimate choice for a picnic surrounded by lush nature. Grab your supplies before your ride or at the IGA in Branxholm. For a break halfway, visit the IMPERIAL HOTEL in Branxholm for a hearty pub meal perfect for a day of cycling. If you'd rather have a variety of options, return to Derby for your choice between delicious wood-fired pizzas at THE HUB, gourmet burgers at MAIN STREET or tasty traditional favourites at the DORSET HOTEL.

Branxholm

Branxholm is a working town that sprawls out across a verdant valley filled with hop fields and timber mills. It's most notable for the red bridge decorated with Chinese symbols. This bridge is a stop on the Trail of the Tin Dragon, a themed touring trail telling the story of the Chinese tin miners who worked here from the late 1800s. Another worthy adventure if you have the time is Mt Paris Dam, a 10-minute drive east of Branxholm. A short walk allows access to the unused dam, where you can catch the afternoon light rays filtering through the wall's concrete columns.

25

St Helens Foreshore & Townlink

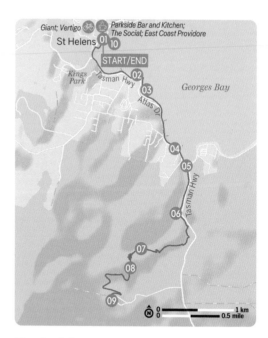

DURATION	DIFFICULTY	DISTANCE	START/END
2hr	Intermediate	13km	St Helens Wharf

TERRAIN	Gravel cycle path, beginner MTB track

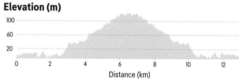

Elevation (m)

Known for its sensational seafood and fiery coastline, St Helens is the largest town along the northeast coast of Tasmania and home to an abundance of outdoor activities. The St Helens Foreshore and Townlink trail will take you on a peaceful journey around Georges Bay before testing your endurance as you thread through the coastal woodland to the St Helens MTB trailhead. The real fun begins on the flowing descent back down the Townlink, which will have you squealing in delight and ready for a lazy afternoon by the bay.

Bike Hire

There are two rental stores in St Helens. Giant has a variety of mountain bikes and e-bikes from $60, while Vertigo offers beginner mountain bikes and e-bikes from $75.

Starting Point

The St Helens Foreshore trail begins at the wharf just south of the town centre. Here, you'll also find a large car park, playground and two delicious seafood restaurants.

01 Your journey begins on a dual-purpose path leading from the sprawling marina, passing the famous floating Skippers Fish and Chip shop and crossing the bridge onto the St Helens Foreshore track. Tall shady trees hang over the path, providing a buffer from the busy Tasman Hwy and affording a beautiful contrast to the vibrant sea-green bay. The shared trail is often bustling with runners, dog walkers and bike riders, all enjoying the peaceful atmosphere that Georges Bay emanates.

St Helens

Tucked beneath the Bay of Fires and above Freycinet National Park, St Helens is the largest town along the northeast coast of Tasmania and provides the perfect base for an extended stay in the area. The seaside town exudes a quirky laid-back vibe that encourages you to slow down and enjoy the small things. Days in St Helens can be spent admiring the many artistic shops and delicious cafes and restaurants, surfing and swimming at St Helens Point or exploring the numerous waterfalls nearby – Halls Falls is a favourite among locals and is located a 20-minute drive from town.

02 Continue weaving along the foreshore path as it hugs the contours of the bay for 1km before briefly climbing behind the Tackle Shop and back down to the water's edge. Around 500m later, you'll arrive at a picnic area equipped with a toilet block, barbecues and a grassy spot to sit and watch as locals and tourists alike fish from the pier.

03 Moving past the picnic area, you'll wrap around a rocky point often occupied by black swans and crested terns diving for their next meal. The views continue to unravel as you ride, revealing the mouth of the inlet and the distant mountains bordering St Helens in the west. After another kilometre, you'll pass by two long piers and a car park – which offers an alternative starting point if you want to shave 5km off the ride.

04 Continuing on, a small rise shaded by towering gums takes you around a set of buildings and delivers you the final 500m to Lions Park. Here, you'll find a sheltered picnic area with barbecue facilities, a toilet block and a playground. This is where you'll leave the peaceful coastal path behind and begin the ascent along the Townlink to the St Helens MTB Park trailhead.

05 Ride along the track sandwiched between Lions Park and the highway and cross the road at the yellow poles approximately 50m ahead. Entering the Boggy Creek Conservation Area and Wetlands, a boardwalk funnels you into a forest of swamp paperbark and tall tree ferns. Keep an eye out for the resident sea eagles flying above and the white-faced heron stalking about in the wetlands below.

06 Leaving the boardwalk behind, the dual-purpose trail takes on a rough and rocky status as you begin winding your way through a vibrant eucalypt woodland filled with enormous blue gums and stringy bark trees. After 1km on the Townlink, you'll arrive at a bridge leading to a sweeping corner ascending out of the dense forest and into a field of colourful ferns peppered with towering eucalypts.

07 The abundance of wallabies and echidnas that call the open woodland home allows you to shift focus from the consistent climb as you try to spot these elusive native animals. The trail continues to traverse the side of a deep gully for 1km until you reach the infamous switchbacks leading out of Boggy Creek Valley.

08 After the switchbacks, you're afforded a slight respite as the gradient softens and the undulating trail continues winding through the shrubby coastal woodland full of bright green ferns. On a few occasions, tree roots rise above the dirt track, requiring a little extra attention as you cover the last 1.5km.

☕ Take a Break

After your thrilling descent down the Townlink, stop in at the PARKSIDE BAR AND KITCHEN for a well-earned break. Indulge in their locally caught seafood as you look out over Georges Bay. Or if you're visiting in summer, stop in at THE SOCIAL on your return to taste their mouth-watering street food and extensive range of Tasmanian craft beer and gin. Alternatively, pick up supplies at the EAST COAST PROVIDORE and set yourself up at one of the many barbecue areas along the foreshore.

LISABENJESS/SHUTTERSTOCK ©

Fish and chips, St Helens

09 Arriving at the St Helens MTB Park trailhead, you'll find a large sheltered area, a car park and a toilet block with a water refill station. On weekends, you'll also be tempted by the delicious coffee and toasted sandwiches served at The Lid cafe. Stay around for a while and explore the various mountain bike trails or get ready for an exhilarating descent back to Lions Park.

St Helens Mountain Bike Park

In the mountains bordering the south of St Helens, a multitude of mountain bike trails can be found carved across the forested slopes. The St Helens Mountain Bike Park has some of the most scenic trails in Tasmania that overlook the breathtaking coastline. This MTB park has been impeccably built with all parties in mind, accommodating the advanced, beginners and every rider in between. You can ride the easy-to-intermediate cross-country trails from the trailhead or book a day of shuttles with Gravity Isle or Vertigo MTB to access the downhill runs beginning at the top of Loila Tier.

10 Return under the giant wooden archway and follow the Townlink stickers on the orange trail marker signs to the right. The fast and flowing descent will have you back on the shores of Georges Bay in no time, where you can enjoy the relaxing 3km back to St Helens Wharf, perhaps even stopping for a swim along the way.

Also Try...

Bay of Fires

TOM JASTRAM/SHUTTERSTOCK ©

North East Rail Trail

DURATION	DIFFICULTY	DISTANCE
6hr	Easy	26km one way

This scenic trail 62km east of Launceston winds through lush farmland and temperate forests, following an abandoned railway line.

The North East Rail Trail begins in the town centre of Scottsdale, on the corner of the Tasman Hwy and William St, and weaves through a sprawling landscape of rolling hills and native woodlands before finishing at Tulendeena Station near Billycock Hill. Along with sheltered picnic tables, interpretive signs can be found scattered throughout the easily navigated gravel path, offering insight into the history of the old railway. Although the trail cuts through deep granite gullies and traverses the hilly countryside, you'll find a gentle and easy ride along the well-built North East Rail Trail.

Bay of Fires MTB Trail

DURATION	DIFFICULTY	DISTANCE
6hr	Difficult	42km one way

For mountain bike enthusiasts, the Bay of Fires adventure trail should not be missed.

A mixture of tech and flow awaits on this 42km intermediate mountain bike trail that takes you from the depths of the enchanting Blue Tier forest, through a stunning coastal woodland to the white-sanded shore of Swimcart Beach in the Bay of Fires. This is a point-to-point ride beginning at the Blue Tier car park between Derby and St Helens. While private shuttling is possible, it's worth booking a tour for the best experience and some additional guidance. The most popular shuttle companies are Up Down Around and Vertigo MTB. Up Down Around operates out of Derby while Vertigo MTB operates from both Derby and St Helens.

CHRIS ISON/SHUTTERSTOCK ©

Golden Valley Ascent

DURATION	DIFFICULTY	DISTANCE
2–5hr	Difficult	38km

This one isn't for the faint-hearted. It is a Hors catégorie (HC) climb, winding its way up from Deloraine, a quaint country town known for its craft fair, through dense eucalyptus forest all the way up to the alpine and desolate region of the Central Highlands.

The climb starts in open country farmland, taking you up switchbacks and quickly changing into a cool temperate rainforest. As you work your way further up you come out from under the forest canopy into the open and amazing views overlooking the entire Meander region. Once at the top of the climb, 1240m above sea leave, you are welcomed with one of Tasmania's rarest trees, the pencil pine. This has to make the list as one of the best HC climbs in Tasmania.

West Coast

DURATION	DIFFICULTY	DISTANCE
Up to 5hr	Easy-difficult	5–50km

We want to put in a special mention for the west coast. Whether for road cycling or mountain biking, step outside your comfort zone and experience the raw, the untamed and undeniably wild west coast of Tasmania

After nearly becoming a ghost town (and region), Queenstown, and the entire west coast, is now experiencing an injection of life with its growing mountain bike parks. Queenstown is surrounded by dramatic hills that provide stark evidence of a history that once made it one of the richest mining towns in the world. Whether you're after a big mountain adventure or an easy rail trail, the west coast offers trails for all abilities, ranging from easy to extreme. You can choose your own adventure!.

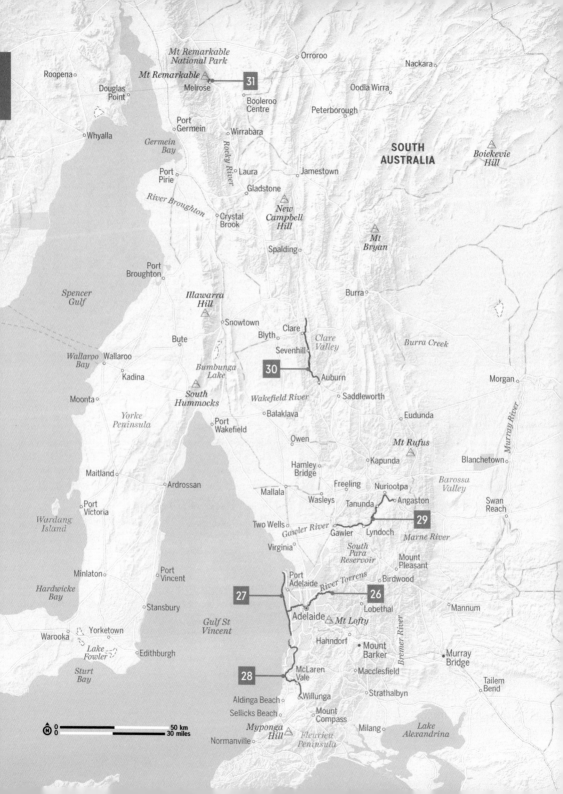

TRAVELLIGHT/SHUTTERSTOCK ©

Winery, Clare Valley (p186)

South Australia

Explore

South Australia

South Australia, with its warm climate and diverse landscapes, is a dreamy destination for cyclists. The state caters for all riding levels, offering winding trails through valleys and straightforward bikeways along beaches. Each year, Adelaide plays host to the Tour Down Under, the opening race of the Union Cycliste Internationale (UCI) World Tour, drawing the world's elite, painting the city lycra and elevating its robust cycling culture to heady heights. By bike is the best way to explore this region's natural beauty, and SA has it all. With a mix of coastal, outback and wine-growing terrain, it's ready-made for cyclists.

Adelaide

As the primary gateway to this corner of the world, Adelaide has something for everyone willing to make the journey. While smaller than its mainland counterparts, the city delivers more than its share of world-class hospitality, with all the necessary comforts to rest and replenish, or resupply, before exploring SA's extensive offerings. Known as the '20-minute city', Adelaide's compact size, clean grid layout and separated bike paths make it a breeze to explore on two wheels. The city is surrounded by 760 hectares of lush parkland and, further out, scenic hills and white-sand beaches, thus providing endless cycling opportunities. Its Mediterranean climate makes for the perfect alfresco dining experience while enjoying a glass of SA's celebrated wine – don't worry, there won't be a shortage; the state is responsible for almost half of the nation's annual production. With a thriving arts and culture scene, countless festivals and events throughout the year, and a growing number of shopping outlets, Adelaide has something for everyone. Visitors can choose to stay in the city centre or venture out to nearby coastal suburbs such as Glenelg or Semaphore for a relaxed beachside vibe.

McLaren Vale

An enchanting town in the heart of the wine-growing region of the same name, and located 45 minutes south of Adelaide, McLaren Vale is known for scenic drives and picturesque countryside. With a mild climate, unique soils

WHEN TO GO

SA's climate is as diverse as its landscapes, from sizzling days in the outback to cooler temperatures along the southern coastline. Adelaide's dry heat can make for challenging conditions during summer, but evening sea breezes offer some respite. Spring and autumn bring comfortable cycling weather, plus the state's festival season leads into March and April, meaning you can party and bike.

and cool ocean breeze producing a diverse palate, the region's 70-plus cellar doors offer an array of tasting experiences. The town hosts an excellent range of dining and bar choices, plus B&Bs and hotels to keep you rested. If you're looking for camping and outdoor stores to supplement that bike trip, nearby Noarlunga presents a great spread.

Victor Harbor

One of SA's most popular holiday destinations, this historic seaside town seduces with its laid-back atmosphere and proximity to surfing beaches and conservation parks. Lying approximately 85km south of Adelaide, 'Victor' is best accessed by car, though buses also run from Adelaide. With ample accommodation options, as well as cafes, restaurants and adventure stores along the coastline, it's the ideal base for exploring the Fleurieu Peninsula.

Clare

A community hub nestled in Clare Valley, just two hours north of Adelaide, Clare offers

TRANSPORT

Adelaide Airport covers both domestic and international flights. Adelaide Metro provides integrated transport, with bus, train and tram services covering the breadth of metropolitan Adelaide. Bikes are allowed on the five suburban train routes (Belair, Gawler, Grange, Seaford and Outer Harbour). However, a car is required to explore freely beyond the metro areas, including SA's wine regions and coastal hubs.

visitors a laid-back, authentic country experience. With a decent supply of goods and services, it's a great choice for a peaceful weekend getaway or an overnight stop before continuing north to the Flinders Ranges.

 WHERE TO STAY

Located on the banks of the River Torrens, in the suburb of Walkerville, The Watson Adelaide – Art Series is ideally positioned for adventures to the hills or excursions into the city – only a 15-minute cycle away. Best of all, vintage bicycles are available for guests to hire free of charge – a convenience worth paying for.

CABN offers off-grid accommodation, creating cosy, sustainable retreats in rural regions of SA to suit both moderate and high-end tastes. With locations near the popular wine regions of Barossa Valley, Clare Valley and McLaren Vale, plus bike-friendly Kuipto Forest, these cabins make for an ideal base camp, well away from the crowds.

 WHAT'S ON

Tour Down Under
(*tourdownunder.com.au;* January) The first race of the UCI World Tour begins in the heat of Adelaide's summer, kicking off the pro-cycling calendar.

Fringe Festival
(*adelaidefringe.com.au;* February, March) The largest arts festival in the southern hemisphere, and the centrepiece of SA's festival celebrations.

WOMADelaide
(*womadelaide.com.au;* March) An iconic open-air festival in the heart of Adelaide, honouring cultural exploration and discovery.

Resources

Broadsheet's (*broadsheet. com.au/adelaide*) coverage of Adelaide provides a dependable online resource for current events, openings and developments.

The website for the **National Parks and Wildlife Service South Australia** (*parks.sa.gov. au*) is a valuable resource, providing up-to-date information on the state's conservation programs and national parks.

All tourist regions, including central Adelaide, provide comprehensive and well-stocked **visitor centres**.

26

River Torrens Linear Park Trail

DURATION	DIFFICULTY	DISTANCE	START/END
2hr	Easy	33km one way	West Beach/ Athelstone
TERRAIN		Paved paths with gentle inclines	

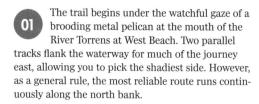

KWEST/SHUTTERSTOCK ©

Pelican in the River Torrens

Stretching 33km from the foot of the Mt Lofty Ranges to the edge of the Southern Ocean, the River Torrens Linear Park Trail is Australia's longest hills-to-coast track. Perfect for beginners, the trail slices through Adelaide's metropolitan sprawl while remaining blissfully detached from the city's frenetic pace. Enjoying mostly flat terrain (aside from the bump towards the hills), this leafy trip through the 'burbs paints a picture of Adelaide's greening ambitions and gives a nod to its National Park City status.

Bike Hire

Spinway Adelaide's self-service station, in West Beach Caravan Park, rents bikes for children and adults. Check at reception for helmets and locks. Prices range from $11 per hour to $33 per day.

Starting Point

The mouth of the River Torrens at West Beach is best accessed by car, with parking at Henley Sailing Club. Alternatively, base yourself in Adelaide and complete a round-trip over several days.

01 The trail begins under the watchful gaze of a brooding metal pelican at the mouth of the River Torrens at West Beach. Two parallel tracks flank the waterway for much of the journey east, allowing you to pick the shadiest side. However, as a general rule, the most reliable route runs continuously along the north bank.

02 Cycle over Seaview Rd and along the Breakout Creek channel, where ongoing restoration efforts are transforming this former drain into a flourishing haven for native flora and

Elevation (m)

Distance (km)

fauna. Beyond Henley Beach Rd, the river returns to its more natural, serpentine form, narrowing and bending gracefully towards the hills.

03 Meandering 6km past a series of reserves, sports fields and playgrounds, the path scythes through suburbia. Keep to the north bank at Holbrooks Rd and pedal past River Park Reserve on your left. Before long, you'll come to a pedestrian bridge adjacent to McDonnell Ave – cross here for supplies at the historic Brickworks Marketplace. Be sure to return to the north bank before continuing to Adelaide's industrial inner west.

04 Dipping below South Rd and Port Rd, you'll soon emerge into Adelaide's largest parkland, Bonython Park. Choose from any of the three bridges crossing the lake, and make your way through the rail underpass, staying alert for hasty commuters. As you ride, take in the heritage-listed Torrens Weir and golf course on your left, then the hospital on your right. Before long, you'll arrive at the northern edge of Adelaide's central business district (CBD).

05 The Adelaide Riverbank is the perfect spot to take a break from the saddle and explore the city. Secure your bike at the rack under the River Torrens Footbridge and climb the steps to the plaza. Continue straight into the train station, then navigate through the underground arcade to Hindley St. Some of Adelaide's best dining

River Torrens

Adelaide's River Torrens Linear Park broke ground as Australia's first fully realised linear park, uniting the river's ever-changing ecologies and characteristics. The Kaurna people, the Traditional Custodians of the Adelaide Plains, revere the River Torrens, or Karrawirra Parri (which translates to 'Red Gum Forest River'), for its impact on their social, economic and spiritual world. However, the fragile river system was devastated following European settlement. It took some 140 years to restore the waterway to its former glory. Even today, works continue to clean stormwater drains, remove weeds and rejuvenate vegetation in order to strengthen and protect the river.

and coffee options are just ahead, on Peel St and Leigh St.

06 Returning to the trail, the river's south bank provides excellent views of Elder Park, Adelaide Oval and Torrens Lake. Expect to see paddle boats in the water on sunny weekends and school holidays. Mind your head as you pass under the Adelaide University Footbridge and continue past the zoo and neighbouring Adelaide Botanic Gardens on your right.

07 Keep an eye out for turnoffs in the east – they can inadvertently lead you into the suburbs. After the zoo, cross to the north bank at Sir Douglas Nicholls Bridge and switch back at the small wooden footbridge beyond Hackney Rd. Stick to the right for 2km as the river winds towards Walkerville – accessible via a footbridge. This leafy suburb offers a refreshing rest stop, and one last chance to refuel before the steady ascent to the hills.

08 As you head back across the footbridge, look for the iconic O-Bahn, which chaperones the trail beyond the city. This German-inspired busway combines a regular bus service with a direct train line, cutting congestion and connecting the northeast to Adelaide's CBD. Follow the O-Bahn fenceline for 250m before crossing a bridge and taking an immediate left up a slight rise. Then turn right at the intersection, where the river reappears in front of you.

09 As the trail progresses, a gentle incline can be felt between Ascot Ave and Darley Rd, where the O-Bahn veers north towards Tea Tree Plaza. The trail's abrupt climbs arrive after crossing Lower North East Rd – don't worry, they're over quickly.

10 As you approach the trail's final 6km, watch for dog walkers and wildlife enthusiasts scanning the river red gums for koalas. The footpath meanders through an open field to Adelaide's northeastern foothills, where the Torrens continues into the Mt Lofty Ranges, and the track reaches its Athelstone terminus. Public transport here is limited, but you can enjoy the opposite side of the trail on a return journey as it meanders gently downhill towards the city.

☕ Take a Break

The ADELAIDE CENTRAL MARKET remains the city's favourite culinary hotspot. Boasting a veritable cornucopia of stalls and restaurants, it's a true feast for the senses. Despite evolving over time, the market has remained faithful to its roots as a traditional produce marketplace that boasts a selection of artisanal products and seasonal fruit and vegetables. Indulge in a leisurely sit-down meal or assemble a basket of delectable picnic fare. Simply follow the well-signed laneways via the market to Riverbank Link to access it.

MYPHOTOBANK.COM.AU/SHUTTERSTOCK ©

River Torrens Linear Park Trail

South Australian Museum

Just a short pedal up the south bank of the Torrens, the South Australian Museum houses the world's largest collection of Aboriginal artefacts. Housing over 3000 curated items, the exhibition offers a unique glimpse into the cultural heritage of the Indigenous peoples in Australia, showcasing an array of ceremonial objects, weapons and artwork, including paintings, carvings and weavings. The collection also includes some of the world's only intact bark canoes. These items hold significant cultural and historical importance, and the museum works closely with Aboriginal communities to ensure their respectful and appropriate use.

27

Coast Park Path

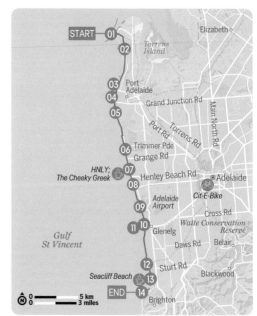

DURATION	DIFFICULTY	DISTANCE	START/END
2hr	Easy	32km one way	Outer Harbor/ Marino

TERRAIN	Flat paved paths and boardwalks, with some sections experiencing high foot traffic

Elevation (m)

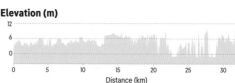

Adelaide's coastline is a captivating blend of sand, sea and history, featuring a gorgeous foreshore just begging to be explored on two wheels. The Coast Park Path is a perfect example of the city's commitment to recreation and sustainability, linking Semaphore, Henley Beach, Glenelg and Brighton's waterfronts through a series of lush revegetation zones. The journey is further complemented by easy access to urban beaches and the charm of heritage buildings. Since its first stages of development in 1992, the multi-use path has been a family favourite, offering everyone the chance to pedal through Adelaide's past and present.

Bike Hire

Cit-E-Bike provide a range of e-bikes with baskets, perfect for gathering supplies along the coast. Pick them up in Adelaide before jumping on the train to Outer Harbor. Prices from $50 per day.

Starting Point

Approximately 20km from the city, the trailhead is a short cycle from the terminus of the Outer Harbor train line. Thankfully, bikes are allowed on Adelaide's trains.

 01 Begin at the Outer Harbor lookout, located at the end of the train line on Lefevre Peninsula's northern tip. Here, you can witness a flurry of marine activity, with ocean liners, cargo ships and yachts all surfing the waters. Your journey starts east, passing Lady Ruthaven Reserve on your right. The shared-use path slowly bends south, rounding the North Haven Marina before straightening alongside a littoral vegetation strip.

Best for

COASTAL
RIDES

KIRSTY NADINE/SHUTTERSTOCK ©

Henley Beach (p172)

02 Running adjacent to Lady Gowrie Dr, the trail is flanked by a row of majestic Norfolk Island pines. These evergreens feature heavily throughout the route. Initially valued for their potential as ship masts, the supple wood of the trees proved unsuitable for ocean voyages. Nevertheless, they have found a home supplying shade and stature to SA's winding coastline.

03 After 4km, the path veers briefly among the vegetation, revealing Largs Bay's white sandy beach and majestic jetty. On breezy days, expect to see a flurry of kiteflyers and windsurfers harnassing the condi-

tions. Beyond the sailing club, the historic Largs Pier Hotel comes into view, its distinctive bluestone facade a highlight of the suburb's art deco architecture. The venue also boasts a rich musical history, having hosted performances from Aussie rock legends Cold Chisel, AC/DC, The Little River Band and The Angels before they made it big. Catch acoustic sessions between 4pm and 7pm on Sundays.

04 The trail eventually diverges from the Esplanade, leading through Semaphore Foreshore, a vibrant parkland that buzzes with summer festivals and an amusement park. Perched atop the dunes is the

Palais Hotel, its ornate tower a distinctive sight. Originally built in 1922, the building now houses a bar and grand ballroom that welcomes patrons dressed in everything from swimwear to stilettos. If you're feeling peckish, treat yourself to arguably the best hand-cut chips in Adelaide at Sotos Fish Shop, just 250m up Semaphore Rd. Continue your detour east along the road to explore Port Adelaide's maritime precinct.

05 Continuing south from Semaphore Jetty, the trail runs parallel to the tourist railway line to Fort Glanville for 2km. Trains depart regularly between 11am and 4pm

☕ Take a Break

At the halfway point of your ride, Henley Beach features a nest of restaurants and cafes to suit all budgets; from fine dining to fish and chips, there's something to delight every palate. With a balcony overlooking Henley Sq, HNLY offers a sophisticated dining experience, focusing on high-end seafood and mouth watering cocktails. Alternatively, grab a generously stuffed yiros from the CHEEKY GREEK.

on Sundays and on public and school holidays. Once you've passed the line's southern terminus, rejoin the Esplanade briefly for 400m before turning left onto Third Ave, then right onto busy Military Rd. Take care – this is the only lively roadway on the trail, so stick to the bike lane. A path extension along the coast is currently under development.

06 Cycle 3km southward, then turn right onto Bournemouth St, followed by a left through residential backstreets. The trail soon rejoins the foreshore across from Cable Station Reserve. You'll soon see the heritage-listed Marine Terraces tucked behind the palms on your left; this comprises the only three-storey Victorian-style terrace ever built on Australia's coastline. Overlooking the immaculate Grange Beach, this block of eight townhouses is only a third of the proposed 24. Fortunately, the impressive Grange Hotel and 140-year-old Grange Jetty – seen ahead – were completed in full. The shady lawn here is perfect for a quick break and a stroll on the sand. You'll find bike racks behind the waterfront cafe.

07 The shared path grows busier as you near Henley Beach, though pedestrians are used to cyclists. Soon, you'll arrive at chic Henley Sq. This plaza is a modern meeting place for

locals and tourists, offering restaurants and cafes, a large recreation area, a rustic jetty and a gorgeous beachfront. For ice-cream lovers, the award-winning salted pecan and maple gelato from Bottega is a must-try. But don't worry if you miss out here – there's a second outlet in Glenelg.

08 Progressing south, the path breaks from the Esplanade at Ozone Reserve, then veers east past the pelican sculpture that guards the mouth of the River Torrens. Climb the left lane up to Seaview Rd, cross the bridge, then turn right, back along the river bank before again returning southbound towards West Beach. Enjoy the peaceful 1.5km ride, taking in the unbroken ocean views, until the seascape momentarily disappears behind a revegetation dune, then returns past the boat ramp.

09 The trail slants gradually eastward before arcing inland and arriving at the pedestrian bridge over Patawolonga River. Be sure to dismount and walk through the lock before crossing the bridge. Wait here for a few moments if the gates are closed – a procession of boats will soon be entering and exiting the marina below you.

10 Once across 'the Pat', you've arrived at the fringes of the coastline's

MILLEFLORE IMAGES/SHUTTERSTOCK ©

Grange Jetty

Semaphore Music Festival

As winter's icy grip thaws, Adelaide's locals flock to the city's beaches in search of warmth. Those looking for more than just sand and surf can be found at the Semaphore Music Festival. Each year, Semaphore bristles with musical energy as the event engulfs the seaside suburb over the October long weekend. Launched in 2005, the boutique festival showcases an array of emerging and established Australian artists spanning alt-country, blues, folk and jazz. With gigs scattered around the town's charming heritage venues, the festival delivers an unforgettable few days by the sea.

Adelaide's Moving Coastline

Adelaide's beautiful beaches are in constant flux. Just take the coastline from Seacliff to North Haven – one continuous beach system – where the sands naturally drift north due to the winds and ocean currents. This process causes erosion on the central and southern beaches, including West Beach and Henley Beach South, while the sand accumulates on the coast's northern shores, including Semaphore. Roughly 100 Olympic swimming pools' worth of sand are trucked and piped along the coast each year, combating erosion and preventing Adelaide's pristine shoreline from completely relocating north.

Glenelg beach

retail hub, Glenelg. Turn left along the boardwalk, then right through Wigley Reserve. Keeping to the footpath, take a right just before the roundabout, then circle it to the left, crossing at Chappell Dr. Skirt the amphitheatric Colley Reserve, then head right to Hold-fast Promenade. Blending seaside charm with urban convenience, Glenelg, or 'the Bay', is another great spot to stretch your legs. You can secure your bike at the racks in front of the Glenelg Surf Life Saving Club. Then, head into Glenelg's vibrant Moseley Sq and up Jetty Rd, or stroll along the jetty. Until the 1940s, the pier stretched an additional 165m into the ocean, culminating in a three-storey pavilion at its end.

11 Returning to your bike, the track splits around a tree-lined reserve. Take the high road to the left alongside the modern apartment towers and heritage villas of Glenelg's foreshore. The 4km track to Brighton is popular with walkers, so be sure to use your bell before passing. The route continues parallel to the sea, deviating briefly through Minda Coast Park at Somerton Surf Life Saving Club.

12 Brighton Jetty will soon come into view, with its distinctive spire rising from the sea. Originally built in 1886, the jetty endured for over a

century before winter storms left the landmark battered and broken. Fortunately, a mobile phone company funded its reconstruction, and a telecommunications tower now stands as a subtle reminder of its benefactor. Take a moment to appreciate the view back along the coastline here, testing your eyes to recognise the distant landmarks.

13 As you cycle past Angus Neill Reserve, the Seacliff Beach Hotel emerges on the left – a perfect spot for a cold drink and a crisp ocean view. The waters here are a hub of activity, so expect to see all manner of vessels battling the waves. Before resuming, stop by the pump station near the beach ramp to inflate any ailing tyres.

14 The trail's final 1.5km continues along the Esplanade and through the Kingston Park Coastal Reserve, culminating just before the hill climb. Further on, a dirt track branches off the road, but it's unfit for bikes due to its cascading steps. Cycling enthusiasts dream of a day when the bikeway will connect the entire southern coast. The state's vision is to develop the path to Sellicks Beach at the start of the Fleurieu Peninsula, creating an epic 70km experience. For now, retrace your ride back up the coast or head inland to Marino Station, where you can catch a train back to the city.

☕ Take a Break

A dip in the crystal-clear waters off SEACLIFF BEACH delivers a great refresher after a sweaty cycle down the Esplanade. This beachfront, nestled along Adelaide's curved coastline, offers a quiet and secluded cove in which to cool down and relax. Alternatively, you can hire a stand-up paddleboard and explore SA's coastline from a different perspective. SUPs are available to rent, with lessons optional for beginners, from the Brighton and Seacliff Yacht Club. Prices start from $35 per hour.

28

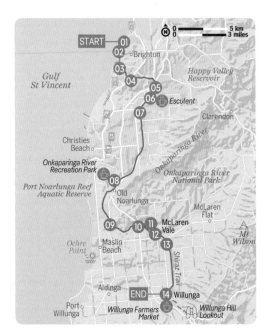

Coast to Vines Rail Trail

DURATION	DIFFICULTY	DISTANCE	START/END
3–3½hr	Intermediate	38km	Marino Rocks/ Willunga

TERRAIN	Paved cycleways with some inclines and road crossings

Elevation (m)

Linking Adelaide's southern suburbs to the McLaren Vale wine region, the Coast to Vines Rail Trail serves up a captivating blend of SA's seaside grandeur, heritage towns and celebrated vineyards, all threaded along the retired Willunga Railway. The paved path begins with coastal views before meandering inland through suburbia and onto the Fleurieu Peninsula's rolling hills. Then, the journey passes through McLaren Vale before finally extending along the Shiraz Trail to Willunga in the shadows of the Sellicks Hill Range. To embrace everything this trail has to offer, consider allowing a couple of days to fully immerse yourself.

Bike Hire

Adelaide Bike Hire is a convenient option for multiday trips. Rentals include free delivery to your Adelaide accommodation, as well as a helmet, tool kit, pump and map. Prices start from $135 for 48 hours.

Starting Point

While you can ride the trail in both directions, public transport from Willunga is limited. Instead, take the train on the Seaford Line to Marino Rocks. From here, it's a short pedal south to the trailhead.

01 As you exit Marino Rocks Station, set your sights south along Cove Rd, watching for passing cars. (Note that this path runs parallel to the Coast Park Path's southern terminus, providing the opportunity to combine the two in a multiday cycle.) After a short 200m, four multicoloured pillars appear on your left, signalling your arrival at the start of the Coast to Vines Rail Trail. It's worth taking a moment to study the information provided and familiarise yourself with the bright yellow caps – these are your wayfinding markers for the journey ahead.

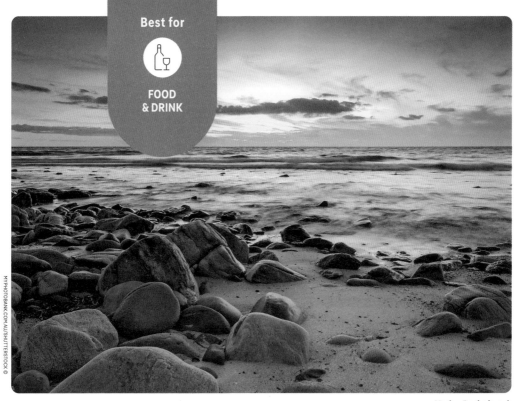

MYPHOTOBANK.COM.AU/SHUTTERSTOCK ©

Marino Rocks beach

02 For the first 2.5km of the trail, you'll continue beside the metro line to Hallett Cove Station. If you're still waking up, feel free to enjoy the seascape from the comfort of the train and disembark here. These are the best ocean vistas on the route. From this vantage point, the sea stretches before you, providing a serene outset for your journey. If you want to feel salty spray on your skin, this short undulating path presents the best opportunity.

03 Walk your bike through the station and up a ramp to your right, leading you across the overpass. The bike path resumes after a right hairpin turn

down the other side of the tracks. The trail then arcs inland along the line of Waterfall Creek gully, tucked in behind the suburbs. You'll soon reach the lively Hallett Cove Shopping Centre intersection, where the wayfinding gets tricky. At the traffic lights, follow the curve of Quailo Ave in front of you before proceeding to cross at the next junction, over Lonsdale Rd. The trail follows the road for the next 1km before swerving right onto the old railway line alignment, cutting through the tree-lined reserves of Sheidow Park.

04 After cycling peacefully along the tranquil suburban laneway for 1.5km,

you may feel slightly jolted by the state's most infamous expressway thundering away ahead of you. In 2001, the M2 Southern Expressway was bestowed the Guinness World Record for the longest one-way road on the planet, stretching 21km from Adelaide's south into the Fleurieu Peninsula. The highway flows towards Adelaide in the morning and switches southbound in the afternoon. The route has since doubled in size to accommodate traffic travelling in both directions at all times.

05 Once over the Southern Expressway, the path rolls down to the cycling intersection with the Patrick

☕ Take a Break

Joining the trail north of the Seaford Meadows Station, the ONKAPARINGA RIVER RECREATION PARK is a verdant pocket of tranquillity amid the urban sprawl. While not large, its peaceful wetland and flat walking tracks provide enough diversity to reset you for the road ahead. For those seeking a more adventurous break from the saddle, the neighbouring national Pprk offers an array of activities, from bushwalking through rugged terrain to abseiling rocky outcrops and kayaking in the river.

Jonker Veloway. This sealed bike-only track runs alongside the M2, providing cyclists with a speedy commuting corridor. The Coast to Vines, however, continues to chase the scenic route. Take the immediate left, dipping under the Reynella Bypass, then climb to the busiest intersection of the trail. At the lights, take a right across Old South Rd. Look for the little yellow marker pointing you in the direction of Old Reynella. Once across, turn right, following the road until it rejoins the path. From here, travel through sweet-smelling pines, gum trees and stringy-barks for the next 12km.

06 Before continuing south, Old Reynella is best positioned for a pick-me-up. Should you need a caffeine boost or a quick bite, the bike-friendly Esculent is a top choice (open every day except Mondays). To reach the cafe, veer right onto the concrete footpath after passing behind the Reynella Bowling Club, crossing Corn St and arriving at Old South Rd. You'll find the cafe on the opposite corner, to your left.

07 Tracking the old railway line, the path follows a linear reserve, gliding through the peaceful outer suburbs of Reynella, Morphett Vale and Hackham. It's a cruisy ride, but prepare to stop periodically at intersections. All major roads

are equipped with traffic lights or islands to ease your journey. Beyond Hackham, the scenery briefly transitions into rural vistas before you descend through the tunnel under the M2.

08 The urban landscape fades from view as you enter Onkaparinga River Recreation Park, giving way to a grassy floodplain. Be careful of the protruding pole as you approach the Onkaparinga River bridge crossing. This traverse provides the perfect vantage point to scan for kangaroos sipping at the river's edge. After 450m, the trail again merges with built surrounds before rejoining the metro line for 1.5km to its Seacliff terminus.

09 After one final jaunt through Adelaide's outer sprawl, the trail finally reaches its residential boundary, giving way to open countryside. Following the rise for 600m, the route swings inland, but not before affording you one last glimpse of the ocean through a break in the fence line. Head east through the underpass beneath Main South Rd, where large swathes of the McLaren Vale wine region unfurl in the valley below. Following the gyrations of Pedler Creek, the scenery completely transforms. The path curves along the gently undulating terrain, delivering a series of shady cuttings and elevated

DARRYL LEACH/SHUTTERSTOCK ©

Sugarloaf rock formation

Hallett Cove Conservation Park

Exploring the best of the Fleurieu's dramatic coastline requires a detour from the trail. From the Hallett Cove Beach Station, take a shortcut through the backstreets to the Boatshed Cafe, where you can secure your ride at the racks. Next door, the Hallett Cove Conservation Park is a geological wonderland, featuring ancient glacial pavements and towering cliffs that showcase Australia's ice age, which occurred around 280 million years ago. The park's crown jewel is the Sugarloaf, a towering rock formation made up of layers of quartzite, sandstone and shale – arrive at twilight to marvel at its iridescent glow.

The d'Arenberg Cube

Standing tall in the heart of the McLaren Vale wine region, the d'Arenberg Cube is the architectural icon of the Fleurieu Peninsula. This structural marvel rises five storeys high, flaunting a fanciful design with a seemingly impossible form. Wandering through the maze of gallery spaces, tasting rooms and bars, it's easy to lose yourself in the whimsy of it all. The Cube's peculiar exterior and interior designs also incorporate artworks and installations from various artists. But don't forget the wines – the cellar door offers an extensive range of d'Arenberg's award-winning drops, each with a story and personality to rival the cube itself.

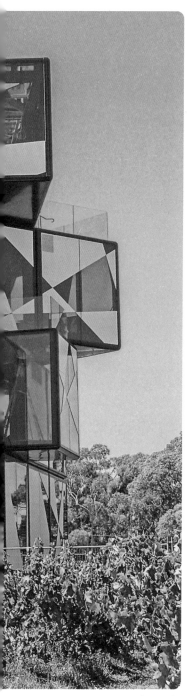

D'Arenberg Cube

platforms to view the vineyards below. Continue east for 3km before swinging north to navigate the ring road into McLaren Vale.

10 Passing under Victor Harbor Rd, you'll soon encounter a turnoff to your right leading to the McLaren Vale and Fleurieu Coast Visitor Centre. This is an excellent spot for a coffee break, and it features a gallery, exhibition space, cafe and public facilities. But remember, McLaren Vale's restaurants, bakeries, cellar doors and wine bars lie ahead.

11 The trail arcs south, popping out onto the town's main street. For the next 800m, you'll have to share the road or travel along the pedestrian path. As always, prioritise safety. The bike path picks up again at the zebra crossing, heading east alongside the historic Almond Train. This junction marks the official end of the Coast to Vines Rail Trail, but only by name, as it transforms into the Shiraz Trail leading to Willunga. If it's break time, pedal into McLaren Vale, where you'll find no shortage of delicious goodies.

12 The vines and the vignerons spring up quickly beyond McLaren Vale. The intersection at Field St is your first gateway to a cluster of the region's world-class wineries. Detour north for local favourites Alpha Box & Dice, Maxwell Wines, Angove Family Winemakers and Chalk Hill Wines, which also houses Never Never Distilling Co. Note that you'll need to venture 2km further to reach d'Arenberg and its quirky Cube. Also, be aware that you'll be cycling on active backroads, so exercise caution.

13 Back on the trail, you'll soon find yourself isolated amid the vines, if you haven't been tempted in by Serafino Wines' inviting trail entrance off to your left. The final 5km stretch leads into Willunga, where the journey ends in spacious parkland alongside the Willunga Jubilee Rose Garden. Head east on Aldinga Rd, then turn diagonally up High St for the town's most extensive spread of eateries.

14 If you're looking for a post-trail challenge, the 3km climb up Old Willunga Hill is a heart-starter. With an average grade of 7.4% over 3km, the ascent to the Willunga Hill Lookout is one of SA's favourite – and most arduous – climbs. If you're feeling sporty, continue along High St for 600m. When you reach the Old Post Office Telegraph Station on your right, a paved strip crosses the road: this is your starting line – deep breaths and good luck.

☕ Take a Break

In Willunga, the weekends are for markets. Showcasing the region's love for local produce, the weekly WILLUNGA FARMERS MARKET boasts farm-to-table delights featuring organic fruit, seasonal vegetables, bread, cheeses and of course, wine. The friendly vendors are the region's growers, who love chatting about their produce and farming practices. The town also hosts the GREEN LIGHT ORGANIC MARKET every Saturday, while every second Saturday visitors can look forward to WILLUNGA QUARRY MARKET and the WILLUNGA ARTISANS & HANDMADE MARKET.

29

Barossa Trail

DURATION	DIFFICULTY	DISTANCE	START/END
2½–3hr	Intermediate	42km one way	Gawler/ Angaston
TERRAIN		Paved paths with some sections of road and gentle inclines	

Trail to Angaston (p184), Barossa Valley

The Barossa Trail may be the perfect way to experience Australia's most revered wine region. With the sweet scent of grapes perfuming the air, time slows to a leisurely pace that embodies country life at its finest. The Barossa Valley exudes a palpable sense of history, culture and natural beauty. Meandering through townships steeped in German heritage, the trail invites you to explore some of the wine industry's most legendary producers. Whether you're an avid cyclist or a casual rider, the Barossa is best savoured over several days.

Bike Hire

With six locations around the valley, Barossa Bike offers hybrid and e-bikes, some equipped with baskets. Delivery and pick-up are available, and helmets, locks and maps are supplied. Prices start from $50 for eight hours.

Starting Point

Trains run to Gawler Central Station, 3km from the trailhead, just outside of Gawler. However, a car is needed if you wish to begin the trail from within the valley.

01 From Gawler Central Station, head south on Murray St for 300m before turning left onto Lyndoch Rd and the beginning of Barossa Valley Way. Just past the intersection, the Gawler Visitor Information Centre is a great base, offering lockers, maps, drinking fountains and bike hire.

02 Barossa Valley Way is the main route between Gawler East and the Barossa Valley, and it can get busy. Exercise caution and, if it's safe, ride on the footpath. After 1.3km, an access road, Eucalypt Dr, appears on your right, taking you off the main

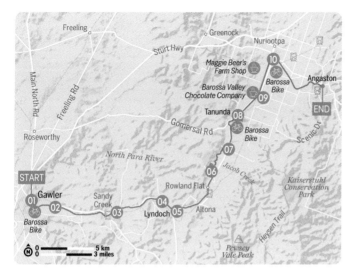

Elevation (m)

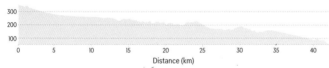

drag. The suburban sprawl gives way to farmland, with paddocks to the north bringing in the decommissioned Gawler-Angaston Railway. Dating to 1911, this line acts as your guide, leading you through the valley's heritage towns. Crossing Sunnydale Ave, the first Barossa Trail sign welcomes you onto the bikeway corridor.

03 Slowing for intersections, follow the path for roughly 6km before diverting left onto Cockatoo Ln, then right after 200m back alongside Barossa Valley Way. Over the next 4km, vineyards fill the countryside, signalling you've entered the Barossa.

04 Exercise caution when crossing at Lyndoch Hill, as the road here can be busy. The trail veers left through a delightful rose garden before curling right and continuing into Lyndoch. Established in 1837, this is one of SA's oldest towns. The village green opposite the bakery is a great spot to refill your water bottle and enjoy a traditional German-style pastry – *Bienenstich* (bee-sting cake) is a local favourite.

05 Winemakers come thick and fast beyond Lyndoch, with award-winning small batch cellars and international heavy hitters lining the route. No fewer than 15 wineries sit on or near the trail before arriving in Tanunda – remember to check cellar-door opening times before venturing inside. Continuing northeast beside Barossa Valley Way, a gradual ascent works its way past Altona Landcare Reserve – detour up Altona Rd to

visit this rehabilitated quarry, and don't forget the camera. The trail briefly reconnects with the railway line before veering towards Rowland Flat. Cycling through the small community, the path arcs left through the vines, twisting towards Jacob's Creek – the site of the valley's first commercial vine plantings in 1847.

06 The following 5km are the trail's most challenging; you'll navigate short steep climbs and awkward switchbacks. Your reward is an immaculate rolling landscape set against the backdrop of the distant Barossa Ranges. Zigzagging around the ultramodern Jacob's Creek Visitor Centre and St Hugo Wines, continue tracking the signage through the undulating terrain. Eventually, you'll reach St Hallett Winery; turn right here, then left back alongside Barossa Valley Way.

07 Follow the highway for another 3km before switching sides at the caravan park, leading to the archway welcoming you to Tanunda. With its rich German history, the town retains its village feel, with shops, art galleries and gourmet restaurants housed in heritage buildings. The main drag also features the well-equipped Barossa Cycle Hub, located at the visitor centre.

08 On-road cycling lanes replace the designated multi-use path for the length of the town, though these are sometimes occupied; use the footpath if it's empty. After the Kroemer's Crossing roundabout, the trail transitions back onto a bikeway, where it's reunited with the train line.

09 A stunning display of red roses accompanies the route for the next 3km, contrasting vibrantly with the surrounding greenery. Heading over the rise into Nuriootpa, Penfolds' fermentation tanks appear above the vineyards. Its classy cellar door, plus a taphouse, pizza bar and distillery, sit just behind the lawns to your left.

10 Crossing carefully east over Barossa Valley Way to South Tce, turn left to the Crescent. This backstreet curves around to the beginning of the rail trail – and the steady climb – to Angaston. The incline increases as you push up the bend into Angaston, but the shady pines overhanging the cutting keep the path cool. Finally, you'll pop out into the Angaston Railway Precinct, complete with refurbished station and adventure playspace – perfect for kids, and those young at heart.

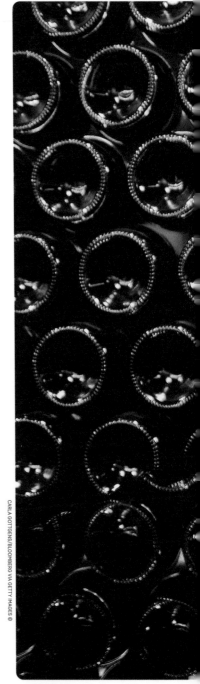

☕ Take a Break

Experience a delectable journey just a short distance from the trail, between Tanunda and Nuriootpa. Take a moment to savour the artisanal treats at the BAROSSA VALLEY CHOCOLATE COMPANY, which, despite its recent arrival on the Barossa scene, is already a crowd-pleaser. And for an authentic Barossan experience, head further north to MAGGIE BEER'S FARM SHOP. This valley institution offers perfectly curated platters, all expertly paired with your preferred tipple by the half-glass. Enjoy these indulgences in moderation; you may still have some cycling to do!

Penfolds wine

Penfolds Grange Hermitage

Penfolds Grange Hermitage is an icon of Australian wine, a legendary label whose influence has rippled across the wine world for over 70 years. It began as the experimental project of Max Schubert, a Penfolds winemaker based in the Barossa, who set out to create a wine that could rival the best of Bordeaux. Despite early criticism, Schubert persevered, and his shiraz (syrah)–cabernet sauvignon blend eventually became one of the world's most revered wines. Today, the Grange legacy continues, with each vintage highly sought after by collectors and wine enthusiasts, cementing its place in the pantheon of Australia's great wines.

30

Riesling Trail

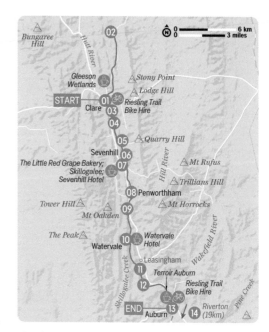

DURATION	DIFFICULTY	DISTANCE	START/END
2–2½hr	Easy	33km	Clare/Auburn

TERRAIN	Gravel paths with slight inclines

Elevation (m)

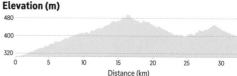

When it comes to Riesling, Clare Valley reigns supreme. The region has a time-honoured tradition of creating exquisite and age-worthy expressions from this noble grape. The Riesling Trail expertly highlights this reputation, weaving its way past the world-class vineyards between Clare and Auburn. Formerly a section of historic railway, this route was reimagined as a recreational rail trail in 1998, becoming the first of its kind in SA. Even today, its past glory lingers among the vines, making it easy to savour the rich history and flavour of Clare Valley without needing to stray far from the path.

Bike Hire

Located at both ends of the trail, Riesling Trail Bike Hire offers a range of bikes and accessories to transport you and your purchases. Prices range from $25 per half day to $40 per full day.

Starting Point

Your journey can start from anywhere along the way. Yorke Peninsula Coaches serve Auburn, Watervale, Penworthham, Sevenhill and Clare triweekly. In Clare, head west on Lennon St for the trailhead.

01 A short pedal from Clare's town centre, the trailhead sits at the old railway precinct. Little remains from the original infrastructure, and the only train you'll see today is the three-quarter scale silhouette of a steam locomotive – the first of many sculptures along the route. In fact, the Riesling Trail is as much about artwork as it is heritage railways and premium wine. The trail features many pieces that reflect the region's cultural heritage and beauty. Expect to pass congregated iron kangaroos, hollowed-out steel sheep and throwbacks to when railways ruled the land.

KWEST/SHUTTERSTOCK ©

Best for

FOOD & DRINK

Clare Valley

02 Beginning from Clare, you're faced with a choice: follow the well-trodden path south to Auburn, or start with the 8km extension to Barinia through the valley's provincial north. This scenic route takes you out of the suburbs, over an old rail bridge on Farrell Flat Rd, and through a shady cutting beneath towering pines. As you emerge from the tree line, you're greeted with White Hut's stunning vineyards before traversing native bushland to the Barinia siding terminus. Depending on whether you've already had your caffeine fix, it'll take around 30 minutes to an hour for the round trip.

03 Running south from the railway precinct along Station Rd, the trail navigates Clare's eastern flank. After a short 250m cycle, you'll discover the first of many trailside wineries by turning right onto Dominic St. Housed in a beautifully converted leather factory, the industrial charm at Mr Mick's Cellar Door and Kitchen is a must-see, even if you haven't worked up a thirst yet.

04 Returning to the trail, the path breaks from the road to join the Hutt River, cycling beside a nest of gum trees. Clare's residential outskirts soon give way to open paddocks, fruit orchards, native scrub and the

region's iconic vines. There are a few intersections here, so exercise caution before riding through. Shortly after Wendouree Rd, you'll feel a slight incline before arriving at the next winery on your left. If you're ready to partake in a hand-selected single vineyard wine and artisanal cheese pairing, Tim Adams Wines has you covered. Turn left along the dirt laneway for this indulgence.

05 Ease off the pedals as you approach the Clare Showgrounds on your right. Ready your camera: the Riesling Trail's most photogenic relic is moments away. Framed by a red bowstring arch, the iconic

☕ Take a Break

Located just off the trail in Watervale, the WATERVALE HOTEL is a true icon of Clare Valley, standing proud for over 150 years. Striding through its historic doors is like stepping back in time, to a place where classic architecture and warm hospitality create an authentic Australiana dining atmosphere. With wrought-iron balconies and a wide verandah, the Watervale Hotel exudes charm and nostalgia, perfect for a boujie break from your saddle. Looking for several dining options? You can't go past SKILLOGALEE, TERROIR AUBURN, UMBRIA or SEVENHILL HOTEL.

Quarry Rd Bridge transports you back to the railway's golden era. Pause briefly at the nearby information board to delve deeper into the landmark's construction and history.

06 Passing 'The Cyclist' near the Sevenhill Cemetery, turn left on College Rd for the oldest winery in Clare Valley, a place of pilgrimage for wine and history aficionados. Nestled beside the stunning St Aloysius Church, Sevenhill Cellars was built by Jesuit priests in 1851. Sevenhill's contribution to Australia's wine industry is significant, with the Jesuit Order acknowledged for introducing new grape varieties and winemaking methods to the country. Take a self-guided tour before enjoying a tasting at the cellar door. As always, remember to drink and ride responsibly.

07 By now, you're probably thinking about lining your stomach. Head back towards the trail, but instead of resuming south, continue straight on College Rd for 750m before carefully crossing Horrocks Highway to the townlet of Sevenhill. The Little Red Grape Bakery is carb-loading heaven, with a reliable range of vegan and gluten-free options. Alternatively, roll in next door to the award-winning Sevenhill Hotel for a longer lunch.

08 Continuing on, you may feel a slight rise as you pedal towards historical Penwortham. Dating back to 1839, this small community marks the first European settlement in Clare Valley and the Riesling Trail's highest point. It's all (mostly) downhill from here. You'll also notice several signs pointing you in the direction of wineries further afield, with many found on three additional circuits: the Spring Gully, John Horrocks and Father Rogalski loops. Be warned – these side trails demand an intermediate level of cycling skill and, ideally, an off-road bike. To expand your journey, you're best off returning with a car or enlisting the services of a friendly tour guide.

09 As you pass under Horrocks Hwy, the Riesling Trail begins its gradual descent towards Auburn. The landscape ahead undergoes a magnificent transformation, presenting a delightful medley of vineyards, pastoral vistas and native flora. This section of the trail is particularly scenic, offering fewer crowds and an ideal opportunity for a relaxed downhill cycle while taking in the refreshing countryside air.

10 If you're ready to return to civilisation, keep your eyes peeled for the detour

JFCREATIVE/GETTY IMAGES ©

Sevenhill Cellars

Down in the Dirt

Clare Valley's reputation for producing outstanding wines can be attributed, in part, to its dirt. The region's hills are home to a range of highly coveted soils, from shallow rocky grounds to red-brown loams, sand, gravel and slate. The area's geological history, once a seabed, has created a unique mix of soils, contributing to ideal conditions for growing a wide variety of grapes, with Riesling the region's trademark. Each subregion features a distinct combination of soils, imparting its wines with unique flavours that have established Clare Valley as one of Australia's most diverse and desirable wine regions.

Clare Valley Art Trail

The Riesling Trail's sculptures aren't the only places to find the valley's artistic riches. The Clare Valley Art Trail celebrates the region's creative spirit, featuring a diverse range of contemporary and traditional artworks, from paintings and sculptures to Indigenous crafts. Take to the road to explore the numerous galleries, wineries, restaurants and pubs that showcase the talent of local artists and artisans. As you wander through the towns, keep your eyes peeled for the vibrant public art installations that adorn the streets and parks, including murals and sculptures that are sure to ignite your imagination.

Vineyard, Watervale

into Watervale in 3.5km, just before the town's siding. Take a left onto Sollys Hill Rd, following the backstreet as it veers onto North Tce. Here, housed in a rustic 19th-century cottage, you'll discover the family-owned Crabtree Wines, whose classic terra rossa topsoils have produced some of the region's finest Riesling since the 1880s.

11 Further along, just beyond the turnoff to Leasingham, O'Leary Walker Wines presents a more contemporary experience. A newcomer by Clare Valley standards, its small batch vintages, sourced from vineyards around SA, deliver regional character by the glass. Perched atop a hill, its sleek cellar door provides unspoiled views from the verandah, dining area or lawn – where a competitive game of Kubb awaits.

12 The stretch ahead continues the tranquil passage through the countryside, where rows of apple trees and olive groves border the trail. If you're looking for an excuse to stretch your hamstrings, stop by *The Gathering,* carved from stones chiselled out of a nearby quarry. These five sculptures commemorate an ancient meeting place of the Ngadjuri people, and are well worth a moment's reflection.

13 As you approach Auburn, the path follows the highway before switching sides and passing beneath *The Archway,* a beautiful tribute to the stunning landscape you've just traversed. On the other side of the sculpture, a leafy park leads to the Riesling Trail's southern terminus at the old Auburn Railway Station, now home to Mount Horrocks Wines. Auburn's charming main street lies just two minutes to the east, featuring cellar doors, B&Bs and a host of historic buildings. Don't miss the Courthouse Museum, the Old Post Office and the ever-hospitable Rising Sun Hotel, built in 1850. For a refined experience, Terroir Auburn offers a sophisticated locavore dining experience, with rustic accommodation options available.

14 If you still have juice in the tank, consider continuing on the Rattler Trail to Riverton. The additional 19km route continues south from Mount Horrocks Wines. The countryside echoes the landscape from the north, passing through vineyards and farming country. The trail finishes by skirting the Riverton Golf Course and traversing a grazing paddock (remember to close the gate behind you to prevent livestock from escaping), before arriving at the end of the line at Riverton Oval.

☕ Take a Break

Just a short pedal from Clare's trailhead lies the hidden gem of GLEESON WETLANDS – a serene reserve where nature thrives. Created as a haven for local wildlife, the wetlands protects and enhances the natural environment, with a particular emphasis on waterbird habitats. As you explore its winding walking trails, meandering waterways and grassy fields, you'll come across a visitor centre brimming with information about the local ecosystem and its inhabitants. This is a must-visit for nature lovers and cyclists seeking a peaceful escape.

31

Melrose MTB Trails

DURATION	DIFFICULTY	DISTANCE	START/END
1½–2hr	Difficult	11km	Melrose

TERRAIN	MTB trails along roads and singletrack

DALLASETTA/SHUTTERSTOCK ©

Track near Melrose

In the shadows of the imposing Mt Remarkable, Melrose beckons as SA's ultimate MTB haven. With a population of just 342, this quaint community offers country hospitality and a thrilling network of trails. Experienced riders can conquer the mountain's renowned black diamond trails, tackling challenging climbs, narrow ridgelines and intense chutes. Meanwhile, beginners can find their cycling legs in the tranquil creek beds and eucalyptus forests, ideal for building confidence. Melrose is the perfect playground for mountain bikers of all levels.

Bike Hire

Located in Melrose, Over the Edge is your one-stop shop for all things MTB. Featuring various hire options, sales, repair, merch and a quirky cafe, rentals start from $65 per day.

Starting Point

Melrose's central trail network is a short cycle west from town. Alternatively, Genesis Transport buses make the weekly journey from Adelaide to Melrose for $80.

01 Note that this route tackles three of Melrose's challenging but achievable black diamond trails from their central network, but plenty of blue and green trail alternatives will help you find your feet. Before setting off, check in at Over the Edge on the main drag for maps, bike hire and a trail status report – oh, and a coffee – you may need it. Cross over to Joes Rd, past the caravan park, and head uphill towards the War Memorial. Beyond the monument, look for an access gate leading up the mountain; this track shares a starting point with the summit's walking trail but veers

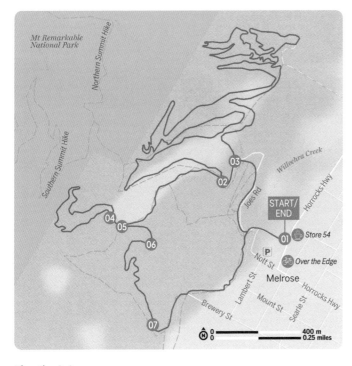

Fat Tyre Festival

Melrose's three-day Fat Tyre Festival is a celebration of all things MTB. This annual event over the June long weekend features the network's epic trails, live music, pop-up bars and plenty of tucker. But the real appeal lies in its community vibe. Riders from all backgrounds gather to trade stories and share the joys of MTB life. For those seeking a challenge, the 18 Hours of Melrose is a team-based endurance event that tests all your biking limitations. Held on the same trail network as the festival, riders aim to complete the course as many times as possible in six or 18 hours.

Elevation (m)

right. The path begins alongside the summit's walking track, but soon turns right.

02 Here lies the first ride of the day: the mighty Dodging Bullets. (Alternatively, continue along the access track and warm up your wheels at Don's Summit.) Offering 6.6km of trailblazing singletrack, this maze of mayhem will test your mettle with its seven climbs and descents, each with its own flavour. Glide through the scrubland, weaving sharply around hairpin berms and navigating bulging tree roots, log rollovers and leaf litter. The course runs through a former WWII shooting range, thankfully a relic of days gone by. Soak in the stunning vista from the top of the sawpit, with Mt Remarkable looming overhead, before hurtling through the forested gully. The track finishes by jumping the bank of a dry dam and breezing through the living room of a crumbling ruin, finally breaking into spacious doubletrack before circling back to the monument.

03 Pedal back through the access gate, but continue straight onto the Farmer's Freewheelin Fun Track – a gentle route. In spring, the mountainside is awash with Salvation Jane's vibrant purple, contrasting starkly with summer's pastel yellow. Continue for 650m until you arrive at the intersection on an open plateau. Follow the arrows right to Hellrose – the route's next black diamond. Cross the connector trail towards a bright orange column, marking the start of the clockwise ascent. (Or reroute left along the Benchin Track for a calmer blue cycle.)

04 Take a breath before pushing up the hill; the climb is slow and technical, giving you every excuse to stop and admire the infinity of Willochra Plain. After a steepling 60m, you'll arrive at the top of the Melrose trail network, where the fun begins. The singletrack slaloms rapidly down a narrow gully, navigating roots, rock gardens, fast jumps and a tight 90-degree switchback before dropping and looping back to the marker.

05 While your adrenaline is still pumping, scrabble back to the intersection, then follow the sign to A Bit Sheepish Track, veering right through the gum trees. This short trail connects the network's other central saddles. Watch for a spread of tracks here, scanning the arrows for the Greener Pastures entrance up and to the right. (Textbook 10%, one of the network's original trails, offers a straightforward ride, reconnecting with Farmer's Freewheelin Fun back to Melrose.)

06 Hucking off the lip of a gum root, the last of the loop's black diamonds is 800m of adrenaline-fuelled Gnarnia. Starting steadily enough through a grassy paddock, the singletrack plunges at around 100m, blasting down the ridge-line. Brace yourself for a series of natural rocky chutes and fast booters before crisscrossing a crooked creekbed towards the end – expect wet feet in winter. The track finishes with a sharp wall exit, so keep your speed.

07 Popping back out onto Farmer's Freewheelin Fun, turn left, following the trail along the creek 200m to Brewery St. Here, you have the option to pedal back into Melrose via backstreets, but the Chicken Run, joining on the banks of Willorcha Creek and reconnecting to Joes Rd, is a gem. This route is also a favourite for dog walkers, so exercise caution down the slope. Then, take a deep breath and go again, or turn right to catch your breath in Melrose.

☕ Take a Break

Nestled among the gums southeast of Melrose, the Weaving Camels Track transports you to a land of fairy tales. The lush greenery and babbling creek create a magical atmosphere straight from a storybook. The 1km trail gets its name from the stands of river red gums *(Eucalyptus Camaldulensis)* that line the track. Your journey ends at a delightful riverside table, the perfect spot to unpack a picnic. For a range of sweet and savoury provisions, head to STORE 54 or OVER THE EDGE before leaving Melrose.

Mt Remarkable National Park

Mt Remarkable National Park

Mt Remarkable National Park is a magnificent geological spectacle that has taken shape over an astonishing 800 million years to reveal towering mountain ranges, steep valleys and striking red quartzite cliffs. It is split into three sections – Mt Remarkable, Alligator Gorge and Mambray Creek – each with a variety of outdoor activities on offer. The park is teeming with a diverse range of wildlife, including endangered species like yellow-footed rock wallabies, tree goannas and echidnas, while birdwatchers will find over 100 species, including vibrantly coloured wrens, Australian ringneck parrots, emus and majestic wedge-tailed eagles.

Also Try...

Cockle Train, Victor Harbor

THOMAS WYNESS/SHUTTERSTOCK ©

Sturt Gorge Recreation Park

DURATION	DIFFICULTY	DISTANCE
2–3hr	Intermediate	40km+

Located 20 minutes south of Adelaide's city centre, Sturt Gorge Recreation Park offers a peaceful hideaway for mountain bikers seeking an urban escape.

Trails, ranging from beginner to advanced, span 40km of the park's rugged terrain. The network winds through native scrub, past rocky outcrops and alongside waterfalls that run during winter and spring.

The park is also committed to conservation. The preservation of the greybox grassy woodland vegetation, once found in abundance across southern Australia, is a priority. Additionally, the park features a unique rock formation, Sturt Tillite, formed 800 million years ago from glacial material that dropped from floating ice in the ocean.

Encounter Bikeway

DURATION	DIFFICULTY	DISTANCE
1½–2hr	Easy	31km

Running 31km along the Fleurieu Peninsula's coastline, the Encounter Bikeway absorbs the stunning waterfront, taking in five distinctive towns, each with its own captivating history and charm.

From the quaint River Murray port of Goolwa to the delightful seaside townships of Middleton, Port Elliot, Victor Harbor and Encounter Bay, every stop is worth further exploration. The trail follows the historic train line – the first public railway built in Australia – occasionally hugging the coast or navigating wetlands, but featuring gorgeous beach vistas at all times.

To complete the outing, a return trip on the restored Cockle Train, which provides a delightful chuffing and puffing throughout your journey, is a must-ride for railway buffs.

GALUMPHING GALAH/SHUTTERSTOCK ©

Emu, Ikara-Flinders Ranges National Park

Ikara-Flinders Ranges

DURATION	DIFFICULTY	DISTANCE
5hrs–3 days	Difficult	200km+

Venturing into the ancient landscape of SA's Ikara-Flinders Ranges National Park is an experience only reserved for the most adventurous mountain bikers.

With its potent blend of isolated outback, wild gorges and lush vegetation, the iconic geography demands respect and (at least) an intermediate level of MTB experience. Rawnsley Park and Wilpena Pound Resort make great base camps, or try camping under the stars to fully submerge yourself in the otherworldly terrain. Due to its remoteness, organising support from a local guide is highly recommended.

To truly immerse yourself in Adnyamathanha Country, there's no better way than to explore by bike, whether on a multiday adventure or a lap around the ranges.

Mawson Trail

DURATION	DIFFICULTY	DISTANCE
2-3 weeks	Difficult	900km

Running 900km along SA's geological spine, the Mawson Trail showcases the breadth of the state's untamed wilderness.

In the spirit of its namesake, the legendary explorer Sir Douglas Mawson, the two-week adventure takes riders on an enthralling expedition through a range of demanding terrain. The rugged route, designed for seasoned mountain bikers, features a network of unsealed roads, forestry tracks, fire trails and farm roads that link the popular cycling destinations of Adelaide Hills, Barossa Valley, Clare Valley, Melrose and Wilpena Pound.

The Mawson Trail requires riders to be well-equipped, experienced and prepared for the challenges ahead. But the payoff is enormous, with SA's captivating landscapes the perfect reward.

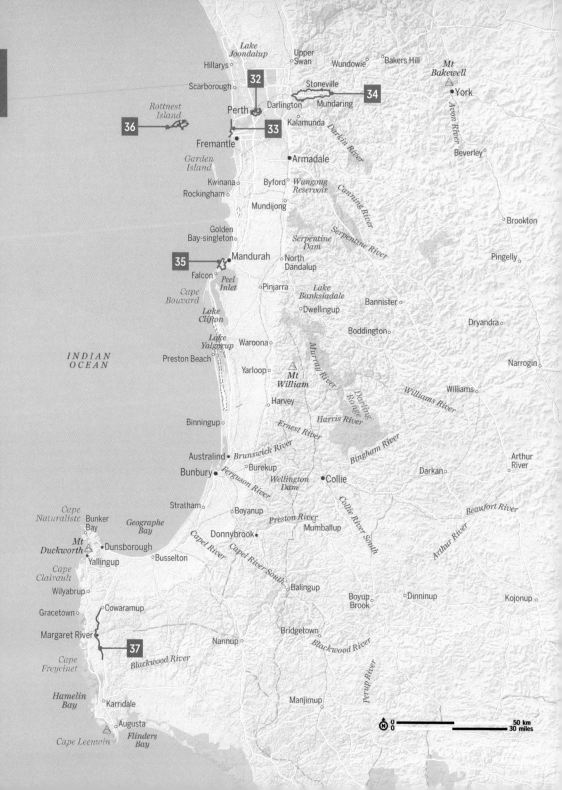

Lake Joondalup

Hillarys

Scarborough

32

Upper Swan

Wundowie

Bakers Hill

Stoneville

Mt Bakewell

York

Rottnest Island

36

Perth

Darlington

Mundaring

34

Avon River

33

Kalamunda

Beverley

Fremantle

Garden Island

Armadale

Darkin River

Brookton

Kwinana

Byford

Wungong Reservoir

Rockingham

Canning River

Mundijong

Serpentine River

Pingelly

Golden Bay-singleton

Serpentine Dam

35

Mandurah

North Dandalup

Falcon

Peel Inlet

Pinjarra

Lake Banksiadale

Bannister

Dryandra

Cape Bouvard

Lake Clifton

Dwellingup

Boddington

Lake Yalgorup

Waroona

Murray River

Narrogin

INDIAN OCEAN

Preston Beach

Yarloop

Mt William

Dorling Range

Williams River

Williams

Harvey

Harris River

Binningup

Ernest River

Bingham River

Arthur River

Australind

Brunswick River

Bunbury

Burekup

Ferguson River

Wellington Dam

Collie

Darkan

Stratham

Boyanup

Preston River

Collie River South

Beaufort River

Cape Naturaliste

Bunker Bay

Geographe Bay

Donnybrook

Mumballup

Arthur River

Mt Duckworth

Dunsborough

Capel River

Capel River South

Cape Clairault

Yallingup

Busselton

Balingup

Boyup Brook

Dinninup

Kojonup

Wilyabrup

Gracetown

Cowaramup

Bridgetown

Margaret River

Blackwood River

37

Nannup

Perup River

Cape Freycinet

Blackwood River

Manjimup

Hamelin Bay

Karridale

Augusta

Flinders Bay

Cape Leeuwin

N

0 50 km
0 30 miles

EA GIVEN/SHUTTERSTOCK ©

Path to Cape Vlamingh (p224), Rottnest Island

Western Australia

Explore

Western Australia

Breathe in the scent of lemon gums and peppermint trees as you hear the chuckle and caw of native birds and feel Western Australia's sun warm your skin. WA seems to be made for bike riding, be it zooming along the straight stretches of a historic railway track through the bush or coasting alongside the Indian Ocean as waves crash on blonde beaches below. The nearly always-sunny weather, mostly flat terrain and impressively well-maintained routes make two-wheeled explorations abundantly accessible. With wildlife sightings a very real possibility, and a pub, cafe or winery never far away, you'd best get pedalling.

Perth

The WA capital city is as bright and perky as the sunshine that coats its every surface. With 3000 hours of sunshine a year, the city's population is predictably outdoorsy, relishing in the Swan River and Indian Ocean, as well as the many surrounding national parks and bush tracts ribboned with biking and hiking trails. The Perth Hills are only 30 minutes' drive from the central business district (CBD), and feel like a collection of country villages that have spread into one another; amenities here tend to be simple, slower paced and close early; Kalamunda and Mundaring have the most shops and eateries. Perth Airport is the main arrival point for visitors, and most base themselves in the city centre or characterful

Fremantle. Hit Northbridge's James St for small bars, 24-hour convenience stores, Asian supermarkets, Italian delicatessens and China Town eateries.

Fremantle

Freo, as locals love to call it, has a distinctive personality: idiosyncratic, creative, artsy and gritty. Many of the port town's residents are famous musicians and writers: from Bon Scott, John Butler and San Cisco, to Ben Elton, Craig Silvey and Tim Winton, there's quite the list. It's the kind of place where heritage facades loom large, small bars fit into former warehouses and art galleries team with garden cafes. While public amenities are good, supermarkets are hard to find; the independent grocer (IGA) inside the new FOMO Freo

WHEN TO GO

From August through to late October, WA's remarkable native wildflowers bloom en masse. Add to that the gushing waterfalls fuelled by winter's rains, and a mild daily temperature with sunny skies and cool winds, and spring is the ultimate time to cycle in nature. Conditions are also ideal from April to June, as summer heat recedes and autumnal colours emerge. Winter can be muddy. Sunscreen is essential year-round.

precinct is your best bet, unless you hit the weekend markets for fresh produce. The family-friendly restaurants lining the Fremantle Fishing Boat Harbour pride themselves on their fish and chips.

Margaret River Region

The southwest towns of Cowaramup and Margaret River sit 10 minutes' drive apart. Cowaramup, fondly nicknamed 'Cow Town', is indeed dotted with 42 life-sized fibreglass dairy cows and calves, enlivening a stroll along the main street, which is also the region's major highway. Only a small village, it has a post office, a butcher, a bakery, a beer taphouse, a distillery, a candy shop and cafes. Accommodation tends to be Airbnbs, farmstays and winery cottages. Margaret River is the bigger sister, with three major supermarkets, three pubs, several cafes and restaurants and all the shops expected of a larger hub. Accommodation

TRANSPORT

With such great distances to cross, WA is a car-dominated state and getting around to specific destinations is easiest with four wheels. That said, the Perth train network is reliable, and gets to Fremantle and Mandurah faster than you can drive. A regular bus service travels to Margaret River, but getting around may be tricky. Rottnest Island is car-free, with an excellent ferry service.

tends to book out in advance and is priced at the upper end of the scale. For each town, the beach is a 10- to 15-minute drive to the west.

 WHAT'S ON

Everlasting Kings Park Festival

(*bgpa.wa.gov.au/kings-park/events/festival*) Some 16,000 wildflower species are planted into region- or species-specific gardens in Perth's central bush naturescape for this month-long annual event. Millions of blooms cover the botanic garden each September.

Fine Vines Festival

(*finevinesfestival.com.au*) Visit wineries that don't normally open to the public, eat native foods in a wine barrel room and gaze at local art in a storage warehouse. This grassroots festival, held over nine days in October, opens up spaces that are normally off-limits.

 WHERE TO STAY

Tiny cabins have popped up around Perth and in the state's southwest, allowing for off-grid stays on farms, wineries and secluded farms. Heyscape has cabins in Serpentine, 55km southeast of Perth, as well as outside Busselton in Margaret River. In the orchard-raked community of Bickley Valley, in the Perth Hills, the heritage Bickley Valley Cottage overlooks an asparagus farm and plunging valley views. More central is Alex Hotel in Perth's buzzing Northbridge, which has a coveted rooftop. Or try Warders Hotel, a tranquil boutique hotel in Fremantle beside the covered markets. Its limestone rooms once housed prison guards and some are said to be haunted.

Resources

Trails WA (*trailswa.com.au*) Nearly every hike and bike trail in WA can be found at this comprehensive site.

Tourism Western Australia (*westernaustralia.com*) Has loads of tourism info.

Pedal and Pint Trail (*pedalandpint.com.au*) Six Perth Hills pubs can be visited on this trail, which is an extension of the Railway Reserves Heritage Trail.

32

Best for

CITY
ROUTES

Swan River Loop

DURATION	DIFFICULTY	DISTANCE	START/END
1½hr	Easy	16.7km	Elizabeth Quay
TERRAIN	Paved bike and shared paths, flat with a few small rises up to bridges		

EQROY/SHUTTERSTOCK ©

Elizabeth Quay

The wide Swan River splits Perth in two, not just physically, but also behaviourally: Perth residents will often stick to one side or the other, and commonly identify as being from 'north (or south) of the river'. This flat, leisurely ride invites you to experience both sides, as it crosses bridges to loop around the central riverfront. The adventure blends looming urban structures with hushed nature sanctuaries, eye-catching public art, playgrounds and even wild kangaroos. You can shorten the ride with a number of bridge crossing options.

Bike Hire

About Bike Hire is on the eastern side of this trail, at Point Fraser Reserve. You can also start the loop ride from here. Basic bikes start from $10 per hour, e-bikes from $19 per hour. Some city hotels also offer free bikes.

Starting Point

We recommend starting at the *Spanda* sculpture, a looping white structure that looks like a skipping rope, crowning Elizabeth Quay. It's a three-minute walk from Elizabeth Quay Train Station.

01 From the *Spanda* sculpture, point your bike in a westward direction and ride past a traditional Venetian carousel. Follow the water's edge past the Transperth ferry terminal, to the start of Elizabeth Quay suspension bridge. Discover a giant silver bird sculpture in a boat, created by a Noongar artist. It represents her ancestors' impressions of the first European settlers arriving in distant sailing ships.

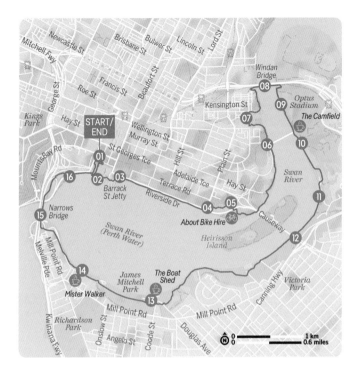

Elevation (m)

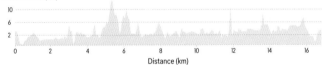

Distance (km)

04 Where Plain St sprouts from Riverside Dr, either keep going straight, or cross at the lights and explore the gardens diagonally opposite. Follow the boardwalk into the wetlands, where you'll see real black swans and other waterbirds. The morning avian symphony is quite magical. The boardwalk leads to a children's playground, free barbecues and a memorial.

05 The billabong is called Lake Vasto – Vasto in Italy is Perth's sister city. Curl around it, then cross the busy road southward towards the river, where you'll see a sign for On The Point. Follow a labyrinth of pathways towards the river and you'll find the cycle path, a water fountain and About Bike Hire. Ride towards Causeway Bridge. Look across the river to see Heirisson Island (p206), home to wild kangaroos that are easily observed at dawn and dusk.

06 After riding beneath the Causeway, the path becomes quiet and narrow and the surrounds feel somewhat like a wasteland. Past Trinity College you'll see Perth's Optus Stadium, a doughnut-like piece of architecture that opened in 2018. The curves of Matagarup Bridge, a pedestrian and bike thoroughfare, lead to it. The shape is designed to evoke swans, and also embodies the Wagyl, a giant serpent central to the Noongar peoples' creation story; notice the deliberate mingling of black and white colours. To shorten this ride, cross Matagarup Bridge and head westward around the river.

02 The bridge is pedestrian and bike friendly; cross with the island cafe restaurant and nature playground on your left, then look to the right where stairs descend to a secret platform with a public bench for quietly watching the world go by. Across the water, Kings Park and its row of iconic tall, straight trees beckons. Back on the path, veer right and pass the Rottnest Express ferry terminal at Barrack St Jetty. The pointy glass structure to your left is the Bell Tower, an 82.5m building housing 14th-century bells from London. Daily tours, bell-chiming demonstrations and the observation deck views are popular.

03 Continue following the U-shaped sidewalk as it turns towards the city. Notice three bronze swan sculptures on your left; the black swan is the bird emblem of WA. Reach the corner and turn right onto the bike path. Follow it through a palm tree tunnel and smell caffeine wafting from the white weatherboard Rurbra on the Swan cafe to the right. It's your last coffee stop for a little while.

☕ Take a Break

As you might expect of a pub sitting 100m from the state's premier sports stadium, THE CAMFIELD is a big, people-pleasing space. Claiming to be Australia's largest pub, it fits 2500 bodies across a beer garden, five bars – including one in a sea container – and a microbrewery. The kitchen dishes up steak sandwiches, wood-fired pizzas and chicken wings as 20 TV screens entertain. Naturally, it's rammed on game days– the people-watching is captivating – and relaxed at other times, with cold beers constantly pouring from its 175 taps.

07 Staying on the smooth and well-maintained east-riverside cycle path, pass public wooden slat lounge chairs, picnic benches and free exercise equipment. You might see a kayaker paddling, or hear the putt putt of a dinghy. Perth residents enjoy a high quality of life, something evident at Claisebrook Cove, a beautiful waterfront enclave of cafes, an alfresco pub and multi-storey homes. To get there, follow the path up a small, but steep hill to Victoria Gardens. This verdant haven was first planted in the 1870s as one of Perth's earliest parks. Take a pit stop and explore Claisebrook Cove, or continue on the route, dismounting to cross Trafalgar Bridge to your right. Spy hundreds of engraved love locks fastened to it by romantics.

08 Return to the tranquil waterfront and continue riding through shady bush. When you see Windan Bridge, take the path up the incline leading to the left, past an enclosed dog walking park. It turns in a U-shaped direction to arrive at the top of the bridge, where there's a dedicated walking and cycling path shielded from traffic. Cross the Swan River, while looking down to see jellyfish floating below.

09 At the end of the underpass, turn right and follow the bike path downhill, towards the river. Take a left and continue following the path through the trees. There's an excellent nature playground to your left, containing Banksia towers, musical instruments, a flying fox, trampolines and more. If you're travelling with kids, this will be a highlight.

10 Just before pedalling under Matagarup Bridge, look left to The Camfield riverbank pub. You might also notice the wire ropes stretching from the bridge to the foreshore. This is a 400m-long zip line that opened in 2021, allowing adventurous types to climb the bridge and zip line down at up to 75km/h (you can also descend using the stairs).

11 Ride on as the Crown Perth casino and resort complex looms to your left, and spot more public art, free barbecues, public toilets, playgrounds and public exercise stations along the path. You're now south of the river, which feels more tranquil than the northern CBD side. Expect to see many locals exercising here.

NIGEL JARVIS/SHUTTERSTOCK ©

Elizabeth Quay suspension bridge (p202)

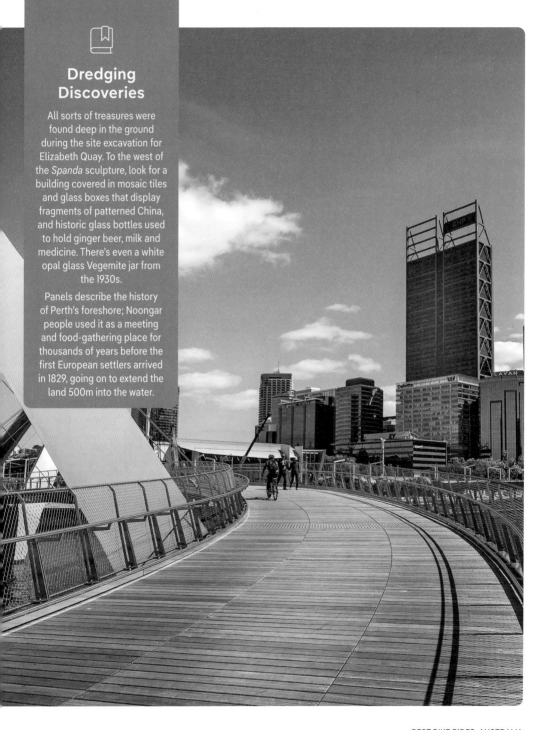

Dredging Discoveries

All sorts of treasures were found deep in the ground during the site excavation for Elizabeth Quay. To the west of the *Spanda* sculpture, look for a building covered in mosaic tiles and glass boxes that display fragments of patterned China, and historic glass bottles used to hold ginger beer, milk and medicine. There's even a white opal glass Vegemite jar from the 1930s.

Panels describe the history of Perth's foreshore; Noongar people used it as a meeting and food-gathering place for thousands of years before the first European settlers arrived in 1829, going on to extend the land 500m into the water.

Heirisson Island

How much money would you put on a bet that you won't see kangaroos bounding in the middle of an Australian capital city? While it sounds unlikely, there are, in fact, a handful of tame roos that live on the western side of Heirisson Island. The female western grey roos live unhindered in a large, contained area of swampland, grass plains and native tree thickets. They're usually dozing and hidden in shade during the day. Your best chance of seeing them is to walk quietly around the sanctuary before 10am or after 5pm, when they emerge to feed and drink in cooler conditions.

Heirisson Island kangaroos

12 Duck under the low Causeway Bridge leading to Heirisson Island and continue along the river's edge. As the city skyline comes into view, you might see fisherfolk in the shade of the trees to your right; like the roos, they usually appear early or late. As you ride, watch for the cute duck and duckling pavement stencils.

13 Cross over Coode St and, to the right, see a row of mini sail boats called Funcats that can be hired for a cruise along the river under your own breeze. Stop at The Boatshed Restaurant for a drink with a dazzling outlook. After Coode St, you'll ride through a beautiful thicket of Australian paperbarks. Look at the way the bark peels off, like reams of paper.

14 Arrive at South Perth where the bike path hits a T-junction. To your right, watch for the driverless RAC Intellibus bus that's being trialled (pre-book a seat to ride). Turn right, cross the road onto the concrete bike path and continue along the riverside, passing a conical shell sculpture. Ride westward towards an old paddle steamer called the *Decoy;* behind it is Mister Walker restaurant. Mends St, to your left, is a leafy shopping strip with plenty to lighten your wallet. Ride through a giant, bright yellow and orange numbat and frill-necked lizard that act as shade sculptures. Don't miss the small emu bronze sculptures beneath.

15 Keep to the path that is closest to the road; the riverside path is for pedestrians only. Continue towards the Narrows Bridge. When the path ends, cross the road towards the Old Mill, a former flour mill built in 1835. Turn right and ride up a small hill onto the start of the bridge; cross it, returning to the city. On the other side, take the path under a blue tiled bridge and through wetlands that are home to dozens of ducks and waterbirds. Continue on, under another blue tiled bridge, and pop out at a T-junction where there's free public exercise equipment and a water fountain. Turn left and head back towards the city. Soon, the Elizabeth Quay Bridge that you started the ride on will loom into view.

16 As you arrive there, curl around the quay again and spot the free waterplay park with fountains and pavement art. Why not splash in?

☕ Take a Break

Casual, welcoming and riddled with epic views of the city skyline, THE BOATSHED RESTAURANT is a great place to stop. The service is friendly, the servings are enormous, and it has an enclosed mini playground with picnic tables inside; parents can sit there, or on the other side of the glass.

For a similar experience with more sophisticated dishes, bustling interiors and celebratory vibes, make a beeline for MISTER WALKER RESTAURANT, perched on the Mends St Jetty opposite the South Perth foreshore.

33

Indian Ocean Explorer

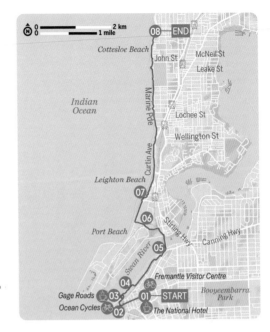

DURATION	DIFFICULTY	DISTANCE	START/END
1hr	Easy	10km one way	Fremantle Visitor Centre/ Grant St, Cottesloe

TERRAIN	Paved shared cycle and pedestrian paths, road and rail crossings, minor rises

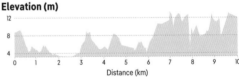

Elevation (m)

Marvel at Perth's glittering coastline on this beach-hugging ride that also takes in the heritage streets and sights of kooky and creative Fremantle. Tick off the port town and nearby Cottesloe Beach while discovering a historic tunnel, large-scale street art and a slew of outdoor sculptures. Aim to do this ride before 11am; it's when the local wind, known as the Fremantle Doctor, often starts to blow. The cycleway described here is a shared path; be sure to give way to pedestrians, ring your bell and travel single file when passing.

Bike Hire

The City of Fremantle offers free bike hire with a refundable $50 deposit. Bikes are limited so go early to the Fremantle Visitor Centre. For e-bikes, head to Ocean Cycles Fremantle (from $70 per day).

Starting Point

The Fremantle Visitor Centre at Walyalup Koort is somewhat hidden behind the large, cream-coloured St John's Anglican Church. Out front is a colourful children's playground.

01 From the visitor centre, push your bike through the High St pedestrian mall. When you reach traffic, ride along High St in a southwesterly direction. Notice the shops changing from mainstream to boutique and the historic buildings becoming ever grander. Cross Cliff St and head to the Round House, WA's oldest public building, built in 1831. Stop to explore if you wish.

02 Follow your curiosity through the tunnel beneath the Round House and turn right along the shared path. Discover the garden

Round House

The Historic West End

Fremantle's West End was largely established in the 1890s gold-rush era and is regarded as one of the best-preserved Victorian streetscapes in the world. More than 250 buildings are contained within the State Heritage–listed precinct, many of them housing chic wine bars, niche book shops and gallery-cafes, blending modern life with portside history. You may notice grand doorways, hefty arches – often used for wedding photography – and a beautifully weathered patina on surfaces. The convivial area has a youthful vibe thanks to Notre Dame University having many classrooms within the former banks, hotels and warehouses.

sculptures fronting the J-shed art studios. A number of artists work from here; pop in and watch them on weekends. You'll also find Bathers Beach, an almost secret strip of sand with calm waters and small waves perfect for a paddle. With the ocean to your back, ride through the J-shed car park.

03 Pop out on Fleet St and follow the road edged by sawtooth-roof sheds until you reach a stop sign. Follow the main road as it veers left, just before the roundabout. Keep the tall building that says 'Welcome to Victoria Quay, Fremantle' to your left – this is the port authority. Continue into a large car parking zone and turn hard left. Cycle until you arrive at the WA Maritime Museum.

04 With the museum at your back, follow the parking lot road parallel to the sheds and past Gage Roads brewery until you reach the E-shed markets, on your right. They're open Friday to Sunday with a mix of handcrafts, collectables and food stalls. Continue northeastward, past C and D sheds. Follow the road as it turns right and join the bike path diagonally across the road. Riding northeast alongside the railway tracks, you might see a cruise ship to your left.

05 Follow the bike path underneath the bridge and turn hard left, following the road's bike path up the gentle hill. Cross at the traffic lights, first southeasterly, then cross northeasterly, watching for oncoming traffic in all directions. Continue up the hill and rejoin the cycle path, marked by green stencils. When you reach the bridge leading to Queen Victoria St, admire a huge street mural depicting an octopus. Allow your eyes to travel further ahead to *Containbow,* a 9m high rainbow of sea containers which acts as a welcome statement to Fremantle by local artist Marcus Canning. Cross the road and cycle the path to get a closer look, or continue on the cycleway in front of you and cross the Fremantle traffic bridge, using the protected lane for cyclists on the western side.

06 As you leave the bridge, look for the bike path to your left, travelling through an industrial-looking area. At the redback spider mural, turn left and ride under the bridge. This is a heavy truck traffic zone for noisy transport trucks, so stick to the shared path. It will cross three roads and train tracks before arriving at the Port Beach Rd traffic lights. Rejoin the bike path on the ocean side.

07 You could swim at Port Beach or wait for the soft, white sand and turquoise waters of Leighton Beach, further along. There, you'll see Bib and Tucker restaurant, owned by former Olympic gold medallist swimmer Eamon Sullivan, and The Orange Box, an open-air cafe with sun-drenched deckchairs. Nearby are public change rooms,

Cottesloe Beach

☕ Take a Break

A hidden-from-view, open-air bar decorated with white parasols sits on the rooftop of THE NATIONAL HOTEL, a redbrick pub on the corner of High and Market Sts. Head up for sensational views of historic Fremantle rooftops. You might also pop into GAGE ROADS brewery, beside the WA Maritime Museum, to watch tugboats, cargo ships and Rottnest ferries glide by as you sip a cold beer. Further along the trail, you'll often see food trucks and caravan cafes in the car parks between Leighton and Mosman beaches on weekends.

toilets and showers. Continue along the coastline, passing fragrant pockets of native scrub.

08 As you arrive at Cottesloe Beach, follow the path up a hill and around the front of the surf club. Be mindful of the foot traffic around Perth's most popular sandy stretch, home to the annual Sculpture by the

WA Maritime Museum

Look up, when you're in the WA Maritime Museum, to see boats strung from the ceiling. The creative display, covering two levels and perched overlooking the Indian Ocean, reveals WA's intimate connection to the ocean and its navigation. From pearl luggers and tin canoes to the *Australia II* – the racing yacht that famously won the America's Cup in 1983 – there's plenty to marvel over. Linger at the silver 'welcome walls' outfront: some 21,000 migrants arrived in Australia through Fremantle port, and many of their names are inscribed here. Finish by clambering through an 89m-long Cold War–era submarine, once used by the Royal Australian Navy.

Sea exhibition (each March) and a protected swimming enclosure with a submerged shark net (in place October to March). Continue along the sculpture-dotted shared path to finish at North Cottesloe. You can either return the way you came, or ride up Grant St, past Daisies Cafe, and travel back on the Fremantle-bound train, departing Grant St Station.

34
Railway Reserves Heritage Trail

DURATION	DIFFICULTY	DISTANCE	START/END
4–5hr	Intermediate	41km	Swan View Railway Heritage Trail Hub

TERRAIN	
	Gravel rail trail with road crossings, some paved dual use trail, a long but subtle uphill climb

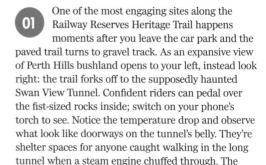

ANASTAS_STYLES/SHUTTERSTOCK ©

National Park Falls

Access to WA's native bush is only a 30-minute drive from the city centre, a convenience local trail riders revel in. Our pick of the Perth Hills bike tracks is the Railway Reserves Heritage Trail, for its frothing waterfalls seething over flat rocks, its sweeping eucalypt views tumbling down slopes and its surprises – from a gaping quarry to a haunted tunnel. More than just a path through nature, this trail follows the scar of a disused railway line; its history adds layers to the cycling experience.

Bike Hire

WA Mountain Bike Adventures rents mountain bikes for $99 for four hours, operates a bike shuttle service and runs guided bike tours of the Perth Hills.

Starting Point

The Swan View Railway Heritage Trail Hub, at the corner of Morrison and Swan Rds, is a great place to leave your car or get a hire bike dropped off.

01 One of the most engaging sites along the Railway Reserves Heritage Trail happens moments after you leave the car park and the paved trail turns to gravel track. As an expansive view of Perth Hills bushland opens to your left, instead look right: the trail forks off to the supposedly haunted Swan View Tunnel. Confident riders can pedal over the fist-sized rocks inside; switch on your phone's torch to see. Notice the temperature drop and observe what look like doorways on the tunnel's belly. They're shelter spaces for anyone caught walking in the long tunnel when a steam engine chuffed through. The

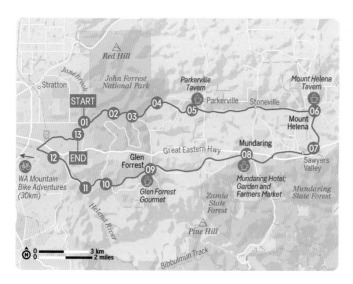

TOP TIP:

When to Go

Aim to ride this loop in early spring, when wildflowers bloom and waterfalls flow; it's the most beautiful time of year in the Perth Hills. If you can't make it then, opt for autumn or winter; summer days tend to be uncomfortably toasty, unless you depart very early in the day.

Elevation (m)

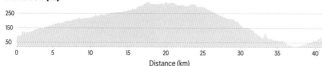

Distance (km)

---

information panels outside are worth reading.

02 Return to the trail, which is as wide as two cars, as it slices through native bush and grants yawning views in John Forrest National Park. A few kilometres on and you'll come to National Park Falls, with bike parking station, picnic bench and bridge. Continue on towards giant boulders, grass trees and native Australian bush. As the path reaches a series of white signs pointing to various sites, the trail peels to the right and descends. Arrive at a free barbecue and picnic area where you'll likely see kangaroos lazing on the ground (if you cook sausages, beware the robber kookaburras). Walk down to the old bridge and look up.

03 The trail leads up a hill and turns left towards interpretive signage. Pass a small narrow bridge; to your left is Jane Brook Dam, where people have swum for many decades. Next you'll come to one of the park's fairy huts, built in tandem with the native gardens in the 1930s. Follow the trail to the left, over an old bridge, then head up a hill. As the trail narrows, ride under a tree canopy and pop back onto the main trail. Ride on, past jagged rock formations reaching up the hill; soon afterwards, spot a sign to Hovea Falls.

04 The next, straight section crosses two bridges. See eight tall, skinny palm trees bordering old Hovea station, the first to be built in 1912. It

served farmers and workers commuting to Midland. Further on you'll come to a low, white gate across most of the path, signalling the border of the national park. Continue straight on the gravel path for some time. After passing a colourful playground, look for a sign on the left, to Falls Park. There are picnic benches and a little waterfall to watch and listen to.

05 The trail narrows as it rises towards a bitumen road. It's one of several roads you'll need to carefully cross. At the third crossing, consider following the hill 500m down to the Parkerville Tavern. Or observe the iron sculpture – one of many memorials of the 2014 bushfires, which decimated 57 homes throughout this region.

☕ Take a Break

There are a number of traditional, heritage-listed country pubs dotted along this trail, without much diversion needed. The PARKERVILLE TAVERN dishes up excellent pizzas, according to locals, and overlooks a creek. The MOUNT HELENA TAVERN specialises in smash burgers and old-fashioned country service with a grassy beer garden. The MUNDARING HOTEL serves above-average pub grub, such as chicken parmigiana, burgers and steak. If cafes are more your thing, try GLEN FOREST GOURMET – a cyclist hotspot with an airy terrace.

Look for the white emergency access gate and follow the gravel trail beyond. The bush now gets shorter and the landscape becomes slightly less hilly. Another white gate signals a break in the park; cross over the bitumen road.

06 Ride until you've got a proper sweat up and cross another road. About 2km on, turn left for a break at the Mount Helena Tavern. This is the kind of warm-hearted country pub where, if they notice you're a cyclist, they'll offer to fill up your water bottle with ice water. Head away from the pub on the trail and follow a green sign pointing to the right. Ride through a cutting and notice the trail narrowing among dense scrub. Chances are you'll still hear traffic on the road that runs parallel.

07 The trail rises; cross at the bitumen road. The next Perth Hills community, Mundaring, is 6km away. Presently, you'll pedal up a small rise with a warning sign about vehicles. Giant twin pipes loom to your left: this is the cross-country water lifeline known as the 'golden pipeline' (see p216). Continue to another white gate and squeeze through the narrow gap, following the slender trail that runs

straight ahead. Do not veer off to the wider track on the right. Ride through several cutaways until the track becomes paved – this is Sawyers Valley. Cross the bitumen road and return to the trail.

08 Eventually you will hit a T-junction. Here, turn left onto the paved trail. Ride slowly up the hill towards the Great Eastern Hwy – cross with care. Turn right onto the gravel trail, go round a bend and up a small rise with wooden railings. Ride on, flanked by industrial sheds and graffiti, then cross a small road. Do not deviate from the trail when it becomes a narrow gravel track. Ride through a number of cuttings and cross the next road. You will see a line of slender trees reaching for the sky, a playground, sculptures, picnic benches, water fountains, toilets and old pieces of machinery to your right. Welcome to the Mundaring Sculpture Park. Beyond it is the Mundaring Hotel, c 1899, a traditional pub with a heaving weekend atmosphere. This point is also the start of the Munda Biddi Trail, a forest cycle route that stretches for some 1000km to Albany, on the southern edge of WA.

09 Ride beneath a tall white sculpture using train wheels. Cross Gugeri St

SUHYB IRAR/SHUTTERSTOCK ©

Swan View Tunnel (p212)

Railway Springs Towns

Old railway lines make for excellent bike trails: they're usually flat, have plenty of straight sections and run through some of the most spectacular bush around. The Railway Reserves Heritage Trail traces the old Eastern Railway, which connected Fremantle with the agricultural town of York. The line was built in the late 1880s, giving life to numerous settlements. For example, the Perth suburb of Bellevue was once a lone farm flanking the railway. The farmer's home was called Belle View and the train began to stop there. By 1900, some 600 people had created a community, leading to a brickworks, a dance hall and a movie theatre.

1895

A Gamble That Paid Off

For more than a century, the Goldfields Water Supply Scheme has been pumping water from an enormous dam in Mundaring to WA's remote eastern goldfields, where freshwater is scarce. Prospectors battling in the desert experienced water famines; a secure supply was vital to continue striking gold. At the time of its construction from 1898 to 1902, it was regarded as a pipe dream with little chance of success. Now described as an engineering marvel and on the National Heritage List, its tree-trunk-sized pipes travel for 560km. When the Golden Pipeline was constructed, it supplied water to 30,000 pioneering folk; today it services some 100,000 people via 8000km of additional piping leading off the main tube.

The Golden Pipeline

and pass another low white gate to the track. This section is quite gravelly, so take it easy. Pedal for some time, cross more roads and pop out at Glen Forest. Stick to the dark brown shared path around a playground and return to the trail. You could veer right, to where you see steel handrails, and pop out at Glen Forest Gourmet. Otherwise, continue for 2.4km towards Darlington. Check out the quaint post office and homewares cottage, or the Little Nook Cafe. Follow the trail through low ranges peppered with hefty grass trees. Cross another road and continue on the gravel path.

10 If you're feeling confident, roll downhill and bounce over a number of bumps. Beware, the stop sign doesn't give much notice of a bitumen road coming up in 10m. Cross over to a car park with a sign pointing to a quarry. It's worth a look, despite the hill climb. There are nice public toilets at the hill's crest, a picnic shelter and then the grand, gaping quarry.

11 Take it easy on the downhill slope and avoid braking, so you don't slide in the loose gravel. Before reaching a narrow stream with steel rails bordering the track,

peel to the right (if you don't explore the quarry, go through the rails and veer left). This next bit has minimal signage and it's easy to get lost. Take the left trail, go up a small hill, then return to the trail, now the width of a single carriage gravel road. When the trail forks again, keep left and pass through the gap at another low white gate.

12 Ride until you pass four square, steel sculptures. Cross the road and arrive at a little playground; spot a sign for Bellevue. At the dirt car park, go right and join the shared suburban footpath, along Miller St. Duck under the bridge and follow the pavement until there's a dip in the concrete. Cross the road and find a dirt trail that leads right, to a cobblestone road that passes underneath a giant steel tower. Cross at Balfour Rd. Spot the Heritage Trail sign and information panel and return to terracotta-coloured gravel. It's now 2.6km until the trailhead.

13 The gravel eventually turns into a burgundy concrete path and passes old Swan View Station, to your left. Ride up the path with steel handrails. Turn right to cross the road and you've finished.

☕ Take a Break

If you're riding the Railway Reserves Heritage Trail on a Saturday morning, allocate extra time for the GARDEN AND FARMERS MARKET. It springs up in Mundaring Sculpture Park each week. Stalls are laden with fresh produce, aromatic coffee, artsy gifts and face painting for the kids. There's also baked goods, healthful juices and sugar-dusted treats. It runs from 8am until noon.

35

Halls Head Coastal Trail

DURATION	DIFFICULTY	DISTANCE	START/END
1hr return, 2hr loop	Intermediate	12km return, or 20km loop	Mandurah Visitor Centre

TERRAIN	Paved cycle paths, road crossings

BHPHOTOGRAPHER/SHUTTERSTOCK ©

Halls Head Beach and Mandurah

About one hour's drive south of WA's capital of Perth lies the coastal canal city of Mandurah – or Mandjoogoordap to the Bindjareb people of the Noongar Nation, meaning 'meeting place of the heart'. The Halls Head Coastal Trail rewards you with views of sweeping beaches, turquoise ocean and salty scrub. If you're lucky, you might also see dolphins, kangaroos and estuary waterbirds. While this is a relatively easy trail with plenty of flat stretches, there are some gentle rises and small but steep hills along the way. Sunscreen and water are essential.

Bike Hire

The Bike Kiosk on the side of the Mandurah Visitor Centre is the only place to rent e-bikes ($40 per hour) and e-scooters (adults $30 per hour). There's also a cargo bike for people with limited mobility ($40 per hour), and guided tour options.

Starting Point

The Mandurah Visitor Centre is the simplest place to cycle from. There is shared cycle and footpath from this point to the official start of the trail, at Halls Head Beach on Halls Head Pde.

01 Head south past Tods Cafe, turn right and follow the path along the estuary, watching for baby stingrays in the water. The floating circular platform for swimmers, named Kwillena Gabi Pool, is illuminated at night; you might see black swans here. Turn left onto the colourful brick laneway. At its end, turn right and mount the Mandurah Bridge crossover. Once across, take the red pathway alongside Mary St, riding over two bridges revealing Mandurah's canals and grand houses, until you reach Victor Adam Park.

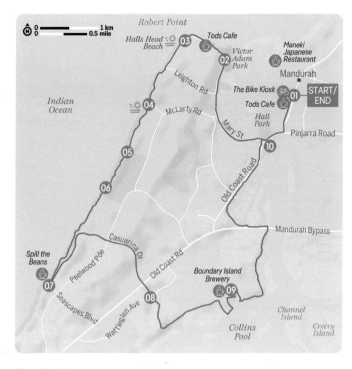

Sparking Joy with Dolphins & Christmas Lights

Mandurah's many waterways are home to groups of Indo-Pacific dolphins, who like to feed, breed and play in the estuary and its offshoots. Anywhere from one to 15 dolphins can be spotted from shore, or from a hired waterbike or on a dolphin cruise. You're most likely to see them between September and May, though they are present year-round.

Mandurah's annual, free-to-view Christmas Lights Trail edges many of the same waterways, with big, fairy-lit installations along the town's foreshore, and impressively decorated residences drawing thousands of sightseers each year. Lights cruises run along Mandurah's canals, and the town takes to calling itself the 'Capital of Christmas'.

Elevation (m)

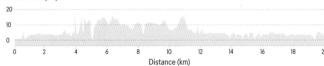

02 Continue on, passing public toilets, drink fountains and another Tods Cafe to the left. Look to your right and see Halls Head (also known as Doddi's) Beach, a calm, shallow stretch with a floating pontoon – on breezy days, it's usually sheltered from the wind. Notice the historic ship anchors on the ground, marking some 150 years of at least 17 different shipwrecks along the coastline.

03 A new cycle path that opened in 2023 links Halls Head Beach with Janis St, hugging the westward side of Halls Head Pde and its dreamy seaside views. As you come to Janis St car park, spot the white-coloured buoys floating on the water – they're connected to rock lobster pots, placed on the coast's many sharp reefs.

04 Ride away from the ocean, towards the row of oceanfront housing, and look for a gap in the limestone wall, with a bollard in the middle. Turn right through the gap and rejoin the cycleway. Observe how the stone wall runs along the two-storey homes, with steps going up and over and gateways grazing the ground. This is how locals deter snakes from coming in – the reptiles live in the scrub land to your right. Be aware but not alarmed – this is Australia.

05 Pop out onto Calypso Rd car park – its epic ocean views make swimming tempting. Keep the ocean to your right and return to the coastal cycleway. Pass another toilet block and a playground, then ride up a gentle hill that leads you to an ephemeral surprise.

06 Tackle several hills then spot the Giant, a huge wooden being constructed from salvaged beer pallets by one of the world's leading recycle artists, Copenhagen-based Thomas Dambo. Head down a small but steep hill and you'll eventually ride alongside a beach covered in a jagged karst system of limestone rocks; the cycle path turns momentarily into boardwalk with stairs to the sand. Cycle up the hill and continue winding along the entrancing coast.

07 Ride past another wooden stairway to the sand and reach what feels like a pathway crossroad. Turn left, then turn right and return to the footpath that edges Boardwalk Blvd. Arrive at a circular grass amphitheatre with a playground and see Spill the Beans cafe across the road – this is the last cafe stop for a while. To your west is Seascapes Beach, an excellent swimming spot with very calm conditions.

08 From here, you can either return to the Mandurah Visitor Centre by tracing the same route back or you can take the loop option by returning to Boardwalk Blvd, now with the ocean to your left as you ride northeast. The road will veer eastward and, at the roundabout, turns into Casuarina Dr. It crosses the busy Old Coast Rd and becomes Bower Dr. Take the cycle path beyond the Bower Dr T-junction, through the bushland. If you're riding early or late in the day, you may spot kangaroos here.

09 Follow the cycle path into Len Howard Conservation Park, a hotspot for waterbirds such as spoonbills, egrets, darters and swans. Reach Marina Quay Dr and pause at Boundary Island Brewery – the best place for a filling meal with marina views from the waterfront balcony out back.

10 On the Brewery's northeastern side, follow the bike path all the way back to central Mandurah, meandering through estuary wetlands, tree thickets and scrub. After passing under Mandurah Bridge, leave Egret Point Rd and join Leisure Way until you see the cycle path that edges Old Coast Rd. Follow it until you come to Mary St, then cross the bridge and you're back in the heart of town.

☕ Take a Break

Pull in for a coffee and a bite at either of the two TODS CAFES along this route; one is in the centre of Mandurah, the other at Halls Head – both are water-facing. Once you've finished your ride, walk north for 10 minutes from the visitor centre, across the footbridge, to Dolphin Quay, where you'll find the small and modest MANEKI JAPANESE RESTAURANT. Consider a bento box and a plate of gyoza; the chef here used to work at NOBU in Perth, and it shows.

ALEISHA ORR/SHUTTERSTOCK ©

One of the Giants of Mandurah

The Giants of Mandurah

Since November 2022, a number of giants have been lurking in the bush, wetlands and parks of Mandurah in a free-to-view outdoor exhibition highlighting sustainability (giantsofman durah.com.au). International recycle artist, Thomas Dambo, says his giants – or trolls, as they're referred to in his home country of Denmark – 'Represent the voice of nature'. Constructed from salvaged timber, twigs and branches, each giant takes about 750 hours to make.

One of them, named Santi Ikto, is found along the Halls Head Coastal Trail with his arms raised, as he calls in the wind. He, and several others, will remain in place until they degrade, returning to the earth.

36

Rottnest Island

DURATION	DIFFICULTY	DISTANCE	START/END
6–8hr	Intermediate	30km loop, plus side trips	Main settlement
TERRAIN		Mostly well-paved roads with undulating hills. Some dirt or sand side tracks to points of interest	

Rottnest Island

It might be best known for its quokkas, but there's so much more to Rottnest Island than just its adorable marsupials. Lying 18km to the west of the mainland, 'Rotto' is beloved of locals and visitors alike for its spectacular scenery, lovely beaches, fascinating history and laid-back holiday vibe. With no private vehicles allowed on the island, it's also the perfect place to explore by bike. Bring a mask and snorkel to explore the sheltered bays and shipwrecks, but don't neglect Rottnest's fascinating historical sites or birdlife-rich salt lakes.

Bike Hire

Pedal & Flipper, in the main settlement, rents bicycles and e-bikes (as well as snorkelling equipment). Daily hire is $30 for bicycles, $71 for e-bikes; reserve in advance online.

Starting Point

All visitors to Rottnest arrive at the main settlement on the island's east side. Multiple companies run regular ferries from Perth or Fremantle. Charter flights are also available from Perth to Rottnest airport.

01 It's possible to ride the circuit around the island in either a clockwise or anticlockwise direction, and which direction you choose may depend on how the winds are blowing when you depart. Leaving in the morning, it's often best to hit the south-coast beaches first, when winds are often lower. From Rottnest's main settlement, head south out of town, following signs towards Kingstown and the Parker Point Loop.

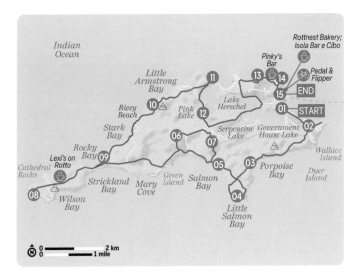

Elevation (m)

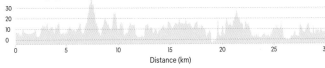

05 Back on the main road, head west along the broad sweep of sand at Salmon Bay. You'll often catch kitesurfers sporting on the waves here – not a surprise, as the winds can be fierce! Near the west end of the beach, turn right and head towards the white Wadjemup Lighthouse, towering on the hill above you. The slope is steep, but reasonably short, and the views from the top of the island are fantastic. You might also spot some quokkas on the way up.

06 Now that you've ascended the hill, it's a good time to explore the top of the island. A 30-minute paid tour will allow you to climb to the top of the lighthouse, but a tour (run daily between 10am and 2pm) of the nearby Oliver Hill Battery is likely more rewarding. Lying a short distance to the east along Oliver Hill Rd, it's the only intact coastal artillery battery remaining in Australia, with two 9.2in naval guns that could fire an armour-piercing shell more than 25km. The guns themselves are visible aboveground, but the tour (run by volunteer guides) explores the underground tunnels beneath the hillside.

07 When you've had enough of the panoramic views, head back downhill to the main road (Digby Dr) and continue west. South-coast beaches like Green Island and Mary Cove lie a short detour away if you're keen to explore; otherwise, approximately 3km to the west you'll hit the isthmus of Narrow Neck. Only 200m wide at its narrowest point, this marks the entrance to the far west of Rottnest Island.

02 The first possible side trip along the route is to the Kingstown Barracks, which lie a short detour to the left from the main road. The WWII-era structures here have been repurposed for visitor accommodation, and are a little down-at-heel. If you're keen to get into the water, park your bike and head down onto the beach at Thompson Bay, where the 1942 military shipwreck of the *Uribes* lies in shallow water just 10m offshore.

03 From Kingstown, head south once again on Parker Point Rd. A short detour leads to the ruins of the historical artillery emplacement at Bickley Battery, whose 6in guns defended the port of Fremantle during WWII.

04 Back on the main road, you'll soon get your first views of Rottnest's south-coast beaches, and they're spectacular. Ride down to the turquoise waters of Little Salmon Bay and explore the small sheltered cove there. A 700m underwater snorkelling trail has been laid among the rocks of the bay; following it, you'll find underwater signage with information about the marine sanctuary you're swimming through, as well pink corals and schools of tropical fish. Even though Rottnest lies at 32° south latitude, sealife like this is able to thrive here because of the warm-water Leeuwin Current, which flows southward down the coast of WA.

☕ Take a Break

If you want to ensure that you're well-provisioned before you head out, a stop at ROTTNEST BAKERY in the main settlement should be on the cards, which has the usual selection of pies, pastries and sausage rolls to keep you fuelled.

After a long and windy ride out to the far west end of the island, the coffee van of LEXI'S ON ROTTO is usually parked near Cape Vlamingh. It's a welcome spot to stop for a cappuccino, a muffin or a cold drink before continuing the adventure.

 08 The west end of Rottnest feels wild and remote, a far cry from the civilised and built-up east side of the island. The seas are wilder here, and are the place for any but the most confident swimmers. Cycle 2.5km west across the windswept landscape to Cape Vlamingh, the island's westernmost point; a boardwalk leads down to a viewing platform overlooking the rocky coast, and the rocky inlet of Fishhook Bay.

09 Turn east along the main road back towards Narrow Neck. To the

north, various short side tracks lead to coastal viewpoints looking out over Cathedral Rocks (which has a resident seal colony), Eagle Rock and Crocodile Rock, among others. Approximately 1km to the east of Narrow Neck, turn left on Bovell Way, which runs along the north side of the island.

10 Rottnest's north-side beaches are often more sheltered from the wind than their south-side counterparts, and are more popular as a result. Nonetheless, the beaches here, far from the main settlement, are often uncrowded – you might even have one to yourself! Cycle past them along Bovell Way, stopping off if the urge grabs you, until you hit Parakeet Bay, approximately 6km to the northeast.

11 The bay and its sister – Little Parakeet Bay, just around the headland – are popular swimming beaches, with calm, shallow waters backed by a photogenic crescent of white sand and ringed by rock cliffs. They're also a great snorkelling spot, with abundant fish life and a long stretch of coral reef to explore.

12 From Parakeet Bay, backtrack approximately 800m to the turnoff to Defence Rd and head inland.

TOP TIP:

Stay Overnight

Though it's great to visit Rottnest as a day trip, the island is positively magical at night, and is best appreciated with an overnight stay. Lodging isn't cheap, and gets booked out months in advance, but you can often find availability midweek, particularly outside of the school holiday period.

MATTHEW CROMPTON/LONELY PLANET ©

Quokkas, Rottnest Island

Quokkas

The emblem of Rottnest, it was these cat-sized marsupials that gave the island its name in 1696, when Dutch Captain Willem de Vlamingh mistook them for large rodents and called the place 't Eylandt 't Rottenest – Rats' Nest Island. Related to kangaroos and wallabies, they always seem to be smiling, and – lacking any natural predators – are naturally tame and curious, especially if they think you have food. While quokkas were widespread on the Australian mainland before European colonisation, their numbers have plummeted since, and today the species is listed as vulnerable, with the largest population found on Rottnest Island.

Island History

Rottnest is part of the Country of the Noongar people, for whom it's known as Wadjemup – the 'place across the water where the spirits are'. Human artefacts dating back 30,000 years have been found on the island, which was separated from the Australian mainland 7000 years ago when sea levels rose. For a century from the 1830s, Rottnest was used as a prison colony for Aboriginal Australians, and in the late 1800s it served for 20 years as reformatory for wayward boys. During WWII, the island became a crucial point for the defence of Fremantle, which was the Allies' most important naval base in the Indian Ocean.

Here, the road leads past an assortment of Rottnest's central salt lakes. The island's central wetlands area covers 200 hectares, and is a key breeding ground for several migratory bird species, including fairy terns and red-necked stints. Head south for 1.5km past small lakes Nigri, Sirius and the otherworldly Pink Lake, then head east on Digby Dr, crossing the causeway that runs through Herschel Lake.

13 At the intersection with Geordie Bay Rd, where wind-whipped foam from the lake often blows over the road, turn north again and cycle around the edge of the lake, climbing uphill past the towering Rottnest wind turbine. At the top of the hill turn east and follow the coastal road approximately 1km east to the beach at the Basin. The underwater limestone reef at the Basin has been hollowed out over time, giving the swimming beach here its logical name. The bay is calm and sheltered, and very popular with families with small children, as well as novice snorkellers. Fish life is abundant, but the biggest draw is the complex of underwater rocks, crags and caves to explore, which can easily occupy an hour or more.

14 When you're done with the water, head 500m east along Strue Rd, where the resident population of quokkas is usually out and about. Turn north on Gem Rd and travel approximately 400m north to the Bathurst Lighthouse, which overlooks the sweep of Pinky Beach to the west. This is one of the prettiest spots for sunset on the island. The bar at Pinky's, perched on the dunes behind the beach, also makes a great place for a sundowner.

15 From the lighthouse, the main settlement lies less than 1km south. Now is the perfect time to hand back your bike and soak in the history of the town itself. Various colonial-era buildings are scattered throughout its streets; head to the Quod, an octagonal jail building dating to 1863, to see the most visible remnant of Rottnest's century-long history as a forced-labour colony for Aboriginal men. Directly to the north of the Quod, walk through the quiet Wadjemup Aboriginal Burial Ground, and learn about the island's history of Aboriginal incarceration and its role in the colonisation of WA. It's a potent a reminder that this incredible island always was, and always will be, Aboriginal land.

☕ Take a Break

Though many longtime visitors to the island will mourn the recent commercial development of the dunes behind Pinky Beach, PINKY'S BAR really is a lovely place for a sunset drink. The cocktails come highly recommended, and the sunset views over the beach to the west are fantastic.

If you're looking for something more substantial than just drinks, ISOLA BAR E CIBO, overlooking Thomson Bay, is the finest dining available on Rottnest. The Italian fare here is big on seafood, and prioritises local WA produce.

The Basin

37

Wadandi Track

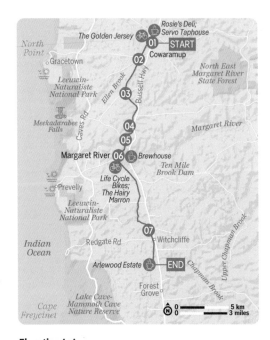

DURATION	DIFFICULTY	DISTANCE	START/END
2hr	Easy	31km	Country Fire Association shed/Arlewood Estate

TERRAIN	Flat bush trail that's a shared pedestrian and cycle way, with river bridges, tree roots and some dirt roads to cross

Elevation (m)

Distance (km)

Located in one of the world's 36 biodiversity hotspots, the Wadandi Track brings together native bush with granite boulders, vineyards and farmland as it traces what was once a railway line. The Busselton to Flinders Bay Railway lives on through remaining cuttings, embankments and bridge crossings; in places, steel lines can still be spotted through the dirt. Its new name recognises the traditional owners of the land: Wadandi means 'People of the sea'. As well as visual diversity, keep your ears open for birdsong along this journey.

Bike Hire

In Cowaramup, the Golden Jersey has bikes for all ages. You can also depart from Margaret River; try Life Cycle Bikes or the Hairy Marron. To incorporate wineries into the trail, book with Easy Ride Tours.

Starting Point

Go to the western outskirts of Cowaramup, to the left of the Country Fire Association shed, and look for the pole signage and paved path.

01 As you pedal from the start of the trail, imagine the huff-puff, shrill whistle and brake screech of the steam trains that used to chug through the dense eucalyptus forest. You'll notice an old train station platform; go to the back of the wooden shelter to see panels of historical information and photographs depicting the many uses of the former railway. You might also see a 'Rails to Trails' sign – this is what the Wadandi Track used to be called.

Old steam train, Margaret River

MARGARET RIVER RAILWAY

Kate
230ft
A.S.L.

ROTARY PARK STATION

MARGARET RIVER

Railway History

When built in the 1880s, the original railway carted timber, felled from the region's majestic forests, to oceanside jetties. Boats couriered wood around the globe until the industry's decline. In 1916 the WA government bought and extended the railway. In the 1920s, the roads in Margaret River were dirt, more people rode horses than drove cars, and most supplies – from bricks to cream to ploughs – were brought to the region by locomotive. Mail day was a big deal. The train travelled between Margaret River and Perth three times a week, picking up passengers en route for the then-overnight journey. It closed in 1957, as paved roads and cars became more mainstream.

02 Ride beneath leafy tree canopies and leave the paved surface for dirt track. The first section of the ride takes you from Cowaramup to Margaret River, bypassing the township unless you take one of the side trails into town. Many locals commute between the towns, both on bike and on foot. This is a shared path, so be sure to give way to pedestrians and ring your bell when passing. At times, you'll feel like you're in a natural tunnel made of slender trees.

03 The track is flat, with a very slightly downhill gradient, so this leg of the ride is easy and enjoyable. It can be done at any time of year, except for winter when it's wet, muddy and best avoided. The show of colourful wildflowers in spring is particularly spectacular. There are about four dirt roads to cross over as you go – traffic is minimal but always look left and right. The track itself is simple to follow, so you can concentrate more on the smells, sounds and sights of nature around you as you ride. You may see kangaroos, emus, bobtail lizards and skinks at any time of the day, along with black cockatoos, blue wrens and native parrots.

04 Expect to ride over a number of bridges; some are curved, and some are flat. Two of the original timber bridges were replaced and one was refurbished in 2022. The shire's efforts were recognised with a first place ranking at the Institute of Public Works Engineering Australasia Excellence Awards. It's wonderfully shady through this stretch, as tree limbs lean over the trail, creating a natural arch. At the Carter Rd car park, have a look for the steel railway tracks peeking through the dirt.

05 Just before Margaret River town, see the sign to the Alfred Bussell Trail to the left (it's marked with a picture of gum nuts and a green line). If you'd like a break at a nearby microbrewery, follow the trail down a slight hill and ride for nearly 1km. Pop out of the forest at the road, cross over the bridge and you'll see it.

06 Staying on the trail, you'll pass by Margaret River town's western side. As you leave the outskirts and continue south, the marri and karri forest gives way to cattle and dairy farms and vineyards.

You'll pass intermittently between scrub, forest and leaf-littered track, and open agricultural land with grassy paddocks, farm gates, fences and big, old trees. At times the track will be thin and narrow, or wide with minor red dirt corrugations, or resembling limestone road the width of a single car.

☕ Take a Break

In Cowaramup, fuel up with coffee and cake at ROSIE'S DELI, or venture next door to the SERVO TAPHOUSE. After perusing the four-page menu of beers (one page is devoted to 'not beer', aka local wine), head out back to sit among grapevines.

In Margaret River, divert nearly 1km off the trail to BREWHOUSE, a lively open-air brewpub. End your ride with the reward of ARLEWOOD ESTATE, a boutique winery that pairs wine tastings with locally made chocolate.

SHUTTERNELKE/SHUTTERSTOCK ©

Cattle farm, Margaret River

07 As you approach Witchcliffe, look up high for red-tailed black cockatoos – you'll often hear their distinctive call before you see them. You may also see cows on the cattle crossing when passing through a farm just outside town. On the southern side of Witchcliffe, spot the signage to Arle-

Witchliffe

The incy-wincy town of 'Witchy', as it's fondly called by locals, is no slouch when it comes to sharing Margaret River's vinous bounty. Flanked by wineries on all sides, the singular main street embraces the region's major lure with not one, but two cellar-door tasting rooms. One is hidden within the historic general store–turned–artistic incubator space; a section of the building is devoted to Amato Vino's traditionally made, lo-fi output. Up the road, McHenry Hohnen's cellar door – a 2021 pop-up that's stayed around – pours their many wines into glasses. Amble between them, the Flying Wardrobe antique shop and the old-school bakery.

wood Estate. Turn towards the micro cellar door and celebrate a ride well done with a wine tasting. The ride can be continued from this point on, but we can't think of a better way to finish it – unless, of course, you return to Witchcliffe for a cycle-crawl of the micro cellar doors and other treasures there.

Also Try...

Narrows Bridge

Three Bridges Loop

DURATION	DIFFICULTY	DISTANCE
5–6hr	Easy	45km

To extend the Swan River and Windan Bridge Loop, set off on this flat and scenic riverside journey.

From the city centre, it clings to the Swan River, all the way to Fremantle, crossing – you guessed it – three bridges. It's popular, so set off early on peak times like weekends. Depart from Elizabeth Quay and cross the Narrows Bridge, heading south along the river, then cross again at the Canning Bridge. You'll pass through the suburb of Applecross, with so many impressive riverside homes you may have trouble keeping your eyes on the path. Continue until you reach North Fremantle, crossing westward on the Stirling Bridge. Then head back to the city in a northerly direction, through the perhaps even more impressive Mosman Park mansions. You'll also pass the convivial university district of Crawley.

Fremantle to Point Walter

DURATION	DIFFICULTY	DISTANCE
1–2hr	Easy	8.2km one way

Suited to the whole family, this mostly flat and easy track runs along the river, kicking off in Fremantle.

Head to the bike path on the northern side of Fremantle Train Station and stay on it as you go up and down a gradual hill, then pass under a bridge before you see the Jetty Bar and Eats – an excellent place to stop for a shared-dish lunch. Continue on the track, cycling beneath another bridge and past the pub, The Left Bank, which bursts at the seams on Sundays. Along the way you'll also pass playgrounds and river swimming spots with small sandy beaches. Keep going until you reach Point Walter Reserve, where you'll likely spot locals picnicking in the sunshine.

Lake Leschenaultia

Ten Mile Brook Trail

DURATION	DIFFICULTY	DISTANCE
1–2hr	Intermediate	15km return

This shared-use bush trail heads east of Margaret River town, along the meandering river of the same name, to a peaceful dam that makes for a fantastic picnic spot.

Depart from the old steam engine at Rotary Park, found beside Bussell Hwy on the outskirts of town, to the north of the river. Nearly 8km in each direction, the track is mainly flat and runs along coarse gravel and compacted dirt, arriving at a weir bridge. It draws its name from the waterway that was dammed in the mid-1990s to create new supplies for Margaret River and nearby townships, all of which were growing fast. There are free barbecues, public toilets and shelters at the dam.

Lake Leschenaultia MTB Trails

DURATION	DIFFICULTY	DISTANCE
1–3hr	Easy	12km

Beside John Forest National Park in the Perth Hills, the Lake Leschenaultia MTB trails are a fun way to try out mountain biking on a number of easy-to-intermediate, family-friendly trails.

The trail network is custom built, linking trails of 1km to 3km, and it includes a pump track. The trails can be sandy in the warmer months, so aim to visit in winter or spring, after rains have made them firmer. This means you're unlikely to be swimming in the placid lake, which is also a much-loved camping spot about 45 minutes' drive from the centre of Perth. The barbecues there are free to use, there's a nice kiosk doing weekend breakfast, and the lake is open year-round.

Arriving

The main ports of entry to Australia are Perth, Sydney and Melbourne. From those three cities, domestic flights reach far-flung towns across the whole nation. But your first challenge will be navigating the stringent customs regulations, especially if bringing your spotless bicycle.

Travelling with a Bike

Flying with a bike requires a certain faith. But if you pack your prized machine carefully you can be confident it will arrive in one piece. First, research the additional baggage costs of airlines. For the greatest security, invest in a special case. Soft cases are lighter (and therefore cheaper to transport) but less robust than hard cases. Both have wheels for easy manoeuvrability. Typically, you'll need to remove both wheels, deflate the tyres, undo the bolts for the handlebars, lower the saddle and perhaps remove the rear derailleur and brake rotors to prevent damage. You may want to pad the frame. In order to enter Australia, your bike will need to be spotlessly clean and it may be inspected for dirt. Fresh tyres are always a good idea. Note that airlines won't transport batteries for e-bikes. You will collect your bike at the oversized baggage area, by the surfboards and prams.

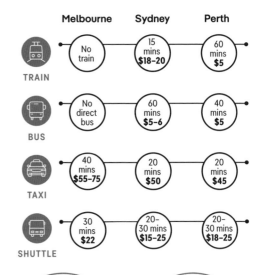

	Melbourne	Sydney	Perth
TRAIN	No train	15 mins $18–20	60 mins $5
BUS	No direct bus	60 mins $5–6	40 mins $5
TAXI	40 mins $55–75	20 mins $50	20 mins $45
SHUTTLE	30 mins $22	20–30 mins $15–25	20–30 mins $18–25

VISAS

All visitors, except New Zealanders, require a visa; remember to apply in advance even for an Electronic Travel Authority (ETA), for which many European and Asian nationalities and Americans are eligible.

MONEY

Plan how to carry cash in advance: pre-loading travel credit cards can be better value than changing money at an airport. Contactless payment is very widespread in Australia.

CUSTOMS REGULATIONS

Australia's rules on what you can bring into the country are extremely strict. If you're bringing your own bicycle, it will need to be clean enough to eat your dinner off. Fit fresh tyres.

FROM THE AIRPORT

Of Australia's three main entry points, Melbourne is the only one without a convenient rail link into the city. A taxi, bus or rental car, especially with outsized luggage, are the disappointing options.

Getting Around

CYCLING RULES

Australian states delight in enforcing a number of laws around cycling, which apply to everyone, including visitors. Nationally, it is the law to wear an approved helmet at all times when riding a bike. Disposable helmets are not a good idea so you may as well bring or buy your own. You can also be fined for cycling too fast, cycling on footpaths or pavements where you're not permitted, using a phone while cycling (in Queensland), cycling without lights after dark and cycling while over the blood alcohol limit.

Train Travel

Australia's rail network is relatively limited and rules for carrying your bike on trains vary according to operator and state. Don't assume it's easy everywhere. Many services will only permit pre-booked bicycles or if there is (limited) space available. Use off-peak trains.

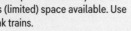

Cycling Cities

Cities vary greatly in their bike-friendliness. Melbourne is exceptionally easy to get around by bicycle, being fairly flat and packed with bike lanes. Sydney is the opposite. Adelaide, Perth, Canberra, Brisbane and Hobart are all manageable by bicycle, with safe routes.

Car Rental

To reach many rural destinations, a private vehicle is best, especially if shared. The rental car market is quite competitive in Australia and if you select a large vehicle you may fit several bikes in the back. Rental firms with large networks may permit one-way rentals.

Navigation Tips

Download base maps in advance to your phone or satnav so you don't rely on network coverage. You can pre-plot routes for GPS both for driving and cycling using websites such as Google Maps, Komoot and RideWithGPS.

COSTS

4WD rental
$100–200/day

Petrol
Approx $2/litre

Melbourne Metro
$9.20/day

Sydney Metro
$16.80/day

Accommodation

BIKE-FRIENDLY HOTELS

Certain destinations in Australia have evolved to be favourites among cyclists. This is usually because there's a concentration of routes or trails in the area. It means local businesses, including hoteliers, B&B owners and other accommodation providers, are often more supportive of cyclists and will offer secure storage, cleaning facilities, sometimes tools and spares and so on. Great examples of bike-friendly towns are Bright, Beechworth and Warburton in Victoria, Derby in Tasmania and the city of Adelaide. The flipside is that in towns without a cycling scene there may be less sympathetic responses to requests to keep your bike in your room.

HOW
MUCH
FOR A
NIGHT
IN A...

Camp site
Free–$15

Motel
$150–200

B&B
From $200

Hostels

Cities and towns popular with tourists often have several hostel options ranging from the grotty to the glitzy. The standard of accommodation, especially at YHA Australia properties, can be high, with the option of dorms or double rooms. Self-catering in kitchens can cut costs and some hostels offer secure bike storage. Don't discount the humble hostel regardless of your age or budget.

Motels

As hit-and-miss as hostels, motels can be a good option in country towns but choose carefully and avoid those near big intersections and on the outskirts of cities. You'll typically pay around $120 to $180 per night and some will be very vigilant about extra guests or keeping your bicycle in the room for security (and others will be much more flexible and welcoming).

B&Bs

For an often-cosier experience, booking a B&B can be a brilliant choice with a huge, healthy breakfast to look forward to. There are some treasured properties in restored cottages, beachside bungalows and the like. But expect to pay for the privilege: prices can be several hundred dollars per night. Weekday and out-of-season deals appeal. Many can be booked on online portals.

Pubs

Pub accommodation ranges from the rough-and-ready in some rural towns to deluxe boutique-style spaces in a few towns popular with weekending urbanites. Both will offer a beer and plates of food for hungry cyclists. Indeed, pubs can be very welcome beacons on longer trips through the bush, though the most basic may only have shared facilities.

CAMPING

Wild camping is typically discouraged in Australia. In national parks you can only camp in designated camping grounds – however, spaces are often free. State forests are more relaxed but always camp well away from a water course and carry out your waste. You shouldn't expect to pitch a tent in a public space without attracting attention.

Bikes

Bike Rental

The perennial issue with bike rental in Australia (and also bike-share schemes in the country) is the law that all cyclists must wear helmets. As a result, many bike rental businesses also include helmets with any bicycle rented. However, these helmets may not be especially good or even fit properly. So if you plan on cycling in Australia, it's always a good idea to bring your own helmet or buy one to keep.

Towns and cities with cycling opportunities in the vicinity will usually have one or more businesses offering bikes for hire. This includes towns on rail trails, towns with mountain bike trails, and cities such as Melbourne. It is less common for hotels to offer bike rental, although a few do.

E-bikes

E-bikes are becoming more widespread, both at the specialist end of the market with high-end mountain bikes, and also for more casual customers with electric town bikes. Typically, they'll cost around 20% to 50% more to rent than a standard bike. You would expect to receive a fully charged battery – take note of its range (this varies according to battery capacity and how you use the bike). Most batteries will be sufficient for a day's light use in eco-mode since few people use the battery at full power continuously (reserving the boost for hills). An empty bike battery will take at least three hours to charge from mains electricity. It is not worth planning to use a public charger: Hobart only installed its first e-bike charger in April 2023.

OTHER GEAR

Some well-established rental outfits also include a spare inner tube, a puncture repair kit and sometimes a lock. But it's wise not to count on being provided with these. Bring your own spares and repairs kit and a pump to be sure. And if you use cycling shoes, don't forget to bring your preferred pedals.

Health & Safe Travel

Hygiene

When cycling longer distances in warmer temperatures, good hygiene is important. Don't wear cotton underwear, because it remains damp: use proper padded shorts and wash or change them daily. Using a chamois cream over contact areas can reduce friction and the risk of saddle sores. Always wash thoroughly after cycling and don't sit around in your shorts. An anti-bacterial cream can clear up irritations.

Snakes

Snakes can be present on even urban bike paths. The chances of

encountering one, let alone being bitten, are small but not zero. Be careful where you place your feet when dismounting onto, for example, a leaf-covered verge. Exercise extra caution near water sources, such as rivers (which many bike paths follow). Snake activity is seasonal and they're especially active in spring. If venturing further afield, carry a snake bandage and know how to use it.

Heat Exhaustion

Heat exhaustion and sun stroke are very real threats when cycling in Australia. With a breeze in your face, you won't always feel that you're overheating. Symptoms of heat exhaustion include dizziness, nausea and a racing heart rate. Avoid cycling on very hot days (or go out early and late). Drink a lot of water. Cover exposed skin and your head.

CARS

The greatest health risk to cyclists will come from people driving cars. In urban areas, beware of people opening the door of a parked car without checking. In rural areas be aware of drivers approaching at speed behind you, whether in a ute or a logging truck, and prepare to pull onto the side. Always ensure that you're visible. Never respond to provocation.

BIKE BREAKDOWN

Before setting off on a bike ride of any distance, ensure that you understand how to fix a flat tyre and, better still, have practised removing the wheel, unhooking the tyre from the rim, checking for the sharp intrusion that caused the flat, replacing the tube and tyre and pumping it up. It's also worth carrying spare links for a broken chain and a chain breaking tool.

Responsible Travel

Climate Change

It's impossible to ignore the impact we have when travelling, and the importance of making changes where we can. Lonely Planet urges all travellers to engage with their travel carbon footprint. There are many carbon calculators online that allow travellers to estimate the carbon emissions generated by their journey; try resurgence.org/resources/carbon-calculator.html. Many airlines and booking sites offer travellers the option of offsetting the impact of greenhouse gas emissions by contributing to climate-friendly initiatives around the world. We continue to offset the carbon footprint of all Lonely Planet staff travel, while recognising this is a mitigation more than a solution.

RESOURCES

Bicycle Network
www.bicyclenetwork. com.au
Has information on where to ride in each state and also bicycle touring and maintenance tips.

Bureau of Meteorology (BOM)
www.bom.gov.au
Up-to-the-second weather reports help you plan cycling trips.

Parks Australia
www.parksaustralia.gov.au
A starting point for exploring Australia's 700+ national parks, with state organisations the next step.

SUSTAINABLE SHOPPING

Stock up on provisions without the food miles and plastic packaging associated with supermarkets by shopping at community food markets, such as Ceres in Melbourne. Also visit weekend farmers markets for local produce.

TRAIN TRAVEL

Extra planning is required but selecting bike rides with a train station at either end is a rewarding challenge. Trains, although running on limited routes in rural Australia, can be an affordable alternative to travelling by car or plane.

INDIGENOUS INSIGHTS

Learn about the Traditional Custodians of the Country you're cycling through by visiting Aboriginal cultural centres such as Brambuk in the Grampians National Park and the Walyalup Cultural Centre in Fremantle.

Nuts & Bolts

CURRENCY: AUSTRALIAN DOLLAR ($)

Cards & Cash

ATMs are widespread throughout Australia but if you're withdrawing cash using your credit card you will incur higher fees and interest than if you find a good deal with a local currency exchange service at home, before you leave. An alternative is to use a pre-paid card such as Revolut.

Contactless Payments

More than most countries in the world, Australia has embraced contactless payments. With a wave of your card you can pay for pretty much anything from a flat white to balloon flight. This is another reason to carry a bank card with a chip and pin that will work abroad.

Tipping

Tipping is common in restaurants and upmarket cafes but certainly not culturally ingrained or necessarily expected. Rounding a taxi fare up is standard. Tipping is not expected at hotels or for most other services.

Mobile Phones

You'll use a lot of mobile data if navigating using your phone so it might be best to sign up for an allowance with your home provider or buy a pre-paid SIM card in Australia.

Network Coverage

Your mobile phone will latch onto a local network, Telstra being the largest in Australia, but don't count on getting 4G for downloading data deep in the outback.

Chargers & Adapters

Australia uses three-pinned plugs, with flat pins (two pins also work fine in sockets). Take a couple of adapters for your phone and other chargers.

ELECTRICITY 230V/50HZ

Type I
230V/50Hz

By Difficulty

Index

NOTES

THE AUTHORS

Robin Barton
Robin is an editor and writer who creates books such as *Epic Bike Rides of the World* for Lonely Planet. @robinabarton

Sofia Tsamassiros
Sofia owns and operates a sustainable focused cycling tour company in Tasmania and is passionate about showing off Tasmania to a larger audience. @tasmaniancyclingtours or @Sofia.tsama

Cristian Bonetto
Cristian is a reformed playwright and TV soap writer who now writes about travel, food and culture. @rexcat75

Jessica Wynne Lockhart
A Canadian living on Australia's Sunshine Coast, Jess writes features for magazines and newspapers about her cycling, paddling and hiking adventures. @WynneLockhart

Josh West
Josh is an avid hiker, paddler and cyclist who can often be found traipsing long distances in search of nature's enlightenment or a well-camouflaged cache. @trekkingwest

Bella Molloy
Travel writer, avid cyclist and host of the Seek Travel Ride podcast, Bella is always on the lookout for her next adventure. @seektravelride

Matthew Crompton
Matthew is a writer, photographer and professional metaphysician in love with hikes, bikes and the mystical solitude of the way-out. @matthew.crompton

Candace Elms-Smith
Candace is a travel writer with a passion for hiking and all things nature; you can read about her adventures on her blog Tracks Less Travelled. @_trackslesstravelled

Fleur Bainger
Fleur writes evocative travel features, mentors freelance journalists who want to nail their craft and teaches podcasting at Murdoch University. @fleurbainger

BEHIND THE SCENES

This book was produced by the following:

Commissioning Editor Darren O'Connell

Production Editor Kathryn Rowan

Book Designer Clara Monitto

Cartographers Chris Lee-Ack, Vojtech Bartos, Eve Kelly

Cover Design & Researcher Marc Backwell

Assisting Editors Shauna Daly, Melanie Dankel, Andrea Dobbin, Michael MacKenzie, Anne Mulvaney

Thanks to Karen Henderson

Product Development Amy Lynch, Marc Backwell, Katerina Pavkova, Fergal Condon, Ania Bartoszek

ACKNOWLEDGMENTS

Digital Model Elevation Data Contains public sector information licensed under the Open Government Licence v3.0 website http://www.nationalarchives.gov.uk/doc/open-government-licence/version/3/

Cover Photograph Elizabeth Quay Bridge, designed by Ove Arup, Perth, Travelscape Images/Alamy Stock Photo ©